"Love entails two intense, simultan⟨ous⟩ and solicitude toward another pe⟨rson⟩ myriad combinations and permutat⟨i⟩⟨on⟩⟨s⟩ – wnat Dr. Friedberg calls 'faces' – are analyzed with insight and empathy in his fourth book, *Faces of Love*. The book includes dramatic case studies of four of his patients, who journey with him toward ameliorating the fears, fantasies, obsessions, and resistances that prevent them from achieving satisfying relationships. *Faces* is not only fascinating, but it provides an essential perspective on contemporary modes of psychoanalytic treatment."

Henry Lothane, M.D., D.L.F.A.P.A., *Clinical Professor of Psychiatry, Icahn School of Medicine at Mount Sinai*

"Anyone longing to better understand how a psychoanalytic analytic mind works will love the wonderfully creative mind of Dr. Ahron Friedberg, as he delves deeply into the phases of his work with four psychoanalytic patients; each case is a pointillistic painting of the many faces of desire and love in myriad forms that unfold over time in treatment. In so doing, Dr. Friedberg captures the essence of psychoanalysis itself and the way treatment addresses the complexities of human desires, longings, and love."

Susan C. Vaughan, M.D., *Director, Columbia Center for Psychoanalytic Training and Research, Vagelos College of Physicians and Surgeons, Columbia University*

"Ever since Freud, case studies have been the lifeblood of psychoanalytic writing. Yet who can write as engagingly as Freud, the winner of the Goethe Prize in literature? Now Ahron Friedberg does, in *Faces of Love*. He reminds us of Paul Dewald's pathbreaking, book-length account of an analysis, demonstrating the lurching, yet reparative paths toward health in treatment. His book richly elaborates on love, and includes not only Plato's taxonomy – sexual, awestruck, playful, self-love, familial – but also love's apparent opposite, 'hate,' which can infiltrate treatment itself. We embark on a fraught journey with Dr. Friedberg and his patients. But we are fortunate to observe as he navigates the troubled waters of inner life."

Nathan Szajnberg, M.D., *Formerly Sigmund Freud Professor, the Hebrew University*

"One of the biggest challenges for any psychoanalyst is to write about his clinical work so as to allow the reader to picture such a complex, fascinating job. This is what Ahron Friedberg does so well as he engages with these patients' troubled approaches to love. We see how the analyst finds a common wavelength, and the best possible theoretical framework in the work he does with each patient, thus profiting from the pluralistic dimension of contemporary psychoanalysis. This allows Friedberg to come as close as possible to the interactive reality of our work – what our patients say, what comes to our mind, and what we tell them. It is as if the reader were in the room with analyst and patient – and, simultaneously, in the analyst's head. We see how psychoanalytic work can still change patients' lives in a way unlike any other form of psychotherapy."

Marco Conci, M.D., *Coeditor-in-chief,*
International Forum of Psychoanalysis

"Faces of Love is an astonishing work. Reading it feels like you're in Dr. Friedberg's actual consulting room with patients. It reminds me of case studies by Freud, Winnicott, Kohut and other luminaries in our field. Its real-time, present-tense unfolding of psychoanalytic cases allows readers to reflect on different facets of love, and the concomitant complexities of human nature. Even with all our faults and flaws, the facets of *Faces* shine as in a gem."

Heather Berlin, Ph.D., *Assoc. Prof., Psychiatry and*
Neuroscience, Icahn School of Medicine

"Dr. Friedberg's *Faces of Love* is an extraordinary, original contribution to the literature of case studies of psychoanalysis. It is more present to what *actually* happens in the psychoanalytic situation than any that I know. By using love as the lens through which to view our clinical work, he identifies and develops an essential element of that work which, until now, has received insufficient attention as we advance the field as a science. Dr. Friedberg demonstrates his clinical mastery, empathy, and ability to capture the therapeutic process in writing."

Harold Bronheim, M.D., *Clinical Professor of*
Psychiatry, Mount Sinai

"Faces of Love offers an unusually clear window through which to view the ordinary extraordinary life of a psychoanalytic therapist at work with his patients. Dr. Friedberg invites us into his consulting room where we see him and his patients in living color, negotiating the challenges of being human in a way that only psychoanalysis provides. These four case studies read like page-turning linked stories, shining a soft light on the vicissitudes of love and intimacy, inside and outside therapy. The studies, anchored in Friedberg's personal reflections on his patients and himself, are free of the distractions of jargon. The analytic relationships will interest therapists and patients of all levels of experience and theoretical persuasion, as we follow this therapist and these patients challenge themselves and each other."

Tony Bass, Ph.D., *former Editor, Psychoanalytic Dialogues*

"In extensive case studies, animated by dialogues that ring true, *Faces of Love* demonstrates how psychodynamic intimacy explores underlying longings for love. Dr. Friedberg's patients discover how their childhood experiences – spankings, bed-wetting, shame – pose problems of love later in life, with transformative and even transcendent analytic solutions. Finally, they achieve what Nobel laureate Derek Walcott calls self-love after love."

David V. Forrest, M.D., *Clinical Professor of Psychiatry at Columbia, Past-President of the American College of Psychoanalysts, and Founding Editor of SPRING: The Journal of the E. E. Cummings Society*

"Dr. Frieberg loves his patients in the deeply stubborn, complicated, and often turbulent way that each of us who do this work must love our patients. In these case studies, he marks his arrival at the forefront of writers who affirm a contemporary vision of psychoanalytic practice. This is not your grandfather/ mother's psychoanalysis. It is a thumpingly creative exposition of how we do what we do, bringing us forthrightly into the analyst's thinking and feeling as the process of treatment unfolds."

Douglas Ingram, M.D., *former Editor, Psychodynamic Psychiatry*

"*Faces of Love* is that rare book that brings the process of psychoanalytic treatment alive for both professional and lay audiences. Patients struggle with unconscious conflicts that result in repetitive self-defeat; the analyst correspondingly feels his way through the fog of the patients' defenses. The narratives thereby capture the essence of the long, arduous analytic work that can bring about psychological growth. In choosing love and its many component emotions, often in a swirl of contradictions, Dr. Friedberg places the reader at the center of the maze that analyst and patient must traverse."

Joseph R. Silvio, M.D., *President, American Academy of Psychodynamic Psychotherapy and Psychoanalysis*

Life Studies in Psychoanalysis

Life Studies in Psychoanalysis consists of four psychoanalytic studies, each representing a patient's course of treatment over several years.

These studies demonstrate how love, in an array of forms, is refracted through the process of psychoanalysis, which unfolds over time and reveals the complexities of human desire. The cases presented here cover topics including repressed homosexuality, a taboo desire for a sibling, obsession with a fantasy, an Oedipus complex, and transferences that become an initial obstacle to treatment. As the studies proceed, each renders the non-linear progress of treatment, as layer upon layer of a patient's issues are brought to light and the patient slowly, often reluctantly, comes to terms with these issues. Dr. Ahron Friedberg offers professionals techniques for encouraging patients to remain in treatment when they become resistant, demoralized, or feel like they have hit a wall.

Ultimately, this book demonstrates how some patients, troubled by romantic, sexualized, fantasized, illicit, and/or uncontrollable desire, learn through psychoanalysis to accommodate their desires to what is possible and permissible in the lives that they otherwise inhabit. In this sense, the studies involve journeys from a place characterized by the epiphenomena of troubled love – grief, guilt, frustration – to one in which, through enhanced self-awareness, patients understand the sources and implications of their motivations. They come to understand why love has seemed like a minefield, and begin to find a more fulfilling path through it.

Life Studies in Psychoanalysis will be of great interest to psychoanalysts in practice and in training, psychoanalytic psychotherapists, and readers looking for insight into the analytic process.

Ahron Friedberg, M.D., is a Clinical Professor of Psychiatry at Icahn School of Medicine at Mount Sinai and served twice as past president of the American Society of Psychoanalytic Physicians. He is editor of American Academy of Psychodynamic Psychiatry and Psychoanalysis *Academy Forum* and book editor of *Psychodynamic Psychiatry*, as well as a regular contributor to *Psychology Today*.

Sandra Sherman, J.D., Ph.D., was a Senior Attorney in the U.S. government and a Professor of English at two major universities. She is the author of four books and over 60 peer-reviewed articles on 18th-century literature and culture and is co-author of several books on neuroscience. Currently, she is a Director at ChildsPlay International. *Life Studies in Psychoanalysis* is the fourth book that she has written with Dr. Friedberg.

Life Studies in Psychoanalysis

Faces of Love

Ahron Friedberg, M.D., with Sandra Sherman

Routledge
Taylor & Francis Group

LONDON AND NEW YORK

Designed cover image: Pablo Picasso, "Girl Before a Mirror" – permission obtained from
Artists Rights Society © 2023 Estate of Pablo Picasso/Artists Rights Society (ARS), New York

First published 2023
by Routledge
4 Park Square, Milton Park, Abingdon, Oxon OX14 4RN

and by Routledge
605 Third Avenue, New York, NY 10158

Routledge is an imprint of the Taylor & Francis Group, an informa business

British Library Cataloguing-in-Publication Data
A catalogue record for this book is available from the British Library

ISBN: 9781032403427 (hbk)
ISBN: 9781032403434 (pbk)
ISBN: 9781003352624 (ebk)

DOI: 10.4324/9781003352624

Typeset in Times New Roman
by Newgen Publishing UK

To my teachers

Contents

Foreword

Contents

Life Studies in Psychoanalysis: Faces of Love is a type of fugue, playing out in astonishing detail the endless variations of a universal theme: how we experience desire for another human being. Its focus shifts and recalibrates, almost moment to moment, as the subjects of these studies struggle with repressed desire, emerge into consciousness of how it has shaped their lives, and – finally – glimpse how they can begin to live in its flow, despite its undertow. Like no other recent book, *Faces* allows us to follow how patients in psychoanalysis undergo this process. It takes years. It can be excruciating. It proceeds through false starts, resistance, retreats, and the discovery of new, diverse, complicating pathologies. But as an illustration of the process, as an explanation of the psychoanalyst's role in its dynamic, *Faces* seems to me unmatched.

Faces demonstrates that the treatment's lack of linearity is an objective correlative of the patient's own conflicted unconscious and compromises. Each course of treatment, as it exposes yet another layer of repression, follows the patient as he or she confronts feelings that have remained unacknowledged (or, at best, barely understood) for their entire lives. The unwonted encounters are themselves troubling. As a result, discussions between patient and therapist are not just about the underlying problem (in all its permutations) but about the *problem with the problem* as experienced in the course of analysis. The effect, both at the narrative level and from a technical, psychoanalytic perspective, is immensely enlightening. We are situated at the outer limits of what psychoanalysis can do – that is, what it is now doing when applied in a contemporary, highly informed, and intensely reflective setting that encourages patients to remain involved even when they resist the process, fall into apathy, or want to quit. We see how psychoanalysis actually works, both in terms of how it operates and how it verges on success.

Faces of Love takes its title from the fact that no two faces are the same. We can never know all the faces in this world the way, for example, cardiologists have a good idea of what hearts look like, or orthopedists can describe one femur and be sure that the next will have similar contours. Faces are unique. So, the four studies in this book capture some aspects of love among all its infinite variations – and among all the infinite ways that people experience these variations. Through his patients, Dr. Friedberg dives into Oedipal obsessions, incestuous wishes, repressed homosexuality, and the need to recover the love of a long-lost father. He deals with forms of transference, where patients project their longed-for or frustrated desires onto him. He deals with love–hate relationships among siblings; romantic love; forbidden fantasies; and problems of self-love gone awry, where it turns outwards into arrogance and inwards into self-disgust. In every instance, desire has somehow distorted a patient's ability to navigate their lives. It becomes consuming, and impedes the capacity to form healthy, fulfilling relationships.

The idea, of course, is to find a way back toward balance, to where love remains at least an option but does not continue to exert the power of irresistible obsession. You may recognize some of these "faces" of love in your own experience. But, even if you do not, in the process of psychoanalysis they are stand-ins for the intense desires that all of us have, and that may at some time – when they become unmanageable – drive us to need psychoanalysis. There is a fine line between passion and obsession.

Of course, as I have been describing *Faces of Love*, I have cited the phenomenon of love and the process of psychoanalysis together in virtually every sentence. So, you might rightly ask: is this book *about* love (albeit by a psychoanalyst) or *about* psychoanalysis (albeit where patients suffer through aberrant currents of desire)? In fact, this book is about both in tandem. It explores the nature of some aspects of love insofar as they are explored psychoanalytically. As we read, we learn about love – how it can obsess us, how it can distort all our other relationships – but we also learn how psychoanalysis can become a third party, as it were, mediating between the subject/patient and the object of love so that neither overwhelms or harms the other. The analyst achieves a certain balance in hopes that the patient will, in time, do so as well.

Those who follow Dr. Friedberg's work know that I wrote the foreword to one of his earlier books, *Psychoanalysis and Personal Change: Two Minds in a Mirror* (Routledge, 2020). That book provided exceptionally candid insights into how psychiatrists think in the moment – that is, in real time, as they are in the midst of treating a patient. It was a book about process and, most importantly, about how the therapist understands it. It was deeply reflective and, at times, even self-critical. It struck me as raising the bar on honesty with regard to a process that is still, notwithstanding the turn toward neuroscience, shrouded in mystery. I agreed to write the foreword to *Faces of Love*, therefore, because I saw it as the natural sequel, exploring in far more detail not just how psychoanalysis works but how psychoanalysts become involved with the process. Moreover, as I looked back at *Two Minds in a Mirror*, I realized that so many of the encounters actually concerned love and its epiphenomena – for example, guilt, anxiety, rage, and jealousy. In *Faces of Love*, Dr. Friedberg's earlier concerns are now present again, this time with an intensity that is immensely compelling.

The four studies in *Faces* are so compelling not just at the level of their subject matter – who does not care about love, who is not fascinated by its exploration? – but also because they are wonderfully readable. Dr. Friedberg has taken years of notes and, through real artistry, turned them into narratives that develop with an emotional logic that replicates the logic of any well-told story. We experience the patient's emotional turns (which are explained, so that we see them full-on), as well as Dr. Friedberg's developing reactions, his course changes, his attempts to deal with instances of transference that, sometimes, seem more like affronts. This is not exactly the stuff of a psychological thriller, but it's close – closer, in fact, than any other series of case studies that I know. If Dr. Friedberg displays his skill as a psychoanalyst, he displays comparable expertise in holding the reader's attention.

While *Faces* is primarily for professionals, it is also intended for any serious reader interested in the healing arts and, in fact, in how aspects of love are illuminated in the healing process. I found it immensely engaging. I have no doubt that you will too.

Arnold M. Richards, M.D.
Former Editor, *Journal of the American Psychoanalytic Association*
Founding Editor, *International Journal of Controversial Discussions*

Acknowledgments

Faces of Love is dedicated to my teachers because it reflects so much of what they taught me. I will name just a few. Michael Porder, M.D., a training and supervising analyst at the New York Psychoanalytic Institute, helped me to deepen my understanding of psychoanalysis and its clinical technique. Arnold Richards, M.D., the former editor of the *Journal of the American Psychoanalytic Association*, encouraged me to think independently and broaden my approach to psychoanalysis. Dennis Charney, M.D., Dean of the Icahn School of Medicine at Mount Sinai and President for Academic Affairs for the Mount Sinai Health System, helped me incorporate ideas about resilience into psychodynamic psychiatry, and bring more rigorous scientific standards to clinical practice. Henry Lothane, M.D., clinical professor of psychiatry at Mount Sinai, enabled me to frame the psychoanalytic situation in terms of the interpersonal approach and its historical context. Richard Friedman, M.D., the former editor of *Psychodynamic Psychiatry*, helped me define my identity as a psychodynamic psychiatrist as he defined the field.

But of all my mentors, none compares to the profound influence of my father, Eugene Friedberg, M.D., who shaped who I am professionally as well as personally. I am forever grateful for his wisdom and immense good sense. I am grateful that he modeled endless patience and understanding, which taught me how to listen to, understand, and best respond to patients, as well as how to be the best version of myself. I am grateful for his example not only as a psychiatrist but also as a husband and father. From him I learned to live wisely and love wholeheartedly. He has been my mentor over a lifetime and, in delicate situations, I recur to what I know that he would do.

While I am not primarily a writer, my writing teachers have sharpened my sensibility. I'd like to cite in particular Donald Pease, the Geisel Professor in the Humanities at Dartmouth College, who supervised my Senior Fellowship thesis, and David Kasden, formerly Old Dominion Foundation Professor in the Humanities at Columbia University. Still, their influence pales in comparison to Sandra Sherman's. In all of my books with Routledge (this is the fourth), she has been invaluable, not just as a co-author but also as a teacher: her presence of mind within a scene, her consideration for the arc of a narrative, and her impeccable attention to detail have literally changed how I approach the task of writing. In *Faces*, Sandra helped me take years of notes and turn them into studies displaying an intrinsic emotional logic.

Finally, since this book is about love and its myriad variations, I would be negligent not to thank my wife, Tania Friedberg, who tirelessly supports my work and our family life.

Introduction

Life Studies in Psychoanalysis: Faces of Love was on my mind for years before I actually wrote it. The patients in these studies went through long courses of analysis. I would write up my notes, reflect on them, then stand back as the whole picture slowly began to emerge. I would think about the connection between these studies – what, for example, did one patient's fixation have to do with another's? How was an Oedipus complex related, if at all, to a repressed desire for one's sibling? Why, in other words, could I group these studies together? I thought about their commonalities, and went back and forth about whether the common denominator was love (in its myriad forms) or the process of psychoanalysis itself (which unfolds over time and reveals the complexities of human desire). Based on the title of this book, you know where I finally came out.

That is, *Faces* concerns both phenomena. It explores the nature of some aspects of love insofar as they are explored psychoanalytically. I consider love – how it can obsess us, how it can distort our other relationships – but also how psychoanalysis can mediate between the subject/patient and the object of love so that neither harms the other (and, in fact, how both might enhance each other's lives). So, ultimately, *Faces of Love* demonstrates how some of my patients, troubled by romantic, sexualized, fantasized, illicit, and/or uncontrollable desires, learn through psychoanalysis to accommodate their desires to what is possible and permissible in the lives that they otherwise inhabit. In this sense, the studies included here are journeys from a place characterized by the epiphenomena of troubled love – grief, guilt, frustration – to one in which, through enhanced self-awareness, patients understand the sources and implications of their motivations. They begin to understand why love has seemed like a minefield, and begin to find a more fulfilling path through it.

Once I realized this book's general direction, I also had to reckon with its boundaries. Clearly, it was not about Love in the abstract. Each patient had a profoundly unique experience that – even when set against all of the others' – still did not present a rounded picture of how we experience love. There was an inescapable pointillistic quality to these studies. They were about some

DOI: 10.4324/9781003352624-1

aspects of love – intense, to be sure, but still individualized. Accordingly, I chose *Faces of Love* as a title because no two faces are the same and we can never see all the faces in the world. I am looking at how love sometimes is expressed, and why it may lead to treatment in psychoanalysis.

Additionally, at the back of my mind was the recent work in neuroscience on facial recognition. In *Origins of Human Socialization* (2021), the prominent neuroscientist Donald Pfaff examined *how* we recognize faces, in context with emphasizing the importance of that capacity to human sexuality:

> A deep neurobiological issue related to the phrase "sexual attraction" is how we are able to recognize faces. If you know nothing else about the science of facial recognition, you know from online dating that a face can be instantly attractive or an instant turn-off. If you don't like someone's face, you won't read the profile that they posted.

"Faces" is a resonant term, suggesting the range and subtlety of human sexual experience, as well as the inescapable fact that sexuality is biological, irrational, and as basic as any other urge controlled by areas of the brain that we are just coming to understand. Dealing with sexuality (as a psychotherapist, as a member of our species) is never easy.

Of course, while I am concerned with versions of love – which, like faces, can be infinite – it is still possible to see how these versions fall into alignment when approached through a psychoanalytic lens. We learn, for example, that repressed desire can continue during analysis, resulting in resistance by the patient to the analyst's attempts to help him (or her) acknowledge and confront such desire. It can result in hostility toward the analyst, who is blamed for causing still more pain. Thus, while each of these studies presents unique problems concerning the nature of troubled desire and its treatment, they nonetheless cohere at the level of certain basic concerns regarding how that treatment is likely to proceed. *Faces of Love* is, therefore, primarily intended for mental health practitioners interested to understand the psychoanalytic process of helping patients to deal with obsessive, conflicted desire.

As will be evident in these studies, the course of treatment is virtually never linear. There is no if-this-then-that quality about them as there is in decision-tree medical diagnosis. Sometimes, it appears that the treatment goes round in circles, returning again and again to where – seemingly – it was months before. Sometimes it appears that treatment moves sideways in directions that – seemingly – have nothing to do with the original complaint. Often, progress is characterized by backsliding to positions that previously seemed to have receded. This is all normal, a consequence of the patient's struggle with conflicts, fixations, obsessions, and ideas about themselves that they cannot or will not confront or at least accept. If they try, they fail, or make progress that frightens them in its implications – causing them, once again, to retreat. These studies convey the difficulties inherent in treatment under these circumstances.

Accordingly, *Faces of Love* is not a how-to prescription for how analysts should approach treatment issues incident to patients' intense, seemingly aberrant desires. It is realistic, an honest depiction of how treatment can seem to stall – until it doesn't. That is, these studies intend to illustrate approaches for helping resistant patients to remain involved in their treatment, even as they bargain, threaten, cajole, hide, and accuse in their attempts to be less than fully honest with themselves. Ultimately, if both parties hang in there, there is a breakthrough. It is not always complete, and not always entirely what anyone could have wished for, but it does represent a decided advance. The patient often emerges with tools to think about themselves even after therapy has concluded, so that whatever self-understanding they gained can continue to develop. Often, this is *all* that we can hope for, but it is significant.

The process is so difficult, in part, because when we speak of love, we necessarily broach the unfathomable issues surrounding human libido. In psychology, "libido" refers to a person's sex drive – that is, his or her desire for physical or emotional connection with another person. Not surprisingly, so basic an urge has etymological roots in Latin, as well as in the Greek term for a life force coursing through the world. Sigmund Freud considered libido as a kind of psychic energy, derived from the sexual instinct. But because his formulation evolved with his understanding of "instinct," it is hard to pin down. In *Three Essays on the Theory of Sexuality* (first published in 1905), libido is a kind of sexual desire in search of satisfaction in terms of objects. A fixation on one object can lead to psychopathology. Later in his thinking, libido was more like a force exerting pressure, tied in with narcissism and the ego. If it was not mastered, it could manifest as anxiety.

In *Beyond the Pleasure Principle* (1920), Freud introduced the notion of Eros, expanding libido into a kind of life force. His disciple Carl Jung virtually ran with this idea and saw libido as embracing a "psychical energy" present in every tendency toward an object. This tied in with Freud's ideas about sublimation, a process postulated to account for human activity motivated by the force of the sexual instinct but with no apparent connection to the expression of sexuality – e.g., art, music, and all forms of creativity.

This capsule history demonstrates that starting with the Greeks, the sex drive has never been regarded as *just* the sex drive. Rather, in one iteration or another, it was responsible for a large share of human action. For Jacques Lacan, the famous French psychoanalyst, unconscious desire was his central professional concern, such that the aim of psychoanalysis should be to help the analysand recognize and articulate his or her desires. In his *Seminar* (1988), he argued that in naming such desire, "the subject creates, brings forth, a new presence in the world" (presumably, not just that of sexual being).

Lacan believed that the need for love is never fully met because no one can fully provide unconditional love. Thus, while desire has its immediate objects, the real – ultimate – object is missing and unattainable. One case study in *Faces* concerns a man yearning for his sister, which might have been taken directly from Lacan's teaching.

In this vein, we have all heard of the Greek notion that we are each searching for our other, missing half – and that "love" occurs when we find it. In our own contemporary mythology, the goal is to find one's soulmate. Dating sites promise to match members across dozens of dimensions (e.g., politics, religion ... everything but the instant chemistry that anyone can recognize at once). Nonetheless, Plato deserves credit for his early, detailed anatomy of love. In the *Symposium* (~385 B.C.), he enumerated different kinds of love, ranging from Eros (sexual) and Agape (whose object is nature and God), to Ludus (playful and fun), Philautia (self-love), and the love between parents and children. While we would add more categories and shadings, his basic approach – that love has many facets – reminds us, once again, that everything is just a "footnote" to Plato.

But important footnotes.

As I suggested earlier, neuroscience has a lot to say about sexuality. What interests me here is its recognition that desire is *always* present; it cannot be confined by moral strictures or binary gender categories. As Donald Pfaff states in *Origins*, sex is "fundamental," a structural element of human identity:

> Men engage in polygamy, women in polyandry. But this morals-defying behavior just underlines my point: *sex persists no matter what* [orig. italics]. It is such a basic impulse that we do not need any cultural approval to throw it into stark relief – that is, to demonstrate how baked into human conduct it is. That is, the prejudice against infidelity is moral – a social construction – and has nothing to do with the continuing attraction of one sex to the other (or, as I suggest below, the attraction of one differently oriented person to another, compatible person). Even when sex is available on the other side of the bed, some go looking for more. ... So, my point is that no matter how we slice up the social construction of sex and gender, some form of initial sexual attraction is a natural form of the fundamental human social impulse.
>
> (Pfaff, 2021)

I quote this passage at some length because it blows past all the taboos and conventions surrounding sex and, from a purely scientific perspective, argues that the sex drive – the libido – is not somehow beneath our humanity but fundamental to it.

In the next section of this introduction, I describe some foundational concepts from psychoanalysis that underlie these studies, and that will help the reader understand how the process operates in context with problematic desire. Of course, neither these basic ideas nor the discussions themselves is comprehensive. I could not even try with a book on each subject. After more than a century of clinical practice, there is no full agreement even as to what constitutes "psychoanalysis."

The Unconscious   For Freud, the Unconscious was both descriptive, connoting mental contents not present in consciousness, and topographical, encompassing a system in the mind whose contents have been denied access to consciousness because they are repressed. It operates with its own set of rules (primary process) in contrast to conscious mental life (secondary process).

Repression (of thoughts, feelings, desire) can produce an array of symptoms, including guilt, depression, anxiety, inhibition, or neurotic conflict. Certain repressed mental contents in the Unconscious become accessible to consciousness (and, hence, the symptoms can abate) only as resistance to the process is overcome. This is the primary work of psychoanalysis, which helps patients to articulate and acknowledge whatever they have repressed.

In *The Interpretation of Dreams* (1900), Freud called dreams the "royal road" to the unconscious. They are expressed through the patient's free associations, and interpreted by the analyst. Dreams, daydreams, and fantasies are often integral to psychoanalytic work.

Free Association   This is the basic method of psychoanalysis. A patient voices all the thoughts, feelings, fantasies, and desires that enter his or her mind as freely, fully, and spontaneously as possible. The method grew out of Freud's hypnotic approach in *Studies on Hysteria* (1895), and developed into the main approach for exploring a patient's unconscious mental life.

But what does "free" association mean? Ideally, voluntary selection of thoughts and other mental productions are minimized, such that patients become freer in their associative process, thereby gaining greater access to their pre- or unconscious mental life. The analyst's observations and interpretation of the patient's verbalizations provide insight into aspects of the patient's mental life of which he or she may have been unaware or conflicted about.

Transference   A process of the mind through which unconscious wishes, fantasies, and other incidents of a past relationship are carried into and actualized in the present. Thus, in the psychoanalytic setting, early childhood relationships are experienced in a strong and immediate way in relation to the psychoanalyst. This provides the analyst the opportunity to observe and interpret the transference and, accordingly, help the patient. Some psychoanalysts would actually argue that a patient can only be cured if he or she develops a transference neurosis, which is resolved in the course of treatment.

Transferences characterize many of our relationships. For example, a boss, doctor, or other authority figure may represent aspects of your relationship with your father. However, the strictness and constancy of the psychoanalytic situation allows a transference to emerge more fully, and to be subjected to inquiry. Understanding the transferences of a patient (and the analyst's counter-transferences) allows the analyst to both parties to grasp elements of early childhood relationships and work through them in the course of treatment.

Working Through   An integral part of the psychoanalytic process, which constitutes much of both parties' work, and which Freud described in "Remembering, Repeating and Working Through" (1914) as a fundamental aspect of treatment. In practice, "working through" allows a patient to more fully accept repressed elements of his or her unconscious that have remained tenacious. The analyst's interpretations are key to unlocking repressed mental contents that are then worked through. Thus, in *Inhibitions, Symptoms, and Anxiety* (1926), Freud characterized working through as a process that frees a patient from the unconscious constraints and conflicts that have caused his or her symptoms. As a patient becomes more conversant with his or her resistances, he or she is better able to "work through" them.

These concepts animate the studies in *Faces of Love*. Thus, in the first study, I examine how a young man works through conflicts that prevent him from dealing with an Oedipal complex that menaces the men in his family. The treatment (which delves into a tangled matrix of obsession) becomes especially challenging because the patient's ostensible obsession with his father is a defense against acknowledging his intense feelings for his mother, which need to be acknowledged as the major source of his anti-paternal obsession. For a long time, we try to see past – or, rather, through – the patient's familial/erotic history, attempting to clarify unacknowledged motivations that shaped his history and still affect him.

In the second study, a woman's quest for romantic love is continually disrupted by self-defeating fantasies. Our objective was to mitigate those fantasies, which kept morphing and recurring as her treatment proceeded. Yet whenever we seemed to be getting somewhere, the fantasy would emerge in some new guise, and we would suffer another setback (albeit still on course to "getting somewhere"). Frequently, I would be blamed, since I was a male and, hence, just as likely to inflict pain as any man she went out with. The study is, in large part, about the influence of transference. But nothing was simple with this patient. At times, she wanted to be my mother and my lover. Her fantasies about men were potent, and helping her to grasp at reality (and remain in treatment) could be challenging.

The third study is named "Gatsby" after the eponymous hero of a great American novel (Fitzgerald, 1925) who, like my patient, organizes his life around a false, inflated image of himself that he displays in public, while in private he lacks self-esteem. Also as in *Gatsby*, my patient is obsessed with the forbidden pursuit of an unattainable woman. The consequences of his obsession are dramatic, and contribute to the disparity between his public persona and his reality. He constructs a persona based primarily on appearance because he cannot face his true, indeed illicit, motivations.

It takes years for this patient even to acknowledge his feelings, much less deal with them. The study examines the power of desire to take hold of us, and our resistance to letting go of fantasies that support our ability to sustain such desire. It is only as he finally acknowledges his illicit desire that the pall it created begins to recede. But the journey is hard, and he suffers relapses. The tortuous course of his therapy recapitulates his conflicts. Ultimately, the study is about the intersection of two faces of love – sexual obsession and our regard for ourselves – and how, in therapy, a patient tries to address them both.

The fourth study concerns a young man conflicted over an aggressive masculinity that his father imposes. He struggles to define his own maleness, complicated by what he feels are his feminizing, homoerotic tendencies. In his more "feminine" mode, he has contempt for his father, especially with regard to his father's indifference to his mother's sensibilities. The family dynamic remains a source of troubling self-doubt, as well as anger at patriarchal figures whose swagger he nonetheless tries to emulate. He finally comes to see me – though I too am a "patriarch" – seeking help with how to be a male on his own terms. But the problem is that as the therapy proceeds, he feels the need to compete with me, to prove me ineffectual and unable to help. Thus, he falls into a contradiction from which it is a challenge to escape. We work through this contradiction, actively analyzing his dreams that reveal an attraction to violence that also distorts his relationships with women.

Of course, all four studies are fine-grained and complex. My goal (to the extent that it is possible) is to situate the reader inside the conversation between the patient and myself as it unfolds over the course of analysis. I provide my real-time reflections. Thus, the studies seek a sense of immediacy because, as psychoanalysts, we are often required to reflect spontaneously on a dream or unanticipated, suddenly recovered memory or association. They hide neither my excitement nor my exasperation.

Finally, in seeking to protect my patients' confidentiality, I have generally followed the principles recently set out by the AMA's Committee on Publication Ethics (COPE), as well as in Glen Gabbard's earlier, highly regarded "Disguise or Consent: Problems Concerning the Publication and Presentation of Clinical Material" (2000). I changed patients' names and deleted or changed any identifying material. The dialogues reflect my conversations in treatment but, again, they have been scrubbed to ensure my patients' privacy.

References

Committee on Publication Ethics (COPE). "Journals' Best Practices for Ensuring Consent for Publishing Medical Case Reports: Guidance from COPE." https://doi.org./10.24318/cope.2019.6

Fitzgerald, F. Scott. *The Great Gatsby* (New York: Charles Scribner's Sons, 1925)

Freud, Sigmund. *Beyond the Pleasure Principle* (New York: Norton, 1920, 1961)

Freud, Sigmund. *Inhibitions, Symptoms, and Anxiety* (New York: Norton, 1926, 1990)

Freud, Sigmund. *The Interpretation of Dreams* (New York: Basic Books, 1900, 2010)

Freud, Sigmund. "Remembering, Repeating and Working Through," *Standard Edition of the Complete Psychological Works of Sigmund Freud* 12, 147–56 (1914)

Freud, Sigmund. *Three Essays on the Theory of Sexuality* (London and New York: Verso, 1905, 2017)

Freud, Sigmund, and Joseph Breuer. *Studies on Hysteria* (London: Penguin, 1895, 2004)

Gabbard, Glen. "Disguise or Consent? Problems and Recommendations Concerning the Publication and Presentation of Clinical Material," *International Journal of Psychoanalysis* 81 (6), 1071–86 (2000)

Lacan, Jacques. *The Seminar of Jacques Lacan: Book II: The Ego in Freud's Theory and in the Technique of Psychoanalysis 1954–1955* (New York: Norton, 1988)

Pfaff, Donald. *Origins of Human Socialization* (London: Academic Press, Elsevier, 2021)

Plato. *The Symposium* (London: Penguin, 2003)

Chapter 1

A Complex Oedipus Complex

The Oedipus complex defines what Freud termed the intrapsychic organization of loving and hostile desires that a child experiences toward its parents. The locus classicus of this idea is Sophocles' Oedipus Rex, *where Oedipus unwittingly kills his father and marries and beds his mother. In a boy, this desire for the death of his father, whom he perceives as a rival, and sexual desire for his mother form the basis of his phallic stage of development (ages 3 to 6, where the infant's libido centers on its genitalia and erogenous zones). During puberty, this phase is revived and mastered to varying degrees through love for another person. In this way, the Oedipus complex is fundamental in structuring personality and desire.*

Psychoanalysis makes the Oedipus complex a center for psychopathology, a nucleus of neurosis, whose pull can produce multiple symptoms and conflicts. By uncovering its hidden structure in terms of personal experience from childhood – love of the mother, jealous rivalry with the father, and all the associated twists and turns – a person becomes more aware of its impact, and correspondingly freer from the conflicts it engenders.

Modern usage of the term "Oedipus complex" derives from Sigmund Freud and, in his formulation, included an element of genital obsession. But while we know what the term describes, we also know that in practice the consequences are often varied and complex. First, Oedipal conflicts like other intrapsychic conflicts are unconscious and play out in ways that may remain unrecognizable even to those affected. Such was the case in Oedipus Rex. *So, a son may just be hyper-competitive with his father on the tennis court or at chess. Or perhaps he turns on himself, with a persistent need – accompanied by guilt and nagging resentment – to live up to his father's professional accomplishments. Ideally, as the son passes through the Oedipal phase of development, he identifies with his father and the rivalry is resolved.*

But what if it isn't resolved? It may play out in negatively competitive ways with teachers, bosses, and other authority figures. And what if, moreover, it escapes the confines of conventional conflict and turns nasty, even self-defeating or dangerous? This can happen, often because a person's underlying conflicts

DOI: 10.4324/9781003352624-2

remain unresolved, causing their Oedipal tendencies to fester and turn into rage. At that point, professional help may be necessary so that the person can become aware of – and finally deal with – whatever is preventing him from resolving his Oedipal conflict.

In this study, I examine the process of how one patient learns to understand the layered, complicated conflicts that have prevented him from dealing with an Oedipal complex that – at least insofar as it threatens the men in his family – comes perilously close to its original, frightening conception. I use the term "layered" advisedly, since as the patient and I begin to explore his history and motivations, his Oedipal urges emerge as deeply rooted in an intrapsychic matrix that needs to be unraveled, exposed, and analyzed. This takes time, as one layer of conflict opens up onto another, submerged beneath it.

The treatment becomes especially challenging because the patient's ostensible obsession with his father is a defense against acknowledging his intense unconscious feelings for his mother, which need to be acknowledged as the major source of his anti-paternal obsession. It emerges that these feelings had always been highly sexualized; that his mother was more stimulating than most in this regard; and that her behavior was oriented more toward attracting her son (which, apparently, gratified her ego) than toward supporting his independence in mature relationships. To succeed with women, he first had to reframe his relationship with his mother.

Thus, while the treatment attempts to probe ever more deeply – bringing up new concerns, which the patient must assimilate – it is hardly linear. That is, we do not proceed directly in expanding our understanding of why the patient feels as he does and how he can address it. Rather, we find elements, factors, pieces of the matrix that will slowly fall into place and provide a picture of how the patient has developed – and how, therefore, he can understand himself and his obsessions, and better resolve his conflicts.

As you read this study, you should expect it to veer into subjects that do not seem directly related to the basic question: how can this patient resolve his Oedipal conflict? This is because I have rendered this patient's treatment with verisimilitude – that is, as it actually happened over the course of several years as we continued to pursue it. Eventually, the raw data begin to cohere but, if you are to see how it does so, then you must follow the process along often unpredictable byways. You may experience the same impatience that the patient experiences. But, at the same time, you will see the treatment actually take hold.

The bottom line is that even a stubborn, deep-seated Oedipus complex is amenable to treatment, provided that the patient and psychoanalyst have the commitment and the stamina to remain engaged.

The treatment described here is an example of classical psychoanalytic technique. It is based in interpretation of a patient's unconscious mental life – e.g., fantasies, wishes, and dreams – so that the unconscious will become available as part of the patient's conscious awareness. In this process, the patient engages in free association, while the analyst provides observations that enhance the patient's insight and understanding. The transferential relationship serves as a "cradle" for the analysis to develop and, as it develops, it is often inflected with aspects of core relationships from the patient's childhood. This provides a context to work through the patient's psychological conflicts, so that healthier compromise formations may emerge. Analysis of the patient's resistance to free association also facilitates treatment.

When he arrived at my office, Bobby was short on formalities. We shook hands, he plopped into a chair, and declared: "I have to be straight with you. Sometimes I want to kill my father. My older brother too."

In the moment, I was stunned. This patient was so literal, as if he'd stepped out of *The Interpretation of Dreams*, where Freud first described the Oedipus complex. I wondered about his motivation. Was I being tested, maybe to see if I'd express surprise, even call the police? Was this an attempt to see if I'm shockable? Maybe this guy was pleading for help, convinced that the only way to elicit a response was to send up flares. I looked for clues in his demeanor.

Bobby was tall and athletic, 29 years old. His brown hair was long. But what struck me was the studded bomber jacket and black T-shirt, with black jeans ripped at the knee. He dressed like a throwback rebel. Marlon Brando in *The Wild Ones*. He looked cool all right, but not quite what you'd expect from a potential murderer.

Perhaps more like someone still dealing with adolescent masculinity and coming into his own as a man.

So, after calibrating Bobby's declaration with the demeanor evidence, I decided that no one was in immediate danger – though that didn't rule out an array of still-scary possibilities. I asked whether he was *provisionally* plotting mayhem, sort of on a long runway, depending on whether or how circumstances in his family developed.

"Well, after you get to know me, you can decide," he said. "But I can tell you right now, I fantasize about doing one of them in. It gives me a lot of satisfaction." Then he smiled, mischievously.

Fantasies *can* precede action. But Bobby was clearly not on a knife's edge. I was reassured he wasn't going to flip out. Still, over the years, I have learned never to dismiss fantasies as harmless. A troubled patient – maybe one who is psychotic – can give in to them (and hide them very well). But the fact that Bobby had sought me out, rather than harboring destructive tendencies, was encouraging. I asked him to describe how he was feeling lately.

He said he was usually "anxious and depressed," especially at night. This led to drinking bouts. He also smoked marijuana, often before his part-time job delivering for Amazon.

"I want to cut down on the pot and booze," he said. "But I can't control it. It's like the fantasies – everything feels out of my control." This sounded like a classic abdication of responsibility – a sort of refusal to grow up. Maybe, harking back to Freud, Bobby was stuck in some genital obsession, unable to accept his own manhood. Maybe he was still competing with his father for his mother's love. Maybe he had come for help with getting his obsession under control.

This seemed a reasonable hypothesis. If Bobby felt powerless to give up drugs, he was (so he acknowledged) just as unable to wash the dishes, shovel the driveway, or take the computer in for repairs.

I was not surprised when he admitted that he'd dropped out of college several times over the past six years. Now he was having trouble getting readmitted. His father, a humanities professor and film critic, was distressed by Bobby's performance. As Bobby put it, "The old man is at his wits' end over this shit." He grinned. But perhaps his academic failure was a way of getting at his father, just as *repeated* failure was a way of twisting the knife.

"Has it occurred to you that failing at school is a way of realizing your fantasies?" I inquired.

"Maybe I am trying to get back at him." Perhaps unwittingly (and just for a moment) he'd grasped the line that I was actually pursuing.

Bobby would start each semester energetically, but then just stop doing the work. There was a pattern, the same one that I suspected with regard to his other to-dos. But here, in addition to avoiding responsibility, was another element: Bobby's father was predictably upset every time he fell behind.

Yet while I cited this pattern to Bobby, he was reluctant to fully acknowledge his role in it. He made excuses.

"I know school's important …" he sighed. "But I get distracted. I waste time reading trashy novels or watching TV. I know I'm avoiding something, but I don't know what." Bobby was "avoiding" responsibility. He knew, at some level that he was hurting himself ("school's important"), but he had to come around to seeing how that was a way of hurting his father as well. So long as he wanted to keep hurting his father, he would keep hurting himself – at least insofar as that kept him from succeeding at school. It was passively aggressive and masochistic.

I had seen this boomerang dynamic before, where in order to hurt those who love us, we unconsciously hurt ourselves. I wanted Bobby to see what was going on, and thought that if he spoke more about his family, we'd turn the conversation toward their investment in his success. If he acknowledged that investment, he'd see how he was hurting them, living out an Oedipal dynamic and his guilt about it.

But at first Bobby described his parents blandly. Even though he had displayed a facility for colorful language, he seemed deliberately to avoid getting beneath the surface. He mentioned that his father was "crippled and wrote" but was reluctant to say more. "Self-involved and successful" served to sketch out his brother, who was also the object of homicidal fantasies. His mother was "a nurse."

He was reluctant to provide a fuller family history. In fact, talking about his family made him uncomfortable. Out of an acute sense of guilt, perhaps, he now seemed anxious to bury the confession he'd made virtually upon entering my office. Instead, he wanted to focus on what seemed to him more immediate issues: his drug and alcohol use, his ex-girlfriend, school. Still, he acknowledged it would be necessary at some point "to look at what all this was really about."

That is, where I saw a profound connection between Bobby's so-called immediate problems and his Oedipal fantasies, he wanted to use these problems to avoid those fantasies. In the worst-case scenario, he would have to perpetuate those problems in order to continue avoiding any discussion of those fantasies. His proposed course was self-defeating, which, of course, would also hurt his father. He'd drawn himself into a vicious circle.

But it was pointless to confront him with what I saw as obvious and he seemed to deny. I decided that we'd try to deal with what he now wanted to consider, in hopes that all of his problems – including his Oedipal fantasies – would emerge as some kind of coherent "complex" that we could finally address. I was at least minimally hopeful, since other patients had attempted to switch gears during treatment when facing their most painful, underlying issues seemed just too painful to endure. Often patients need to develop confidence that they can deal with at least *some* problems before facing what seem like really tough ones.

The rebel

In discussing my fee, Bobby brought up his modest savings and low-wage job as a delivery guy. He'd previously been employed as part of a film crew, where he'd earned considerably more, and he'd also been offered a respectable salary writing for a local paper. But neither career path initially interested him. He claimed to like the "hands-on" quality of his current, blue-collar work, and felt "pumped-up" by the manual labor. It also, he said, gave him time to read.

But I didn't buy it. I thought he was just avoiding pressure. If he took a newspaper job (he liked to write) he'd have had an editor to answer to; he'd have to deal with criticism of his work; and he'd be on deadline. In other words, he'd have to *perform* and be judged on his performance. Delivering packages put him under no such scrutiny.

The low wages were, moreover, just another excuse to avoid growing up. Bobby lived in a studio apartment with his cat Motor, who would make an engine sound when he purred. Bobby and his girlfriend, Sally, had broken up several months earlier. While he kept the cat and the apartment, she made plans for medical school.

But beneath this down-market compromise, Bobby was seething with rage. Dressing up like a bad-boy biker is a classic gesture in American culture signifying defiance. "We're the one-percenters," a Hell's Angel told Hunter

S. Thompson, "the one percent that don't fit in and don't care." But my guess, even early on, was that Bobby *did* care; that he felt the bad-boy role didn't quite suit. Perhaps because he felt rejected, he was now rejecting the middle-class status – and the comforts of a middle-class family – that he actually wanted. So, he projected the image (and adopted the behavior) of a defiant adolescent, rather than an adult. Lashing out at his father was a way of cementing his position, stunting his maturation.

Surrounded by dead and wounded

As we proceeded with psychotherapy, a fuller picture of Bobby's family history emerged. His father suffered from multiple sclerosis and, from the time Bobby was 5, his father's physical condition had progressively deteriorated until he was wheelchair-bound. A well-built man who'd always drawn attention to himself, Bobby's father had gotten louder and, according to Bobby, more obnoxious as his illness progressed.

"The way he cries out for help is pure melodrama," Bobby said. "It's embarrassing."

As Bobby was growing up, the two got into frequent arguments.

"Once, when I was 17," Bobby reported, "we actually came to blows."

"How did that happen?" I asked.

Bobby shrugged. "He tried to keep me from going out. I'd had enough of him telling me what to do, trying to control and manipulate me. I reeled back and punched him in the face. He fell to the floor and broke his nose. I felt terrible."

Here was an unmistakable instance of Bobby's rage. How could anyone, let alone a son, punch a cripple? The punch was a kind of warm-up for all the mental mayhem to follow. In a way, it was less about his father's "control," and more about Bobby's proving to himself that he could get back at his father decisively. If he could throw a punch and hurt his father, he could find other ways. In fact, he did.

His brother, Rick, blamed Bobby for aggravating their father's physical problems.

Judging by Bobby's description of Rick, who was four years older, his brother was narcissistic, selfish, and ambitious. Growing up, Rick had been the center of their parents' attention and was used to getting his way. In one incident that remained stuck in Bobby's mind, Rick muscled Bobby into a corner of his bedroom, filling it with exercise equipment and making it into his personal gym.

"I'd sit on the bed, watching him, and think how I wanted to put a barbell through his fucking head. My parents did nothing."

In young Bobby's mind, his father had failed in his most basic function: to protect his child. His mother had failed too, but Bobby's rage was reserved for his father and secondarily for Rick, toward whom he felt hopelessly inferior.

In addition to the four-year age difference, plenty of other things made Bobby feel like the lesser light. Both had studied Shotokan karate, an aggressive form of the martial arts. But while Rick became a third-degree black belt, Bobby got injured and dropped out. Both had chosen writing as their field. Bobby, however – an English major and aspiring screen writer – couldn't even complete his B.A. Rick had excelled as a journalism major and now had a column in a daily paper. He had even published a popular novel.

Bobby envied Rick's success, claimed to hate him, and reiterated his desire to do him in. But he was obviously conflicted, even if he didn't say so. He had lent Rick money and, together, they bought their mother a birthday gift (when he charged Rick a few dollars extra for his share, he felt remorse). He even gave Rick a favorite chair "so he'd be comfortable" in college. What was up here? Did Bobby really hate his brother, or was Rick some sort of straw man for their father? I wanted to tease him out on this.

But Bobby's motivations were elusive. He seemed filled with generalized fantasies of murderous rage. At one point, he stared at the wall, recalling a dream, "I'm a warrior in battle. Most men around me are dead or wounded. I'm out of ammo and facing my deadliest opponent in hand-to-hand combat." He made it sound as if it was Bobby vs. the World.

When I pointed out that this was not exactly an answer – how was Bobby's anger at his brother related to that toward his father? – he became defensive about his brother, saying how he'd always do the right thing for him. The cognitive dissonance was surprising. All I could conclude was that Bobby's resentment toward Rick was derivative. That is, because his parents favored Rick, and let him get away with murder (so to speak), Rick was a kind of weaker stand-in for his father and had to be put in his place (that is, put in his father's place and done away with just like him). Whether Bobby understood this dynamic at this point in treatment was doubtful. How I could help him understand it was also an issue, not least because he resisted when I even tried to explore his relationship with Rick.

A wake-up call

One man whom Bobby admired was a great-uncle who'd "done his own thing," a rebellious intellectual who'd fraternized with gangsters and bigwigs during the 1950s and '60s. Bobby's preoccupation with Uncle Milt mapped onto his romanticization of the biker and perpetual outcast.

Several months into Bobby's treatment, Uncle Milt died. But when Bobby went to visit his apartment, he was instantly disillusioned. The place was infested with roaches. There was pornography around, and it was filthy. Bobby was suddenly terrified that he would end up the same.

Up to this point, Bobby had been mourning the loss of Sally. They had taken drugs together, and blown past social and sexual norms. Yet while she'd now moved on with her life, he remained stuck. This inability to let go, plus the sight of his uncle's degradation, plunged Bobby into near-paralysis. He was at once terrified and unsure of what to do.

He thought that if he could only get Sally back, he'd want to "perform" up to her standard. But he also knew that Sally was now on a trajectory of her own. We decided that he'd try coming to see me twice a week. The discipline – arriving at a certain place at a certain time – felt reassuring. "If I can show up for you, maybe I can show up for class." This was progress, in a way. At least he understood where he didn't want to end up.

Just finish

Yet while Bobby was in school again, he was (as always) falling behind. He had survived the midterms but, with finals looming, he was in danger of failing. He became increasingly obsessed about his failing to do the work.

I interpreted this failure as part of his continuing complex: competing with his father, rivalry with his brother, and the associated masochism. When I said so, he typically responded "Yeah, but ..." or "So what?" Correspondingly, he began to come later and later, arriving for one session when it was halfway through.

"You see what you're doing, right?" I asked. "Coming late is passively showing anger toward me. You're trying to defeat my efforts to help you just as you've frustrated your father. He wants you to do well, so to spite him you flunk a class." If Bobby had shown some signs of progress, he was now pitched into reverse. He had a pattern of putting himself out there and then knocking himself down. It was all in the service of avoiding responsibility, not least for himself. It was a way of remaining stuck in the early stages of an Oedipal conflict. Bobby wanted and didn't want to grow up.

When I said he was out to defeat me, he didn't disagree. But nothing changed.

Like Bobby's father, I was becoming frustrated.

"Why don't you think about why you need to thwart people who are trying to help you?" I asked. "Let's see if we can get at that underlying problem."

As though his most pressing concern was where he'd rally with some bikers after putting up with his shrink, he said, "I don't feel like talking about it."

I half expected he'd add *dude*. Losing my patience, I said, "Look, frankly, I couldn't care less how you do in school. Just *finish*."

Ultimately, he did complete the semester and got A's. This was an act of will on his own behalf. I thought that my sudden outburst – however intemperate – had set me apart from his father, who seemed stuck in a disapproving rut. Yet when I complimented him, he was dismissive, lumping me and his father together. "I just wanted to get you and my dad off my back." Clearly, he did not want to own his success, perhaps because he was afraid he couldn't live up to it. Also, perhaps, it confused him. He knew on some level that he wanted to undermine his father, so why did he take a step that would please his father? His Oedipal conflict still seemed in place. I hoped we could still explore it.

Into analysis

As summer approached, Bobby started talking about dropping out of treatment.

"I've got problems," he admitted. "Doesn't everyone?"

I felt like saying, *No, everyone doesn't want to murder a parent and, for good measure, a sibling* (well, maybe on some level). But instead, I observed that analysis was called for – more sessions per week, not cessation of treatment (classical analysis requires three or four visits per week, preferably even five). Bobby was put to a choice between virtual polar opposites. It felt like another tug-of-war between us. Finally, however, he said "Okay, you win," and agreed to up the ante on his treatment.

But even in agreeing, he apparently needed some male authority that he could cast in opposition, probably because he needed a foil that, he could tell himself, was keeping him from taking responsibility. It seemed that every time he made progress, there was some built-in mechanism to curtail it (i.e., to make it part of his unrelieved Oedipal complex). I was happy for his choice and I wasn't. He had put me in my place – as part of a hierarchy of male oppressors – even as announcing that I'd put him in his as the defeated, helpless victim. It felt frustrating. But I thought it best, on balance, to try to move ahead.

Yet even after clearing this hurdle, Bobby resumed showing up late to sessions. In addition to the Oedipal conflicts, I wondered about issues with intimacy and trust.

Once, when he was half an hour late, he apologized.

I said nothing.

We sat in silence. He rubbed a long scar on his left forearm. I glanced at it.

"I was 6," he offered. "Vacationing in Paris. My father was giving a lecture. Rick and I stayed at the hotel, playing. I was the lion and leapt from the chair. I broke my arm in three places. A bone stuck through my skin. It was in traction for two months."

After discussing this horrific accident, Bobby recognized that his resistance to analysis was associated, in part, with childhood experiences in which he'd gotten hurt. It was as if analysis infantilized him, made him feel vulnerable – just the way his brother did, let alone his father. That he also *wanted* to remain in a state of childishness, avoiding responsibility, didn't factor into the equation. It was just another contradiction.

So, we began a course of analysis.

Bobby had quit his delivery job and had talked himself into a writer's position at a local paper. Of course, he was quick to say that he'd only taken the job because it paid better. "This has nothing to do with my father," he added, apparently trying to retain his anti-patriarchal options and warn me against getting too close to his Oedipal fixations. Nonetheless, he was now a full-time student with a white-collar job. He had assumed more responsibility and asserted more control over his life, even as he sought to deflect from the significance of the change. He said he also needed the money to pay me.

In this position, he (legitimately) had less time to spare. I agreed to see him three times a week with the understanding that we would reevaluate the frequency as his schedule allowed.

The good father

Bobby returned from summer break depressed over a series of minor incidents – being blown off by a woman he'd asked out, backing down from a street fight, losing some of his fiction due to a computer glitch – which he experienced as injuries to his pride and sense of competence. I thought that the incidents translated into a sense of weakness, as if he lacked the moxie and manliness to stand up to his father. He remarked that the girl had "castrated" him.

Then Bobby made an association. "It's nothing. Just ... something to do with sleep-away camp. It's really not worth talking about."

But in his next session, as if he were confessing, he brought up a memory from his first summer at the camp.

"Everyone else was out of the bunkhouse. I had to go to the bathroom and was pissed about being away from home. I took a crap on the bunkhouse floor."

When the other campers and counselor returned, his specimen became an object of fascination.

"One kid wondered if it was animal or human. Another asked whose it was. I was embarrassed and excited at the same time."

I asked whether Bobby ever acknowledged his action. But Bobby pointed to another aspect of his dilemma: a complex of exhibitionism and hiding that he'd identified as one of his basic characteristics, starting as a young man: "I do and at the same time *don't* want you to see my anger as an object of fascination." Was everything in his self-presentation just a game, even a dare, that would entangle and untangle the participants according to his whim? Was his father in danger and not in danger? Was treatment making progress only to fall back into uncertainty and confusion?

I had a sense of breakthrough – here was a real motivation – accompanied by sensing the conundrum that Bobby created, that surrounded everyone involved with him. He was there and he wasn't, seeking help and avoiding it, fantasizing mayhem but ultimately chickening out.

Of course, there are times when a psychiatrist wonders where a patient is headed and whether treatment will ultimately be effective. This was one of those times. But I didn't tell him.

Still, Bobby's recollection of the incident – even if he did not fully appreciate its significance – helped him to speak more freely about his less-appealing tendencies, the ones he preferred to keep hidden. He mentioned a prostitute with whom he'd put himself at risk, and regressive sexual behaviors with Sally.

Sally

Although Bobby's relationship with Sally had ended more than a year earlier, he maintained the connection through a fantasy of the cat as their shared child. They'd adopted it together and, as I noted, he got custody when they split up. He identified with it as another helpless creature in need of love (whom Sally, of course, had jilted).

I had to point out that Motor was not a shared child or an aspect of himself. Perhaps that helped him begin to separate from Motor's "mother" and, in a sense, from his own since Sally (in his mind) was a version of his idealized mother – devoted, eternally inseparable from him, confirming his manhood through sexual conquest. I wanted to explore this idea of the sexualized mother since, of course, it was at the heart of Oedipal obsessiveness. In fact, Bobby seemed to lead us in that direction by depicting Sally as a version of the elusive mother whom he had described.

"You know," Bobby said, "Sally's self-involved. She's not responsive enough, not committed."

Bobby's concern with Sally's insufficiency reflected his mother's apparent unavailability to him as a child. During his childhood, his mother's attention had been taken up by her nursing career, her husband's disability, and Rick's achievements.

Yet I wondered, would any amount of his mother's attention have satisfied Bobby's Oedipal longing – that is, short of some fully sexualized involvement that could only have occurred in a fantasy that he might (but probably wouldn't) acknowledge? If he could talk more explicitly about Sally, he might become more open about his mother.

Sally was a tantalizing entrée into Bobby's Oedipal longings but, based on his reticence about his mother, I thought we'd have to wait for the connection to become clear to *him*.

However, Bobby did acknowledge that he'd seen Sally through the rose-colored prism as a wished-for version of the mother for whom he longed. Neither version had existed in actuality. But both such versions played a part in longings that seemed to give shape to, and intensify, the other.

So, I thought that if Bobby could admit that his fantasized Sally was gone, then he might jettison his obsession with his mother, and hence the Oedipal obsession with his father and brother. The Sally/mother figure was pivotal. But as Bobby kept playing yes/no games around Sally, he'd be stuck in a pattern that extended to his family – and the murderous fantasies surrounding them. Was he making an effort to stop holding onto this woman who, in effect, he had turned into an agent of his self-infantilization? Did he *see* where such perversity was leading with regard to his family dynamic?

In one session, while lamenting the time he'd wasted, Bobby mentioned a scenario of his cat dying: "I call Sally to ask whether she wants to see Motor one last time. We come together and cry."

"So, a child's dying brings the parents together?" I asked.

Bobby nodded. He thought that being in pain would make him attractive to a sympathetic woman.

"When I was a kid," he explained, "I had this fantasy that my parents would quit squabbling and come together over my pain. They'd drop their differences to take care of me."

Although that never happened, Bobby still sought a mother to comfort and care for him. When he should have been laying the groundwork for what he claimed to want – "a mature relationship" – he was wallowing in despair.

A Freudian slip demonstrated Bobby's sense of how his feelings for Sally were largely a carryover of earlier feelings toward his mother. While talking about how Sally could be unduly trusting, he said, "My mother needs me to take care of her."

"*Who* needs you to take care of her?" I asked.

"Did I really say *my mother*?" Bobby grinned sheepishly. Then he told me how he'd wanted to protect his mother from his father's verbal attacks. Working through the Sally/mother connection helped to clarify *why* he still fantasized about Sally (albeit in his fantasies, Sally was as much his protector and he was hers). In effect, Sally was the current incarnation of his mother, the acceptable female equivalent. Thus, it became increasingly clear that Bobby's mother was on his mind as much – if not more than – Sally, and that his *mother* was as important to him now as she had ever been, even if only subconsciously.

Sally was a kind of stalking horse. I still wanted to talk more directly about Bobby's mother. I was still waiting for the right opening.

In another session, he reflected on what the Sally of his obsessions meant to him in terms of his need to be loved by a beautiful woman. His associations were to his mother's turning her attention to "the star" of their family, Rick. Bobby had never been able to keep up with Rick. Feeling inferior, and suffering on account of it, became a means of gaining a woman's love. At least this was true insofar as stereotyped women want to care for men and, in this sense, exercise power over them. He described a fantasy of being hurt: "A female hand reaches through my spine and cuts it. For some reason that's pleasing."

Bobby was cultivating weakness, hence a lack of responsibility, hence a lack of maturity, as a means of attracting a woman. He just didn't count on most women's impatience with needy men. But even more to the point, he didn't see how such willed immaturity was based in his Oedipal desires. Could I help him understand the complex, layered motivations that were at once conscious and unconscious, willed and predetermined?

Bobby interpreted his fantasy in his own terms: "Ah, I see – *paralysis*. That relates to my dad."

Since his father was partially paralyzed, he got his mother's attention. Thus, it wasn't having his spine cut that was pleasing, but the motherly attention Bobby would receive if he too were paralyzed. Moreover, his Oedipal guilt was intensified by his father actually becoming progressively crippled during his childhood, which on some level he saw himself as causing.

In one dream, he was a decrepit, decaying city. In another, he was a lizard dying of thirst. He recalled how during early adolescence he'd feigned a series of illnesses to get attention from his mother. When CAT scans for his headaches and the GI workups for his stomach ailments were negative, he found other ways to be handicapped, which usually involved problems with schoolwork. Pain was his default position in his quest for love.

The moral masochist

One afternoon, I discovered that Bobby's hit list, which until now consisted of the closest male members of his family, had grown: he also wanted to kill Holocaust deniers passing out literature in the street. It wasn't so much outrage for the mass-murders the Nazis had perpetrated as for those perpetrated on him – Bobby saw his personal history reflected in the history of oppression against Jews. Rick's taking over his room with exercise equipment, for example, was a grave injustice committed against him. It was the Warsaw Ghetto. What began to emerge was the pent-up rage under Bobby's masochistic identification. That is, he wanted to be victimized as an outlet for his fury and violent tendencies. Another way he curtailed his aggression was by identifying with his crippled father.

Over several weeks, Bobby also recounted a series of dreams that displayed his intensely competitive feelings toward other men in his family. In one he was marrying his brother's wife while his brother looked on impotently. In another, he was sinking jump shots with a basketball while his wheelchair-bound father watched with envy. In other dreams, the competitive and aggressive content was slightly more veiled, such as those in which he is peeing on a typewriter or sitting in a chair that looks like mine.

As we continued to examine Bobby's family history, it became clear that Rick had inherited the Oedipal mantle from their father via their father's disability. That is, Bobby's aggressive feelings toward his brother contained aspects of Bobby's rivalry with their father.

With few if any paths to victory over Rick, Bobby's adolescent battle became a moral one: he vowed to be a better person than his brother. He would be "the good son" who was not concerned with money or "superficial trappings," who rejected the fame-and-fortune route that Rick had taken (of course, never acknowledging that Rick had simply made the most of his talents and gotten a responsible job).

"Congratulations on your triumph as the moral masochist," I quipped. "Good guys finish last but they get mom's love, don't they?"

Pain motivated Bobby. "Pain," his father insisted, "makes a man out of you." Being in pain took on a heroic quality, as Bobby tended to make his life into a battle. The psychodynamic was an extension of a childhood in which Bobby fought his needy father – as well as his self-involved brother – for his mother's attention.

Bobby recognized how he identified with his father's attitude toward pain. He didn't quite believe that his father "used" pain, the way he did, in an attempt to hold a woman. But he saw the effect that pain had in his father's relationship with his mother. That is, while his parents fought, his mother still devoted herself to his father's wellbeing. The difference, of course, was that Bobby was only a voluntary cripple. Could he give up being in pain as an approach, and compete for women by, say, acting like a mature adult?

This brought us to the topic of Rick. Bobby thought about his competitive feelings toward him. Some of these were healthy and motivating. But the toxic feelings were, like those toward his father, merely a means to keep him involved in an immature obsession. Maybe he could be persuaded or have more insight to see what a waste of time it was to hate Rick. Maybe he could just try to establish himself on his own turf.

I raised the possibility. At least, Bobby was coming to understand the source of his motivations, even if he hadn't yet found the will to deal with them effectively.

Problem student

After getting through the previous semester, Bobby was once again a problem student. He avoided doing assignments until absolutely necessary, and then worked frantically to hand them in. Maybe it was the pressure of school, his job at the paper, and seeing me three times a week. But maybe Bobby was just reverting to type. He came in one day with his old biker garb, sporting a pony-tail. I thought "here we go again."

In relation to missing a paper deadline, Bobby described a fantasy about his father's getting killed in a car accident, noting that it was "only a fantasy" but that it provided an excuse. Rather extreme, I thought.

His father was still on his hit list.

"You *still* feel that by not graduating, you're hurting your father," I said. It was also a passive solution to Bobby's competitive anxieties (he too wanted to be a writer).

Bobby conceded the point, but his behavior hadn't changed – or, rather, he had reverted after making progress. He went on finding ways to avoid doing schoolwork and writing. Once again, he started coming late for sessions and asking to cut back on their frequency.

What was it that kept pulling him back? He seemed unable to break free of a self-defeating compulsion, a fundamental contradiction of wanting and not wanting to get on with his life. He clung to an Oedipal conflict that was crippling, just as his father was crippled.

When I suggested that he was rebelling against me as a patriarchal disciplinarian, he agreed.

"Yeah," he said. "I infuriate a lot of people trying to help me."

Then he recalled the Saturday mornings when his father would wake him up, shouting "Get out of bed! Don't be so damn lazy!" He'd repeat the sentences like a pounding on Bobby's bedroom door.

"I fucking *hated* being woken up like that," Bobby said. "*Of course* I found ways to get back at him." I was providing another patriarchal wake-up call, equally resented. He also admitted trying to sabotage our work together by undermining himself academically.

When he did make an effort to come on time, he said he was frustrated by how slowly he was progressing.

I knew the feeling – about his lack of real change and his difficulties working through what he'd learned about himself. More than once I wanted to yell, *Don't be so damn lazy!*

But it wasn't laziness so much as a seemingly intractable resistance to letting go of obsessions with his former girlfriend, his mother, and, ultimately, his father. If pain was the only way (at least in his mind) to satisfy his need for love, then it would remain his MO unless we could displace it with another.

No doubt sensing my frustration, he repeated something else his father used to say: "Enough of this bullshit. You have to show more discipline. Do the work."

"You want me to yell at you for not being motivated," I asked, "the same way your father criticized you for not working harder?"

Bobby smirked. "I get a kick out of pissing off the old man." So, I was the Old Man.

He got a kick out of telling me how infuriating it was to commute to my office and pay me to invade his privacy.

Still, Bobby completed the coursework.

The only problem was that he'd failed to get a required signature from the Dean of Students (another patriarchal bully?). By neglecting this detail, he'd nearly prevented himself from attaining the goal that had for so long eluded him – he was like a mountain climber turning back within sight of the summit – but at the last minute, he secured the signature and permission to graduate.

When we discussed this incident, he claimed that his near-miss had been unintentional. The truth, however, was that with no other outlets, his Oedipal aggressions often turned inward, resulting in self-sabotage.

In any event, Bobby's decade-long struggle with academe was over, and he finally had his diploma. Now what?

The aspiring author

With school behind him, Bobby's Oedipal conflicts were refocused toward his writing or, rather, *not* writing. He talked about different ideas for stories, character sketches, and a novel, but perpetually found ways to frustrate any effort to commit them to print. He obsessed about not having enough time to sit at the computer, but there were plenty of other standbys – work, karate, psychotherapy ... fantasies about women.

"Writers write, Bobby. If you really wanted or needed to, you wouldn't make excuses," I said. "You'd make time."

Bobby finally admitted he avoided writing, usually by watching TV, eating, sleeping, or masturbating. Rick, meanwhile, was hard at work on his next book, which frequently alluded to their family. Their father had been busy as well, publishing a critically acclaimed action drama.

Bobby was envious. He ranted about how his brother had stolen ideas from sketches that *Bobby* had written. He raged against his father's hypocrisy in writing about potent males while depending on everyone around him.

"When I publish," he asserted, "it will be honest. Real literature. Totally original."

Putting this kind of pressure on himself made it hard for Bobby to write *any*thing. His dreams helped us unravel the writer's block. In one, he broke a ceramic while rearranging pictures in his father's house. He associated the incident with Moses' breaking the tablets of the Ten Commandments, and considered how, except for "do not kill," he'd broken every commandment (and he'd *wanted* to kill). In the dream, the house looked like a cathedral – God's house – with stone carvings on the walls. One relief depicted a sacrifice in which the head of a male was severed and bloody. Bobby saw himself as the sacrifice.

"Your violent inner life," I observed, "is connected to your writer's block. You imagine that if you express your anger openly, someone will get hurt. You see writing as an aggressive act that will further incapacitate your father."

Bobby felt that his father was dependent on him, and saw becoming more self-reliant as abandoning his father. Thus, in coming into his own, he could no longer be the "good son" who stayed home to care for his father in contrast to his selfish brother, who went out and made his name.

Opposing forces were at work here: Bobby resented his father, liked pissing him off, and went so far as to fantasize about killing him *even while* he wanted his father's love and approval. As we began to parse these conflicts, he had been struggling with the first chapter of a novel. It was to be a semi-autobiographical account of the New York writing scene. Though he still found ways to avoid working on the manuscript, the pages were adding up.

Somehow, appreciating the conflict as an actual approach/avoidance syndrome involved with writing a book was helpful. It concentrated his mind, at least in the moment. So, maybe he could use this enhanced awareness as a paradigm, and try to understand the conflicts underlying his love/hate relationship with the men in his family as well as his underlying desire for his mother's love.

Bobby gave a public reading that attracted a number of critics and literary professionals. A publisher expressed interest in seeing the finished work. Just maybe, he was on his way to becoming an author.

But then Bobby stopped writing.

Given his track record, I wasn't so surprised. With only a few chapters of his novel finished, he'd gotten everything he could reasonably have expected, but still acted as though he'd been dissed. The problem, it seemed, was that Bobby identified with his father-the-cripple, not the successful writer. The primary way he competed was to be a bigger cripple, which was vastly easier than being a better writer.

I ran this past Bobby.

He admitted, "You're right. This is something I need to get over."

Gingerly, he started writing again. He said he'd finish the novel.

Biker no more

Shortly after Bobby's thirtieth birthday, a little more than a year after he'd begun therapy with me, he walked into the office and I was taken aback.

"Something look different?" he asked with a sardonic smirk.

His hair was short.

"So ..." I smiled. "You decided to look like an adult?"

He'd mentioned the prospect of cutting his hair several times over the previous couple of weeks, but I hadn't expected him to do it. His hair, in spite of his mother's protestations and Rick's ridicule, had been shoulder length since he'd let it grow out as a teenager. For years, he took pride in it, along with his black garb, as a part of his bad-boy persona. He saw long hair as a classic sign of frontier virility, a sort of Davy Crockett emblem of strength and power.

About the same time the year before, he'd toyed with the idea of getting it cut, speaking of it as a rite of passage into adulthood. But he hadn't been ready to sacrifice the biker identity, which he'd defiantly nurtured for so many years. Yet another conflict, though unlike his many others, this was about a feature of personal identity with strong cultural resonance but no implications for his relationships. When he spoke about his hair, therefore, I realized how easily Bobby could slip between personae – e.g., victim and warrior – without trying to maintain a stable sense of himself. Just like he was Oedipally obsessed while asking me for help with his obsession.

I suspected that getting his hair cut was a form of castration in which, psychologically speaking, he felt he would lose his virility, becoming impotent and weak like his father. When I asked, he seemed to convey that not opening up was typically male. He evaded my inquiry and, instead, focused on frustrations at work, the scoundrels in the literary world, repetitive fantasies about various women, and his writer's block. There were long silences, as if he were holding onto his (version of) maleness which he'd reified in Oedipal obsession.

Finally, out of frustration, I said, "Getting you to talk is sometimes like pulling teeth."

Bobby looked surprised and laughed. "You know, my mother used to say the same thing."

Here we identified another aspect of our relationship – that is, how he withheld his emotional life as a way of depriving me. Similarly, he'd withheld himself in order to get his mother's attention and love. He'd also withheld doing what he was supposed to in order to punish his mother for turning her attention to other men in the family.

But after Bobby's haircut, other aspects of his self-presentation began to change. The black in his wardrobe gave way to color – first, a mustard yellow T-shirt, then an Oxford-blue button-down, and eventually other outfits with a mix of hues and patterns. He had become, so he said, less abrasive and more compliant in his dealings with other people, his boss in particular.

Apparently, as we covered the same conflictual ground again and again – albeit from slightly differing approaches – he'd achieved a deeper understanding and decided it was time to grow up. Or, rather, to affect the outward signifiers of adulthood like a proper haircut.

It was harder to translate his insights into behavioral change that culminated in giving up his Oedipal fantasies. He knew that he *needed* the conflicted self-images he'd clung to – victim, warrior, persecuted son of a powerful but crippled father. These roles made him feel special. But they were also profoundly limiting, intrapsychic constructions that did not correspond to any life that he *could* live (if he let himself). Perhaps, if he acknowledged the possibility of living without these constructions, he could further create a new self-image.

Two steps back

After partially recovering from writer's block, Bobby started coming late again. He even mentioned dropping out of treatment. Why? In his mind, he'd overcome a huge obstacle – not allowing murderous fantasies to gum up his schoolwork and other matters – so that he could now proceed on his own. It wasn't as if he had actually ditched those fantasies; it was just that he now felt entitled to act as if he had. I suggested that he was getting ahead of himself and, possibly, putting at risk the progress he'd made. But he was adamant. He announced plans to travel for six months, then take a job with a major newspaper out of state.

"Don't you think you might just be escaping, cutting the Gordian Knot, as it were, instead of resolving persistent conflicts?" I asked.

Bobby didn't answer the question, but kept on the same track: "Look," he said, "I appreciate how you've helped me, but I'm a lot better, and now I don't want therapy holding me back."

So, therapy had flipped 180 degrees, from "help" to an impediment. It was as if Bobby was trying to create a much firmer distinction between a needy Before and a potent Future than actually existed. He was declaring himself empowered, effectively a man – ironically, by disavowing the psychological work it would take to get past his preoccupations more fully. When I didn't seem impressed, he took me on, insulting the work that we'd done together after he'd just praised it.

"All right," he said. "I still get a kick out of fucking up all the work we're doing. And, yes, it goes back to the anger I feel toward my father – but it's not worth my trouble anymore." Apparently, he could indulge his Oedipal fantasies without me – that is, the thrill was gone (or, at least, diminished).

"Okay, so you're done taking revenge on your father by hurting yourself?"

He nodded. "Yeah, I get it, but I still want to quit therapy."

"Maybe you're acting out," I suggested.

"What do you mean?"

"Maybe you're asserting yourself about leaving as a way of asking for my further attention. Which would mean, perhaps, staying in therapy."

He shrugged. "Could be."

He acknowledged that he was torn, and agreed to "try" therapy for a while. Try? What did he think he'd been doing all along? Was this another shot at me, as if what we had done together had barely happened? I felt that Bobby's anger at his father was raw and exposed, just sublimated slightly as he addressed me.

Back in analysis

Bobby was now in a position to commit to a fuller psychoanalytic experience. Four times a week would be consistent with our initial arrangement. He said he was willing but could not possibly pay for it.

"Suppose," I said, "we up you to psychoanalysis four-times-a-week but at the same monthly fee you're paying now? If your finances improve, we can always renegotiate."

He seemed touched by my offer, remarking that it distinguished me from his father, who, from Bobby's perspective, tried to control him with money (his father had once tried to bribe him to get good grades), and from his brother, whom he saw as cheap.

We had a deal, and he'd continue psychoanalysis at the increased frequency when he returned from his post-graduation vacation.

Fear and loathing of the blank page

Once again, writing had become the arena of Bobby's conflicts: "I call myself a writer," he said, "but I don't feel like writing."

I diagnosed the same old problem – getting back at his father by disappointing him. But there was also something more. Bobby was testing his father, seeking to be loved for who he was, not for what he could do.

Yet once again, Bobby's attitude was in a way perverse. He wanted to hurt his father by performing poorly, but he also wanted to out-compete him (and his brother) by producing superior literature. "Do you realize," I said, "that until you more fully resolve your Oedipal issues, you'll keep tying yourself in knots? You'll either tend to be paralyzed or stressed."

He didn't answer. Had I stumped him? Of course, even if I had, I felt stumped as well. How could I help Bobby when, in effect, he had trapped himself coming and going? I was accustomed to patients who made fitful progress, but this one made and unmade progress over and over again. It was a kind of vicious feedback loop. Finally, I just said "Bobby, you can help me help you more. You see the contradictions, but the question in our time together is how to help you move forward." There, I'd said it. I had issued a supportive challenge in favor of our work.

Rationality was Bobby's kryptonite. He hated when I dissected his behavior and left him no excuses – except for the sullen cop-out which, he knew, was unworthy of a co-equal interlocutor. Bobby confronted me.

Sheepishly, he said he'd set aside time each day to write. But, as it turned out, he'd write for an hour, then knock off. "I'm bored," he'd say. "I don't have any ideas." Could I call it to his attention or confront him for being disabled, ineffective, nobody special?

He was hanging around his apartment, reading. He especially liked prison literature, in which a man who was trapped managed to escape. The basic plot line affirmed Bobby's sadomasochistic fantasies of battling a powerful foe.

"Maybe," I commented, "to break out of your emotional bind, you need the vicarious experience of being bound. You can close the book, and you're free." The bind was his personal history with family, his writer's block, and the debacle with Sally.

"Sounds about right," he said. But just knowing this background and rehashing it was ineffective as an approach to treatment. Bobby was no Houdini.

He obsessed about ideas and storylines, but they never cohered. He put me in the position of his father, who was telling him to write, so he fought me by not writing. These were pyrrhic victories. I concluded that until Bobby felt sufficiently "manly" to stop opposing his father, and me as a stand in, he wouldn't be able to sustain a writing project; but *unless* he could produce some respectable writing, he'd keep feeling like an adolescent stuck in an Oedipal conundrum.

In a way, his entire case history kept circling around failed objectives that stood in the way of his escaping his Oedipal conflicts – the love of a woman, graduating college, writing something good. This was his life story, at least insofar as it was grounded in anger at more powerful, successful men. He kept repeating his attempts to shake off his murderous feelings because he kept failing at what might have been a mature and productive way out. When he did graduate, his escape couldn't last because then he needed something to "do," something defining that would prop him up against his lingering self-doubts and obsessions about the men in his life whom, he believed, had held him back.

As I thought about it all, I realized that what seemed like a personal narrative with no plot, and a course of therapy with little direction forward, was actually tethered to a common theme: serial disappointment, which gave rise to sustained anger and resentment. To help Bobby get past his Oedipal fantasies, we would have to find some way of helping him feel good about what he was doing and how that defined him in the world of men.

We had to do some heavy lifting.

"Okay," I said. "You see me as *trying* to get you to write. Truthfully, I'd like to help you understand your resistance to living a less encumbered life. Your choices are your own."

Bobby replied by going into detail about the process of writing, the themes and the introspection. "Half of writing is thinking," he said. "I'm thinking." How could I quarrel with that? Well, I could, because Bobby had left himself an open-ended excuse. "You can make an outline. You can write drafts and tear them up. But you can *begin*."

Apparently, he expected to produce a fully formed masterpiece on his first pass at the computer, suggesting to me that he had little notion of how actual writers write. Sometimes, he'd draft a few pages, but because they seemed so rough, he'd give up and toss them out.

Worse still, his lack of anything to say on paper made it hard for him to open up with me.

"You're living out your struggles in your head," I said. "In your professional life, there's not much *there, there*."

"Tell me something I don't know," he snapped.

Perhaps correlative to his taunt, he resumed spiting me by showing up late. It was a reversion, as if analysis were a course that he'd decided to flunk.

Yet while Bobby imagined himself as engaged in battling me – and his brother, his father, and his boss at the paper – his internal conflicts continued to disable him from competing with anyone. He needed to fail at writing so as to anger the men in his life, but that just kept him from finding his own path.

Bobby remained paralyzed. While he envisioned life as a writer, he was terrified that his work was deficient. By producing nothing, he ensured that nothing of his would compete. He could remain resentful, nurturing Oedipal antagonisms toward Rick and his father – both successful writers – without having to endure the risk of not measuring up. In effect, he'd created a perpetual motion machine that kept spinning around, going nowhere.

Sometimes, he'd actually write stuff that wasn't immediately discarded. He'd read me passages because he was still in a phase of preferring not to talk. I'd indulge him, assuming that even this provisional work might lead to progress. But Bobby was dissatisfied, acting as though his life had deteriorated. He belittled what he'd done, reprimanding himself as a failure. The better he did, the worse he felt.

I could only interpret the Oedipal conflict and hope that some of this working through was a part of the process. His complaining also had an element of being for show. That is, perhaps it was a means of protecting himself from derision in case these unedited (but undiscarded) passages didn't add up to a great novel. Perhaps Bobby was securing his flank, imagining that he'd finally burst out when he felt ready. I had to hope that he was making some gains from our conversations rather than playing some further game, since it's often hard to know the real purpose of a person's apparently self-effacing moves.

Art imitates life

Bobby began to agonize over the suspicion that the central character of his book wasn't "fully alive and there." Just as Bobby's voice was often missing from our sessions, the voice of his main character, a lost soul who just observes other people, was also missing. The novel's basic conceit was that it took place in a room lined with mirrors; what we read is a description of the characters' movements. The passages that I heard felt like a silent dreamscape.

"I feel like a switch has been shut off in my brain," he told me. "If I could flip it, I'd have a lot to say."

"Does the name of your protagonist, Isaac, have any significance?" I asked.

"Well, there's the biblical story, but I don't think that has anything to do with my choice."

I pushed him.

"Okay, there's some relevance, I guess. Abraham is all about discipline and teaching respect for the Lord, but he's a difficult father, who unbelievably tried to sacrifice his son."

I nodded. "You see yourself as being, like Isaac, almost sacrificed by your father. So, the silence. But don't you think there might also be a scream? That is, maybe it was both – terror and protest, together."

His face became flushed. Apparently, he'd never made the connection to a complicated victim at once paralyzed and furious.

There was another: Abraham's near-sacrifice of Isaac related to Bobby's infatuation with prison literature, his habit of seeing himself as emotionally tied down by his father. Bobby's fictional protagonist was an extension of himself.

So, even though I'd had access only to disconnected fragments, Bobby's writing offered a window into his psychology, his state of being. Of course, he sensed that from our discussion, and backed away. "You're making me uncomfortable," he said. "I read you stuff just to prove that I wasn't a total bust. I didn't expect you'd use it to dissect me." Well, wasn't I supposed to do that?

Using my own arguments in favor of work against me, Bobby claimed that any talk about his writing kept him from doing it. "You're making me self-conscious," he insisted. Also, he genuinely seemed to think that overcoming conflict would diminish his drive to express those conflicts in writing. He quoted the poet Rainer Maria Rilke, who declined Sigmund Freud's offer of psychoanalysis by saying, "If you rid me of my demons, my angels may also take flight." I could only hope that Bobby hadn't found yet another excuse to nurture his Oedipal conflict, using writing as a means to confront the object of that obsession – his father.

The Jesus delusion

"I can't stand the idea that I get off on being sacrificed," Bobby announced in one session, returning us to the theme of Isaac and Abraham. This time, however, his association was to Jesus. "You know he was Jewish," he added.

In fact, Bobby described himself as "sacrificed," "nailed to the wall," and "pinned down." He now had time to write, but saw himself as "paralyzed" and "martyred."

"Kind of hard to capitalize on writing opportunities when you feel like a martyr," I said.

"Oh come on," he protested. "I don't have a martyr complex."

But he just said that he *was* a martyr.

Apparently, he accepted the parallel to Isaac but resisted one to Jesus. Yet when he mentioned that his thirty-second birthday was coming up, he pointed out that Jesus had died at the age of 33.

"So, don't you see a parallel here," I asked, "in terms of God the Father and His only son?"

Bobby shrugged.

Actually, he hated being caught in traps set by his own logic.

He missed his next session, saying he'd hurt himself and needed to go to the hospital. I raised an eyebrow but, when he came to his next session, his right foot was bandaged.

"I drove a nail though it." He suppressed a smile as if the wound were my comeuppance for having doubted him.

What had happened was the he'd stepped on a nail while making some repairs to his apartment.

"It hurt like hell," he said. "But there was this weird feeling of relief. Maybe a little satisfaction too. I guess because my father's in pain every day, I feel guilty that I'm not. This assuaged the guilt."

"Yes, you felt guilty about your father's pain," I commented, "but you also identify with it. You see yourself as suffering too."

"Oedipus had something driven through his foot too," Bobby said.

He was sort of right: as an infant, Oedipus' ankles were pierced.

"Maybe," I said, "you imagine yourself as Christ-like in being sacrificed by a powerful father for some greater good. But then you want to get back at your father, Oedipus-like. You're maxing out on martyrdom, but you've got your own agenda."

Bobby thought for a while. I imagined his sorting through the peril of Isaac, the injuries of Oedipus, and the martyrdom of Christ to determine how they coalesced in his own narrative (oh, what a heavy burden to bear, if only to keep all the stories straight). Finally, he said "I think you're right. Injury and martyrdom are recurrent themes in my fantasies. Actually, in my life. I tend to martyr myself, I undermine my success."

"Exactly," I said, "Pain permeates your psychic life, and those masochistic needs play out in the real world. The thing is, however, it's a response to pain that you actually feel – or think you feel because of how you respond to your father."

"So if writing effectively dethrones my father – if it causes disorder in the natural order of things – then writer's block is a pre-emptive punishment, it's why I'm imprisoned, why I feel paralyzed."

Translation: if Bobby suffers on account of his father, and wants to dispose of him by writing, then not writing keeps him from violence (even though this not writing pains his father). He carries around both urges at once, and each upends the other.

Bobby's narrative of who suffers, and why, and how, kept evolving. Sometimes the emphasis was on spiting his father by writing a better book; other times, it was by not writing at all. The latter contained elements of self-punishment – even martyrdom – which now seemed to be gaining prominence. The constant was that, whatever the latest formulation, Bobby was still obsessed with what seemed like an eternal intra-family rivalry that controlled Bobby but that he sought to control. He understood this rivalry and its pernicious consequences. But he struggled to get past patterns that had defined his life for years and that influenced the course of his therapy with me.

The nurse

As Bobby spoke about his physical pain, however, I was reminded that his mother was a nurse. In the Oedipal triad that we were exploring (and that he'd acknowledged), I thought there must be some connection between the cycle of suffering and healing that he idealized, and his relationship with his mother. I didn't ask him to describe that relationship directly, but I hoped that gradually he might clarify it. After all, if Bobby needed to re-enact occasions where his mother's nursing – or, more generally, her love and attention – would be expected, then its absence would provide grounds for resenting his father. But if, conversely, he could acknowledge *why* yearning for his mother still obsessed him, then his anger at his father (who'd had her mainly to himself) might be more explicable. That is, was his anger at his father a defense against an infantilizing, even illicit, desire for his mother that he harbored but could not consciously accept? If he *could* finally acknowledge and deal with it, would his anger at paternal figures ultimately subside?

It seemed to me that if Bobby could talk about his feelings for his mother, and put them into perspective relative to his family dynamic, then he could better understand their effect on him as he struggled to behave like an adult. That included the ability to form an adult relationship with a suitable woman.

So, I said to Bobby, "I know you think your father monopolized your mother. But still, she was around, so you must remember some interactions – I mean, she was your *mother*."

I wasn't sure what would stand out in his mind. But it turned out that in being so reticent earlier in his treatment, he had apparently withheld – or, apparently repressed – a lot. "My mother," he said, "was beautiful. I'm sure my father acted more crippled than he was just so she would hover over him, and he could look at her close up." According to Bobby, his father put on an act to be close to his mother just as Bobby did in his imagination. Bobby *understood* his mother as responding to a man's neediness – with himself just a pale imitator of the champ, his father. You could hear the desire for physical closeness.

I thought that part of Bobby's fear about entering into a relationship now, as an adult, was that he recognized his tendency to desire a relationship where the woman would take care of him – as his mother had. What sort of woman wants to be a mother replacement? It seemed that Bobby understood, if only subconsciously, that his desire for his mother (and the fantasy relationship with her that he had nurtured) would be an impediment to his growing up. Ultimately, Bobby would have to convince himself that a fantasy was not his default orientation, and that he would not demand that a real woman participate in his fantasy. That was a tall order, especially when the fantasy had dominated his familial and extra-familial relationships for so long.

So, I brought the conversation around to what started my speculation about Bobby and his mother – the way he had wounded himself. "That nail must have hurt," I said (stating the obvious). "Did you wish that your mother could have 'nursed' you?"

He came right out and said that he had. "It hurt, of course, and if my mom was there, I would have liked it. When I was a kid, even when she was busy with my dad she'd still fuss when I was sick in bed." Bobby could get his mother's attention when he was indisposed – not as "hurt" as his father, who was perpetually hurt, but hurt enough so that his mother would devote herself to him at least for a while. Bobby defined his relationship with his mother in terms of his intermittent displays of need, and her necessary response. But more importantly, he still wanted it, with all the close physicality that being

nursed through pain and suffering implies. He resented this same physicality –
this continual need to be nursed – in his father.

I wanted to pursue this aspect of his thinking, since it brought together his
resentment toward his father and its basis in his own need (his physical need)
for his mother. I asked, "So, physical pain was a way of getting your mother's
attention, which you could interpret as a mother's love?"

"I suppose so," he said. He seemed uncomfortable.

I waited. After a protracted pause, he started talking almost non-stop,
stream-of-consciousness fashion. "I remember her getting ready to go out
to a party. She's in front of a mirror, brushing her hair, and she's in her bra.
She asked me to get her barrette, which was in the bathroom and, when I got
up, I noticed her gown on the bed." He recalled other memories, like when
his mother would be taking a bubble bath and would ask him to bring her
a towel. On Saturday mornings, when his father would be downstairs, she
would ask him to cuddle with her in bed – at least until he was about 8 years
old. He'd get excited and, later, when his father would say "I heard you two
laughing upstairs," he'd glance at his mother and they'd treat the whole incident as part of their private running joke.

Except it wasn't funny, because he knew – just because of his father's reaction – that it was somehow wrong.

"So, when your mother gave you her undivided physical attention, it was
stimulating. There was a sexual element about it, even if you couldn't really
register it at the time – the feeling stayed with you."

Then came the acknowledgment I had been curious about. "Well, it's not
like I was beating off in her bed," he said sort of defensively. "But I do like
MILF porn." (That's Mother-I'd-Like-To-Fuck porn or, more generally, porn
that shows older women and younger men).

I stopped for a moment. It was like a crevasse had opened up. I realized
that to a substantial degree, Bobby's anger at his father was the awful – but
still more acceptable – face of an Oedipus complex where Bobby kept trying
to experience closeness to his mother. His mother had allowed this MO to
develop. She had created little frissons where Bobby would physically want
her, probably to flatter her own ego but clearly to maintain control over
Bobby. She had encouraged his arrested development, at least insofar as he
would shrink from sexual independence and any desire to look beyond her at
other women. Of course, Bobby *tried* to be with other women, but there was
always the unconscious undertow of his mother.

Until now, when he seemed to finally have become conscious of how his
mother was, in effect, a continuing object of desire. Bobby had articulated his
continued need for his mother's love, so perhaps we'd now be able to address
his issues as epiphenomena of that need.

I asked him, "Do you understand the import of what we've just discussed?
Do you see how your other relationships – that to your father, your brother,
women – reflect your unresolved feelings for your mother?"

"Well, I guess it makes sense," he said, "but isn't there an element of incest in every family How am I so different?"

I explained that whether or not most men desire their mothers, they outgrow it. They certainly don't cultivate the feeling, enacting little traumas that keep it alive. He had to agree, especially when I pointed out that his brother showed no signs of similar inclinations.

So, we agreed about his impulses and overstimulation growing up. "I probably admitted to those feelings because I wanted to be caught," he said, though I think it was hardly so deliberate. Most likely, he had been reflecting on his motivations because that was just another way to inflict pain on himself. This time, however, the effect got short-circuited, resulting not in another occasion to fantasize about his mother, but in our shared realization of how his particular Oedipus complex operated.

As if to confirm my interpretation – really, almost on cue – Bobby recalled another sexualized encounter with his mother. "Once I was on the floor in their bedroom. I'd sneak in to sleep there, maybe when I was no more than 5. I'm pretty sure they were having sex, and I'm sure my mother knew I was there." It was that last phrase, about how his mother knew he could have seen and heard, that struck me. Once again, what had stuck with Bobby was the image of his mother as a sexual performer. "It wasn't like I was excited, in some mature sense of sexual arousal, but I was excited because my mother had made herself available to me in some special way."

Bobby looked at me, obviously recognizing that his formative exposure to sexuality involved his mother. From my perspective, he was beginning to see that he currently expressed a desire for his mother in terms of hostility toward his father, even while that same desire stood in the way of a mature relationship with a woman (who wasn't just a substitute care-giver).

We still had a lot of work to do. Would Bobby commit to it, or would reliving more such incidents be too painful? Bobby remarked that "Okay, I'm sort of into my mother – I mean figuratively – and I'm going to try and catch myself when it shows, but I still have these negative feelings toward my father. They're not just going away, and I need to resolve them."

He seemed to move off the topic of women. But we kept talking.

Grad school

During one session, Bobby confessed that he'd never graduated from high school. "I got a GED." Did he feel guilty about not telling me, the father stand-in, sooner? Whatever the case, we saw a pattern of studied reticence. Bobby had taken money from his father's dresser, following an impulse "to have what the big man had," and he'd swiped papers off his father's desk. Was there some lingering guilt?

His revelations suggested a childhood guilt that had hung around, just as his Oedipal preoccupation was a childhood urge that never resolved. Bobby was still fighting old battles, recovering from past inclinations to punish himself. Essentially, he needed to grow up and, if necessary, further work through old traumas. He had to live more freely in the present.

During these discussions, he tried to write. "I dared myself," he said. But there was still this childish, Oedipal persistence insofar as he could only envision his life *relative* to his father's. He felt that the best way to write was to go to graduate school; following his father's footsteps was the only career he deemed acceptable. He was the child who would do what a parent did rather than consider the full range of options.

I was skeptical. "After dropping out of college six times, why would you sign on for more formal education?"

The answer soon became clear: he'd found a new and masochistically satisfying focus for his conflicts. Rather than filling out applications, he obsessed and procrastinated about whether to go. When he finally got around to the paperwork, he delivered the applications to the post office at midnight on the day they were due. I had a premonition that whether or not he was accepted, there would be trouble. Grad school seemed more of a tactic to postpone any serious writing. In the meantime, his conflicts would continue.

While he was waiting to hear back, the paper where he worked had some cutbacks and laid him off. Initially, Bobby saw himself as a victim, taken advantage of by the rich owners. He imagined fighting them in court and threatening to reveal their questionable practices. But rather than dwelling on such fantasies, as he'd done in the past, he was able to accept the economic reality. "There are other places," he said.

But he was now unemployed, and anxious about it. He imagined that if he was late with my fee, I would let him go too. He promptly found a position at another paper ("on the rebound," he grinned), though by comparison it was the equivalent of delivery-driving. He didn't know whether to complain or feel relieved. "I took the first job that I could find," he said, "mainly because of you." Okay, blame me. We bumped along.

Then, however, came his acceptance into a prestigious writing program.

"I'll be starting in the fall." All was forgiven.

Ostensibly, going to grad school was supposed to take his writing to the next level. But, as Freud points out, there are "good reasons" for doing something, and there are the "real reasons." Behind Bobby's rationale was old Oedipus: with a degree from a prestigious university, he could pursue an academic career like his father's. In all likelihood, it would also make further treatment impossible, providing a hard stop to a long-distance run that he could never quite muster the will to quit.

At first, however, Bobby avoided discussing his fantasies about quitting. But finally, he proposed ending analysis. As a full-time student, he'd have no time or money to continue. He claimed that writing (first stop, grad school) was his true calling, and that he would make whatever sacrifices were necessary.

I was sure that he did not consider quitting a "sacrifice," but I didn't want to antagonize him.

However, I also felt that if he was actually going to write, he'd just write. Grad school was just so much temporizing.

During one session, he rambled on about previously "dropping out of school."

"Your dropping out of analysis is like your behavior with school."

My comment apparently stung. "Maybe," he said. "I mean, I can see how I'm doing to you what I did to my professors."

Nonetheless, he kept to his decision to start grad school in the fall. I felt that in terms of his Oedipal conflicts, he still had a distance to go.

Old habits

Bobby enjoyed a burst of creativity for the next several weeks. He considered himself on the right path in life – a path that was now clear – and he was determined to follow it. He talked about how intently he was writing as if to say, "I'm better now and don't need treatment anymore." He acted like he was cured rather than admitting that certain aspects of his life had improved while others still needed work – in particular, his tendency to revert to masochistic, self-defeating behaviors.

At this point, he tended to see psychoanalysis as holding him back rather than as a self-enhancing endeavor that might help him achieve his potential. As for me, I was standing in his way and had questionable motives.

"Now *you're* the one undercutting my success," he remarked. "You just want to keep me in analysis."

In effect, he was claiming that my concern for him was tantamount to acting unethically. It was a new level of hostility, and I interpreted it as a kind of terror on his part that he might not actually go through with his plans unless he broke decisively with everyone who might still talk him out of it. But rather than confront him, I simply observed that to stop therapy now – when there was obvious work remaining – would be an act of rebellion, and might redound to his detriment: "Okay, you've improved. But we've been here before. *It has tended not to last.* You still have certain conflicts, which are likely to keep morphing until you get ahead of them. If you simply leave analysis for grad school, you may be acting out your aggressive fantasies."

"Christ," Bobby moaned, "now you're as nagging and negative as my father."

But his writing had slowed down, and it was looking ever more likely that grad school was just another escape from dealing with the issues that kept him straitjacketed. He may even have known, and may have been lashing out because I was trying to help him understand and explore what he seemed very much to want to repress.

In fact, he continued finding ways to undermine himself. He was offered a decent position at another paper. Taking it would have helped pay his expenses, and given him time to write even while studying. But without any discussion, either with me or the paper's manager, he turned it down.

His masochism placed him in a precarious position. He could no longer keep up with his bills. I offered to lower my fee, but he quickly reminded me of how his father used money to manipulate him.

"You just want to control me," he said, "like him."

It seemed as though we had reached a stand-off. I wasn't sure I would ever see him again. But, true to form – and, obviously, bothered by fantasies that he couldn't shake – Bobby called a week later. "I'm afraid that all I'll write about is my father, and they'll kick me out of the program as boring and obsessed." He was obviously afraid, even as he tried to save face by insisting that graduate school was a done deal. We agreed to resume his analysis provisionally, at least until the semester began.

Combat

One of the first things we discussed was a dream in which Bobby was in a department store with his parents: "They were buying me clothing. I'm going up an escalator in a wheelchair, holding the rails to keep from falling back. The polyester pants my parents pick out for me are garish. I say they're hideous. My mom says they're expensive."

Bobby's association was to a painting in my office that he found "too colorful, like a pair of pants from the seventies." He also remembered the sound his father's corduroy pants would make as he attempted to walk and his legs rubbed together.

"So," I said a bit playfully, "my office aesthetic is a reason to give up treatment you can no longer afford."

"Sounds about right," he agreed and recalled more of the dream. "I feel ashamed that my parents are buying me clothes in front of a nurse."

His association was to how his parents would have to help him pay for treatment if he decided not to drop out, though he doubted they'd be willing.

"Then the nurse turns into my brother," he continued, "and I'm explaining what my mom and dad did. Rick turns into this guy who's off his rocker. He's from the same Shotokan karate school I go to but he doesn't know what I'm talking about. I think this is about you. Sometimes I feel like you don't get me. It makes me think of some of my fights with Rick too."

"You see me as being like Rick," I said, "and feel that I'm not getting your reasons for quitting. The image on my wall, which you find garish, reflects the difference in our sensibilities."

Bobby's relationship with his brother and the corresponding aspect of our relationship was coming into focus. During childhood, Bobby had practiced

Shotokan karate alongside his brother. But, as I mentioned, while Rick became a third-degree black belt, Bobby was injured and had to drop out. He took up karate again a few years later but, instead of Shotokan, he chose aikido, a "softer" martial art that turns the force of an opponent's attack against him.

During the previous year of treatment, he became more committed to aikido, and was now working toward his next belt. At practice sessions, he would fantasize about pummeling a formidable foe. As he had so often throughout his life, he imagined himself the pivotal figure in a great battle that was on a par with the cosmic clash between good and evil. Intertwined in these fantasies of combat were thoughts about how his brother or father might be killed in an accident. While Bobby did not fantasize *my* death, my affinity with his brother meant that I had to be stopped and, perhaps, that it was best if he could break free of me.

Bobby's complicated series of dreamed equations merely literalized how he actually felt. That is, his dreams were not some bizarre, cryptic, funhouse distortion of his world. Rather, they expressed a kind of narrative about how he actually felt. Rick was a menace. By association, so was I.

Obviously, Bobby's violent fantasies toward the men in his family had been crippling, and now they threatened to derail his treatment. The karate dream offered an opportunity to exact revenge for what, he felt, he had suffered at their hands. What I tried to help him see was that revenge was not simple. Rather, it became the fuel for the substrate of his ongoing guilt and neurotic inhibitions. In focusing on the revenge fantasy in his dreams – and how it ultimately reached into quitting therapy – I emphasized its dire effect on Bobby himself. "It's not like you step out of the ring, bow to your partner, and just walk away. You carry your hurts and injuries with you to the next encounter."

The image struck him. Again, this was no abstraction, like feeling jealousy and rage. You could get hurt in karate, you could land on the floor and ache for a week. If I had been searching for a metaphor – for years – this one seemed to grab Bobby's attention. He knew, quite viscerally, that when you finished a karate session you had to recover, even if you knocked your opponent down. If he could understand that he paid a price for all his murderous fantasies, and that it would undermine his performance even outside the ring, he'd have a powerful way in to reflecting on his issues. He might break the vicious circle of his own self-defeating logic.

We kept talking.

Bobby noticed that whenever Rick had good news – a summer home, a raise, having a baby – the frequency and intensity of his fantasies increased. Bobby was increasingly aware of his aggressive feelings. Rather than simply seeing himself as the victim of a powerful rival, he explored his feelings of envy toward his brother. He had a whole childhood and many years of negative thinking to work through.

A dream in which a young, up-and-coming fighter beat Muhammad Ali, a living legend who had recently died, was indicative of Bobby's ongoing internal conflict. While Bobby's growth was associated with his father's demise, it was his brother who beat the champ. But Bobby was Rick's ring man, his willing second. Bobby's association was to his parents' recent anniversary party, which he'd arranged, but for which (he felt) his brother had gotten most of the credit. He saw his life as a fight in which he wasn't fully able to fend for himself, particularly against a formidable opponent. Yet he was also resentful about needing someone else to step up and fight for him, and who then got all the credit.

That is, Bobby felt he just didn't have the goods to stand up for himself. In fact, he feared failing the test for his next aikido belt. He thought he lacked the experience to do it on his own. He was embarrassed because students who had started after him had already passed their tests. The test became a "test" of his manliness, which seemed on the line whenever he was under pressure.

We spoke about his anxiety of lagging behind Rick, who'd long ago earned his black belt in an even tougher form of the sport. Bobby's associations were to analysis and his sense that he hadn't yet gained the tools he needed to progress independently. He became more motivated to renew his commitment to treatment.

His mother again

I thought that all of this talk about pain and injury was a good segue into how Bobby's maternal fantasies still had a hold on him. Why, after all, was he even speaking about pain if, subconsciously, he didn't still crave his mother's presence – her physical attention? I asked him about this, and he tried suggesting that *I* was obsessed with his mother. "I've been working on how I think about her," he said, "which just proves that my feelings about my father and my brother are not just cover-ups for my feelings about her. They're real, and I need to deal with them."

So, I asked about how he'd been "working on" his feelings toward his mother. "Do you think that she has become less of an impediment to your having a relationship? Has someone taken Sally's place, but less as a stand-in for your mother?" I was challenging him to describe whether he was living in the real world of real women, or attempting to conscript such women into his fantasies. If the latter were true, I had hopes for how he might – in time – display less hostility toward his father, his brother, and even me.

Maybe the lines of force were beginning to merge.

So, in a tone that almost seemed like a counter-challenge, a sort of I-told-you-so, Bobby described his new girlfriend, Denise. It didn't seem to occur to him that if he was, in fact, attempting to get past his sexualized mother fantasy, then the treatment that he loved to deride was actually having an effect.

It turned out that Denise was very much like Bobby's mother. She was a nurse, whom Bobby had met online. "Are you looking for women who remind you of your mother?" I asked. Bobby said that he wasn't, but that he did want someone who understood what it meant to care about another person. "Nurses are empathetic. My dad and my mother fought a lot but, deep down, she cared about him – he was a hurting human being." He said that he thought he could best suppress his fantasies if he could meet them halfway in a real-life woman who resembled his mother. "The problem with Sally," he said, "was that she'd disappear into her own obsessions sometimes, her careerism." Bobby wanted someone more traditional.

He said that he had actually described his therapy to Denise, and that she was encouraging. "Denise doesn't think I'm weird or anything. She just says that I need to grow up and that she thinks she can help." I wondered whether Denise hoped to "mother" Bobby even while offering herself as a mother alternative – a pathway to a grown-up relationship. But Bobby seemed excited. "Look," he said, "I know what you're thinking. But if I can focus on a real woman who isn't my mother, and if I can get my mother and my brother and my dad to like her, then maybe we can all be one big happy family."

Bobby was dealing with his obsessions in his own way. He had obviously learned something about himself, but felt that going cold-turkey on his obsessions wasn't going to work. He would ease out of them. He would create an alternative family structure, based not on fantasy and hostility but on acceptance and understanding. I couldn't fault him.

"Well," I said, "this sounds promising. Why didn't you bring up Denise before?" He said that he needed to concentrate on his father and brother because he wanted to "warm them up to Denise." Okay, I thought, it's an explanation, even if it sounds a little *ex post facto*. I asked that he continue to keep me informed about what we decided to call The Denise Project.

Accomplice to murder

Having become noticeably more self-confident (or, at least, deliberately upbeat), and having dropped any residual objection to continuing analysis, Bobby broached what he termed "dark secrets." One involved the killing of a friend's brother by someone that Bobby knew. Since he was aware of the circumstances, he thought he was an accomplice and feared the legal repercussions.

But I countered. "What you really don't want to discuss are your own murderous feelings toward Rick. I know you want to get past them, but I think you're still afraid of them – maybe that they'll derail your hopes for Denise."

Yet despite his associations to childhood slights, Bobby couldn't explore his hostility toward his brother, and he rejected my interpretation.

During this phase of analysis, Bobby's aggressive feelings toward his brother surfaced (again) in *our* relationship. When I hung up some new art in my office, for example, that meant I was becoming more successful, and Bobby expressed an envy that obviously implicated his brother. He had a dream in which Rick was singing a song by a rock star with the same name as their father. In other words, his brother was heir to his father's voice.

As we focused in on the origins of Bobby dark, semi-fratricidal feelings, as well as his unwillingness to fully acknowledge them, he nonetheless returned to his brother's effect on his own ambitions. His own writings would show how Rick just churned out pulp.

A dream helped to clarify some of the persistent issues: "I was at my parents' place. I was supposed to have been doing stuff for them, getting a prescription filled. I had bad diarrhea. No matter how much I wiped myself, I couldn't get clean. Smelly, watery shit got on the bedspread, and it wouldn't stop. My parents came home and were mad because I hadn't done what I was supposed to. Then my brother and I are fighting over two scarves our grandmother made. I think both are mine. My mother says to let me have one. I run an important errand, deliver some documents, and return to my apartment. I get into an elevator but it's in free fall."

His initial association was to painting his parents' apartment over the weekend, getting paint on his hands and clothes, and being unable to wash it off. But after a pause he said, "Sometimes, I can't believe the shit that comes out of my mouth when I talk to you."

"Well," I reminded him, "earlier in the analysis, when you had trouble talking, your association was to a sleep-away camp, where you left a gift for the other campers on the floor of the bunkhouse. Now you feel embarrassed by what you've said, perhaps about ending analysis."

"Yeah, I know what's coming," Bobby said, "a prescription for more analysis. You're pissed off because I didn't follow through the way I was supposed to, right?"

"That's a good interpretation of the dream," I said, "but not an accurate assessment of my attitude toward you. I believe in psychotherapy and, ultimately, I think it can help you further."

He brought up his father's criticisms and verbal assaults, which he himself often provoked. While emotionally wounding, they were also a show of concern on his father's part.

"My passive-aggressiveness gets authority figures to act like my father did."

No argument from me. But I also pointed out that Bobby's aggressiveness had a flip side in admiration. "Why don't you at least acknowledge that you admire your brother's profession, and your father's? I mean, in some ways you want to *be* them."

Perhaps he could just recalibrate the levels of anger and admiration, and even recognize elements of both men in himself. It would be further progress, I told him. He said he'd think about it. Tellingly, he said "I'll talk it over with Denise. She's good about how I should feel." I perceived an element of developing emotional dependency but, at this stage, we could overlook it if it helped to mollify his rage.

Author! Author!

Even coming to psychotherapy twice a week was difficult for Bobby. Aside from the time, there was the money. He'd taken a substitute teaching job, but it didn't pay much. He was done with his delivery work, and wanted a job as a writer or in the arts.

He was reluctant to speak with Rick about freelancing.

"You know what Rick will say?" he asked. " 'You're lazy, you fucked up, and you have a bad track record.' "

Nor did he want to feel indebted to Rick or give him the pleasure of bailing him out.

"A while ago you were talking about starting to see Rick as a resource," I said, "an experienced writer who could point you in the right direction. Now you'd rather have to downsize your apartment and give up therapy than go to him for help."

Bobby was forced to confront the depth of his animosity. "You're right," he said. "I'm cutting off my nose to spite my face. I mean, he's my brother, right? Not somebody out to wreck my life." But, of course, Bobby had constructed a fantasy around Rick in which he *did* help to ruin his life – whether or not he did anything.

There's a children's book in which a boy wakes up in the middle of the night and creeps downstairs to explore the cellar. He's terrified to encounter a fire-breathing dragon in a murky corner and runs back up. But his ordeal's not over. After he falls asleep, the dragon invades his dreams, and the boy has to placate the beast with a gallon of milk and a box of cookies. When he wakes in the morning, he asks his parents why there's a dragon in the basement. His father laughs and takes the boy into the cellar. He points at an old wood-burning stove and asks, "Is this the dragon you saw?" The boy is relieved but also bewildered. He was *sure* he'd seen a scaly, fire-breathing menace.

When Bobby finally did approach Rick and his father about his financial predicament, it was out of necessity and with pent-up trepidation.

Their willingness to help, however, surprised him. It was not lecture-free, and there were conditions (like not wasting money on beer). "They had to get their digs in," he said, albeit half-heartedly, defensively. He was surprised at the relative lack of control. "It could have been a lot worse," he admitted, "my fantasies might have been exaggerations." He thought perhaps they may have "mellowed," again implying that he hadn't been *so* off-base all along. Apparently, he felt disoriented, at least a bit. He'd spent so much time seeing them as outsize rivals, enemies – dragons to be slain. Now they seemed human scale.

Within a couple of weeks of his sit-downs with Rick and his father, Bobby received an assignment – his first paying gig as a writer – for a well-regarded magazine. He even began discussing collaborating with Rick on a screenplay. I was well aware that he could sabotage this plan but, nonetheless, the fact that he'd even agreed to work with Rick – instead of just trying to out-compete him – was promising.

Bobby also showed signs of not viewing me as a competitor, that is, as yet another patriarch that he had to vanquish/humiliate/conspicuously outperform. He said he actually appreciated our work together. "You know," he admitted, "you made financial sacrifices to treat me, and I want to acknowledge those. You're not just a variant of my dad or of Rick." I must have been visibly moved because he followed up by saying "Sometimes, I didn't treat you properly – as one man to another." His message (however flattering to himself) was that we were peers, that I was a person instead of a proxy for a mythical stereotype. I was encouraged. We had finally worked through (at least some of) his Oedipal obsessions. He didn't quite say that he had come to love me, but his overall transference to me as the alpha male was much less negative.

Bobby and I agreed to continue our work, which got a late-breaking boost when Bobby's magazine article led to more (and more lucrative) assignments. It had taken three years, but Bobby was finally willing to explore his mind's basement, and start to discount the dragons that he had created. The defensiveness he had displayed as to his old animosity – now called into question by the objects of that animosity – signified that, while ready to admit but perhaps not fully embrace it, he was preparing to move on. Maybe this time with even greater commitment.

After a pause, another phase

Bobby had wanted a "hiatus" of a few months, mainly to collect his thoughts about what to focus on next. When he finally returned to treatment, however (after longer than I thought he'd need), he was determined as to where we should go next. "I've been thinking about those Oedipal obsessions. I realize now that they're messing up my relationships." It's not that we hadn't explored the issue, but there is often a disjunction (in comprehension, in terms of time) between defining a problem and a patient's readiness to address it. So, we started talking more about relationships.

It turned out that The Denise Project had fizzled. Apparently, she had surmised early on that, to an uncomfortable degree, she was an "acceptable" replacement for Bobby's mother. She had hoped, she told him, that he might ultimately see her in her own right, as a sympathetic woman who just happened to remind him of his mother – not replace her. But finally, she felt that it would never happen. "She told me," he said, "that my whole 'one big happy family' routine was creepy. She said it was polygamous." The progress that Bobby thought he was making on the girlfriend front had disappointed him. "I tried to tell her how far I'd actually come, but it wasn't enough. A day late and a dollar short."

So, for several months, Bobby hadn't dated anyone. He said he'd been humiliated, and didn't want to risk that again. He also said that he tried to get a grip on his feelings. "I wasn't sure how much I could reveal to a woman, and I wasn't sure how they'd react if I revealed *anything*. I think women like to be sympathetic, but not if the underlying reason may be an impediment to a relationship." That struck me as a shrewd perception, and suggested that Bobby had been engaged in some serious reflection.

We kept talking, and Bobby said that perhaps he'd wait for his luck to change. "I've been stuck in a pattern, and I need to be wrenched out of it. Maybe something will happen." I told him that while there was no value in just remaining passive, and allowing "luck" – or anything else – to wrench him out of his comfort zone, he could increase his receptiveness to possibilities.

And then Bobby met Liane, just the sort of possibility he might have imagined, assuming that he *could* have imagined her.

Liane had come to one of his readings, and unambiguously pursued him. "This woman slips her card under a stack of books I'm signing. Then at the reception, she asks 'Did you find it?' I really liked her style – okay, and her flaming red hair." They'd been dating for five months now. Yet as they got closer, Bobby sensed himself adrift. "No joke," he said, but when I see Liane in an up-do, I see red flares." This was a little too vivid, a little too literal for comfort. Of course, he was associating between Liane's hair color and those red flares, but my question was "Did he realize it, or was the equation unconscious?"

So, the question was how to treat Bobby during this phase of our work. He had asked if he could see me in twice-weekly sessions (instead of a full-on analysis), ostensibly because he was busy. I was skeptical, since it seemed as though he was resisting further analysis. Moreover, I wasn't sure that two days a week would suffice. However, as we spoke, I recalled other patients with relationship issues for whom two sessions a week had been surprisingly effective. Also, I wasn't wedded to the traditional view that three to five sessions per week is the gold standard; developments such as cognitive behavioral therapy clearly call this assumption into question. So, I finally said, "I'm not necessarily a more-is-better guy when it comes to treatment, and I'm not committed to the couch if sitting face-to-face suits a patient better." We could always change things later, if necessary. So, we continued.

"What comes to mind," I asked, "when you think about Liane?"

Bobby was quick to respond, as if he had been puzzling over the problem for weeks. "I really like her – maybe I love her by now – but something holds me back. I'm not sure what." I asked whether there were issues around sex (the shoals on which many relationships founder) but he said that the sex was "good enough." "It's not out of a fantasy," he mused, "but she doesn't have

Sally's hang-ups, and we both get orgasms." After a while, he added, "You remember how she first took the initiative – well, a lot of times she still does, and it excites me." So far, so good, but was there something else worrying him?

"You know," he said, "Liane's Catholic. My father, who's nominally Catholic, married my mother despite her being Jewish ... maybe that contributed to their problems." This seemed like a rationalization – a need to find something reality-based – so I probed further. "Do you and Liane discuss religion? You and I rarely talk about it." He admitted that they both had fallen away from faith. "We joke that it skipped a generation," he said. "I was bar mitzvahed, but am totally secular, and she is totally lapsed." He even acknowledged that his parents liked Liane, and never said a word against "mixed marriages." "I guess I've just caught myself clutching at straws," he said. The list of potential problems kept shrinking.

I saw why his unaccountable resistance bothered him, his sense that he wasn't fully in control of his feelings. There seemed to be no *there, there*; that is, nothing tangible. He had *reasonably* concluded, he said, that subconscious motivations were "messing up" his life.

So, we started by reviewing his old failed relationships, on the assumption that eventually they'd connect up with his Oedipal issues and – ultimately – help us deal with his subconscious resistance to getting close to a woman other than his mother.

There was Sally, of course, and we went over that whole tale again while Bobby blamed himself. "If I'd been half the man I should have been, we'd be married," he said. But he hadn't and they weren't. When Sally had finally gone her own way, Bobby fell into bouts of nostalgia. "I still think about her," he said, "and I realize how I mentally run to her when I can't make a commitment elsewhere. It's a sort of if-only response (a retreat) that I know is pointless." He'd told Liane about Sally, and she had listened. "But I wonder," he said, "whether she hears me making excuses for myself. I think she's beginning to sense that I'm worried that I've hit a wall." Probably, Bobby was projecting his fears about commitment onto Liane, but the projection itself was concerning, reflecting a lack of self-confidence. Did he feel stuck?

We talked as well about the Asian girls he'd pick up, who always seemed like they'd be sexually submissive and perpetually surprised him with needs of their own. "I'm not even sure what I want," he admitted, "so how am I supposed to ever make a commitment?" I said that was his resistance talking, and that we should try to understand more about it. "You do want a relationship," I said, "but you're conflicted about your ability to sustain it."

He thought that made sense.

Eventually, our talk about women (several of whose names he'd forgotten) led back to his parents' relationship. "Getting closer," I thought. His mother had taken care of his father, and now Bobby worried about lopsided relationships where one partner feels beholden to another and suffers a loss of self-esteem. "Suppose that happens to me?" he asked. "I've seen it. I know it can happen." He was touching on something important. Often significant relationships that we grow up with are templates for later relationships. How could they not be, since it's what we know? I suggested he put his parents' circumstances in perspective. "You and Liane are young," I said. "She's pretty different from your mom."

"What's really the issue?" I asked.

It finally surfaced. Bobby closed his eyes, creating a sense of drama. I asked him to think about his parents from another perspective, less in the context of their relationship and more in terms of how each parent affected him. Since we had talked endlessly about his father, I said "You were close to your mother – you also stood *between* her and your father."

Bobby opened his eyes (literally, emotionally). He talked about his feeling of obligation toward her. He was, he said, concerned that getting deeply involved with someone made him disloyal to his mother. "It's like it's a zero sum," he mused, "as if there is only so much love and I have to apportion it. That's nuts, right? I mean, there are different kinds of love." He seemed afraid that he hadn't developed sufficiently to make that distinction. "Other people don't have this problem," he sighed. Of course, to varying degrees we all do.

He began to reminisce about his childhood, perhaps to locate the cause of what he saw as his limiting (if not aberrant) emotional connection. He said he'd always been his mother's "emotional" favorite (despite her fascination with Rick), and that she'd told him many times. "When she and my dad would fight, she'd turn to me for support, and I'd be there for her. I was her confidante, like in a secret club." This reflex, apparently, was hard to control. It had become ingrained – part of how Bobby defined himself, even if he could barely acknowledge it. "Once when I was about 10, my mother climbed into bed with me and hugged me. I think it felt weird, but somehow also necessary." In a way, Bobby was suggesting that commitment to another woman violated the natural, "necessary" order of his family, which privileged loyalty to the woman whom he had protected. He would – he should – always be there for her.

But the picture was still more unsettled. As we spoke, Bobby further recalled gazing at his mother while she got dressed; bringing her a towel after a bath; sneaking onto her side of the bed when she lay next to his father. His loyalty synched up with a type of repressed eroticism, the *sine qua non* of an Oedipal obsession. I thought that if he could finally accept and acknowledge the pull that these feelings still exerted, which contributed to his exaggerated sense of loyalty, we could finally address his question of *why* he felt an undefinable resistance toward women who, at least ostensibly, might make good mates.

So, I asked Bobby, "Do you think that you see a commitment to Liane as disloyalty toward your mother?"

"Probably," he admitted. He said that growing up, he'd thought he'd never love any woman more than his mother. "When I had crushes on some of my teachers, say, when I was 8 or 9, they felt threatening. But then I'd laugh because I knew my mother would always take first place in my heart." Well, that was then and this was now – could he get past his yearnings and sub-conscious feelings for his mother, now that more plausible women were a possibility?

Bobby said that the dynamic between his mother and himself had always "haunted" him ("I mean I actually think about it – still"), but that the consequences had seemed too long ago to have any practical effect. Treatment, however, was making him feel differently. He realized that his psychological reality was not bounded just by what seemed tangible, definable, and unalter-ably present-tense. The past was still present. "I guess I am who I once was, as well as who I am now," he said in a burst of clarity. "I have to move the needle further toward Now."

We continued talking. Bobby wanted to try committing to Liane (by which he meant moving in with her to see if there might be a potential for perman-ence). It sounded promising. "I'm fighting a rearguard action," he said. "I've got to see if I can move ahead." Bobby was testing whether he had enough self-confidence – based on an emerging self-awareness – to put his Oedipal conflicts further behind him (or, at least, to manage them).

Now, after a year or so, they've begun talking about getting engaged. Bobby has never fully explained to Liane his fears about falling back into a cloudy, resistant bafflement. "I've told her there's no rush," he said, "because we know that we love each other. I think she trusts me, and that itself is encouraging." So, things are moving in the right direction. We still talk twice a week, but it's mostly about Bobby's sense that his life can't stay on hold forever. "I am not going to repeat what happened with Sally," he said. "So, the only alternative is to grow up and be happy." That sounds like progress.

Chapter 2

The Little Match Girl

In this study, a woman's quest for romantic love is continually disrupted by self-defeating behaviors and entrenched fantasies. Our objective was to mitigate those fantasies, which kept morphing and recurring as her treatment proceeded. As in the Oedipus study, the struggle between fantasy and reality became our central focus. But in this instance, the patient was not in thrall to some mythic character but, instead, to a 19th-century fiction, Hans Christian Andersen's Little Match Girl. To the patient, this little girl, who was orphaned and poor, and dies on the street, becomes the persistent embodiment of what she senses as her own likely failure. As she psychologically resonates with this fiction, she enacts its life-cycle over and over again, defeating herself whenever she starts to show progress. Her deep underlying wish is that by being helpless and in need, a man who loves her will save and rescue her. The effect plays out in her romantic relationships, which she pre-emptively disrupts before the man can cause her emotional distress.

Whenever we seemed to be getting somewhere in the course of treatment, the fantasy would emerge in some new guise, and we would suffer another set-back. Frequently, I would be blamed, since I was a male and, hence, just as likely to inflict pain as any of the men she went out with. Frequently, she viewed me as a father figure, at once able to help her but, because her father had left her, just as likely to cause harm. This study is, in large part, about the influence of transference – that is, when the patient treats the therapist as if they were someone significant from the past – and associated feelings ranging from love to hate. But nothing was simple with this patient. At times, she also wanted to be my mother and my lover. When she wanted to end her treatment, she was afraid of the result. Her fantasies about men were as potent as those that she derived from fiction.

Finally, the patient begins to cope with her obsessions, but the outcome is always uncertain. She wants to improve as she becomes more self-aware, but she clings to fantasies that provide her an excuse in case she should fail. We watch her toggle between these two poles. What we learn, of course, is that psychotherapy is never linear. It is frequently fraught. It deals with intangibles, like

DOI: 10.4324/9781003352624-3

fantasies. The patient and I have to find out how these fantasies originated so that we can begin to deter them and they lose their hold over her psychic life. I have to help the patient examine their origin and function, so that they are not – merely by inertia – allowed to become some fallback substitute for living in the real world.

Of course, my immediate focus had to be with helping the patient cope with the realities of her life determined by her proliferating fantasies. We were necessarily drawn into the myriad ways that she experienced love – or the lack of it. The patient lacked self-esteem – that is, love of self – which was why she identified with the match girl and allowed that fantasy to supersede real-life factors that could have contributed to self-esteem. It was a vicious circle that we set out to break and turn into a virtuous one.

Additionally, we had to address the patient's difficulty with romantic love which, in turn, led to earlier problems that she had experienced with her parents. She loved her mother, but also disdained how she had lived. She longed for her absent father and loved her stepfather, but the relationships were immensely complicated and continued to affect her adult relationships with men. Her experience with her stepfather even precipitated a sadomasochistic desire for punishment. She would provoke men into issuing punishment – if not physical, then psychological – and, as might be expected, attempted to provoke me.

So, broadly considered, this study involves how the varieties of love are influenced by earlier relationships and can precipitate diverse fantasies relating to sex and love. Unlike the preceding Oedipus study, which examined the influence of an unconscious fantasy, here we consider how a fantasy, even a conscious one, can undermine both romance and a patient's own self-esteem. We have to determine why the patient clings to this fantasy, even while she understands it and finds new ways to increase its potency.

We all know that love and fantasy can be delightfully intertwined. However, when their involvement becomes pernicious, we have to untangle them. Here, I demonstrate how the patient struggles toward that end.

This study is an example of self psychology, a theoretical orientation conceived by Heinz Kohut (1913–81) and now integral to psychoanalytic treatment. It focuses on developing and maintaining a solid, cohesive sense of oneself – that is, what is commonly called self-esteem. Thus, where Freudian analysis focuses on the drives (sex and aggression), and drive derivatives in fantasy and unconscious mental life, self psychology considers one's inner experiences – for example, sensitivity to failure, disappointment, and slights. It recognizes empathy as essential to human development and growth and, significantly, to the psychotherapeutic process.

The patient in this study grew up with an absent father and unavailable, narcissistic mother. Her needs for love, care, and attention were unmet. Thus, she did not have the chance to develop a reservoir of basic self-love and self-esteem that she could have drawn on later in life. During her analysis, I provided the type of empathy that had been lacking. That is, rather than simply interpreting her unconscious mental life and the transferential aspects of our relationship, I tried (within the parameters of the psychoanalytic setting) to compensate for what was missing and, thus, help her to gain a sense of her own value. I tried to mirror that value, helping her to see her positive traits and abilities.

This approach helped the patient to develop resilience, as well as a sense of herself as independent – that is, one that did not require someone else (notably, a man) to make her feel sexually desirable or professionally competent. Toward the end of her analysis, the patient uses the metaphor of giving "birth" to a new self, different from that with which she entered treatment. The metaphor is particularly potent because, from an early age, the patient felt diminished by a mother who flaunted her own ability to attract men. Such narcissism literally left no room for the patient, whose sense of self (and of her own femininity) never fully developed. This inadequacy festered, expressing itself as a generalized inadequacy that the analysis had to address.

At our first session, Carol was fidgety. She pulled at her hair, then at a thread on the placket of her blouse. A button came off in her hand. "See," she said. "What's left to say?"

That little accident, I guess, was supposed to be a version of her life. A sort of pantomime. In fact, as we talked, the button fixated her. "I kind of feel sorry for it," she mused. "It was hanging on, and then it wasn't." She cradled it with a kind of empathy. "My life is headed in the same direction."

I wondered how she would have introduced herself had the button not popped off.

"Well, at least you're animate," I said, in contradistinction to that poor little fixture. But my actual objective, assuming that we could think about that button usefully, was to get at why she identified with an inanimate object inadvertently deprived of its purpose.

The rest of her outfit provided a tip-off.

She was not groomed like a woman hoping to reverse a downward spiral. Why, for example, would she wear an army surplus skirt? It just screamed grunge when, actually, she taught English literature at a local university. It was as if she imagined her next stop was handing out spoons at a soup kitchen. This was potentially an issue, since we always dress for where we *think* we're going, as much as for where we are.

Nonetheless, here she was – fidgeting – complaining that her professional life was collapsing because of personal setbacks (the down-market skirt had begun to make sense). She said she felt distracted. She couldn't write; her classes were boring; students got on her nerves; she yelled at a colleague. "What's left? I have no patience for any of it," she sighed. She also fretted because her daughter, who had moved out, had left her alone in the apartment they had shared. "I know she's got to be on her own," Carol said, "but it feels like another abandonment."

I had a sense of what was coming.

Carol had never married, and had begun feeling that her string of star-crossed relationships would now end in her feeling disappeared. "You know how they treat middle-aged spinsters in Victorian novels," she said. "It's like they don't exist."

"But this is the 21st century," I observed, modestly, reminding her that life does not imitate *outdated* art. "Okay, then forget the novels," she conceded. "I'm afraid that I'm turning into my mother." In many of my middle-aged female patients, this claim was a gasp of despair.

Carol's mother, she said, was "depressed, negative, and infantile." The woman had grown up among Southern gentry, but stunned her family by eloping with a handyman. Her life had been hard and manic. She couldn't keep a husband, though she tried four times.

Carol's father (guy number 2) was, she said, "a phantom." He'd been career military and was on active duty when Carol was born. He never came home, and her parents divorced when she was 3. "Between my mother's scattered life and my father's disappearance, I was practically an orphan."

From an early age, she referred to herself as Hans Christian Andersen's little match girl.

"You know that story?" she asked.

"I think so," I said. "A little girl from a poor family winds up on the street one night. It's very cold, and she's barefoot in the snow."

"Yes!" Carol seemed delighted. "It's one of my favorites. My mother read it to me at bedtime."

Over the course of analysis, I came to realize how important that story was to Carol's self-image. But, at this point, I understood that Carol – as she had with the button – liked to associate herself with alternative actors who exemplified aspects of her life too painful for Carol to describe. The trait evinced a kind of displacement, an avoidance of direct encounter with pain that could directly be interrogated. It was an effective strategy if you wanted help but still couldn't bear to face your life head-on. I'd seen it before, though not, perhaps, as clearly worked out as in Carol's case.

Carol kept returning to the idea of being orphaned. When her parents legally separated, her mother started dating again. One of the men committed suicide when Carol was 5, an incident that she vividly recalled.

"I thought it was my fault," she said. "Like he knew he'd hate to be my stepfather."

She began to think that other men would never like her.

When her mother finally remarried, her new husband was Catholic. Carol was sure that he resented that her own father was Jewish, and that she'd been raised in that tradition.

"I'm sure it wasn't my imagination. My mother played along just to keep the peace." When they'd invite her to decorate the Christmas tree, Carol saw it as antagonism.

"Maybe they were trying to include you," I suggested, but Carol interpreted it as part of a larger, incipient pattern. "I've always been on the outs with men," she told me. "We've always had mutual antipathies." Her insistence on "always" resonated with "forever," as if there was no hope. What did she expect from me – that I would somehow prove her wrong? I felt she was boxing herself in, discounting our potential work together. Perhaps we'd have to breach the defenses she had erected.

As if on cue, an unsettling picture of self-deception emerged during our initial sessions. Carol had been sexually active in her teens and early 20s ("You can see my mother, can't you?") but, when she wanted a child, she used a boyfriend as a stud and then badgered him to leave.

This was not, however, a mere repetition of her mother's fecklessness. It was calculated, provocative, deliberately hurtful. Carol had used the boyfriend, then discarded him. Her action was inconsistent with the idea that she was just unlucky around men. It was inconsistent with her as a pathetic little match girl. It was as if Carol wanted to think of herself in one way so that she'd have cover to act in another. I began thinking that the problem she presented when she came to see me – that she was somehow unlucky in love – was not the real problem. Perhaps, instead, she *sabotaged* her relationships, not least because she distrusted men. Perhaps she pre-empted men from destroying their relationships with her by acting before they could.

There was a lot I needed to learn. But I felt right away that if "sabotage" was Carol's tactic of choice, there had to be a psychic, not just empirical reason. It seemed to me, therefore, that a person *might* act this way if they lacked sufficient self-esteem, and couldn't bear what they assumed would be another blow. It reflected an "I'll show *you*" mentality, expressed as a first-strike pre-emptive defense, albeit one that hurt the person employing it as much as the one on the receiving end. I latched onto this possibility because why else would Carol have identified so closely with so poor a specimen as the little match girl, who never lived to become a grown up, sexually successful woman? The little girl (a.k.a. Carol) was cut off at the pass, perpetually unfulfilled. I wondered whether, in holding onto this fantasy, Carol was channeling her mother, whose blatant self-involvement and failure to adequately nurture Carol had left her feeling undeserving and inadequate. Perhaps Carol justified her behavior toward men because – in her view – she believed that she was perpetually, irremediably, the underdog.

In fact, if this were the case, then the whole course of treatment might involve examining Carol's relations with men (as well as the other objectives she had short-circuited) for the purpose of helping her achieve a level of self-esteem consistent with her value as a real-life (as opposed to a fantasized) individual. But this was in the future.

As we talked, Carol revealed that she saw nothing troubling in how she had behaved. Instead of seeing it as exploitative, she claimed (as I had surmised) that it was "defensive," increasing my suspicions that she reconfigured her actions to conform with a pathetic, orphan-like self-image. In effect, she wanted help but she didn't. She feared that she would never have another relationship, but kept making excuses for herself as to why she harbored such fears. She couldn't bear to dislike herself, so she blamed the men. She defined them as chronically prone to abandon her. So, who could blame her for trying to forestall the ensuing pain?

She recited a litany of departed boyfriends. She'd had a brief, ecstatic romance with an accomplished poet and fiery socialist named Javier. The relationship ended in tears when Javier returned to his native Ecuador to live out his politics. Then there was a seven-year relationship during her late 30s, which abruptly ended, she said obliquely, in "psychiatric problems."

This led to a relationship with the therapist who tried to resolve her problems. When they had gone as far as they could, they mutually agreed to end her treatment and their relationship.

Carol criticized herself for getting involved with a therapist, and suggested that he failed to address her issues by way of encouraging her to break things off. "We mutually agreed to stop seeing each other, but he precipitated the break. In the end, he was untrustworthy." While I couldn't be sure, I thought I heard the same old refrain.

It was the obverse with Javier. Although they'd seen each other for only a few months before he returned to Ecuador, and they had no contact for years at a time, she went on imagining herself in the relationship.

Their connection was totally contingent on his whims, but she made excuses for his absence. That is, her defense against being hurt was that it was all for art.

"He wrote like Pablo Neruda," she sighed. "Just beautifully." It was impossible to be angry.

When she sometimes came across his name, her whole body seized up. "I remember," she said, "that it was hard to breathe. He got into my autonomic nervous system."

Once he came to New York for a reading, and she actually *saw* him again. But that was all that happened. He never saw *her*. After the reading he was whisked away.

Then she heard of his marriage and was devastated.

"For days I could barely eat or get out of bed. I'd had this fantasy we would somehow end up together. I couldn't give it up."

Apparently, she had convinced herself that this fantasy lover was her destiny. *This eliminated everyone else as a possibility.* The fantasy was her defense against real intimacy with someone else.

When we talked about her relationships, the conversation always came back to Javier. Even three decades after they had met, she spoke as if she had seen him only the previous day. She recited his poetry sometimes, which she apparently knew by heart. For her, he was Che Guevara, forsaking everything he could have had in America – including Carol – to fight for social justice. It was as if she could not morally, emotionally ever forsake *him*.

"We were passionate about the same things – poetry, politics, each other," she said.

Yet while that may once have been true, I thought that Javier (or, rather, his fantasy double) was now Carol's romantic gatekeeper, instantly turning other men away as unworthy, untrustworthy, unattainable except for a short fling. Only Javier endured, at least in her mind. He was the durable rationale for Carol to resist other men, and avoid attempting to form stable new relationships. When men approached her, they were not Javier, and she would attribute to them whatever anti-romantic gestures that, in fact, she had initiated.

Yet despite Carol's self-defeating obsession with Javier, she was knowledgeable about the process of psychotherapy (she had, after all, been involved with it before, however disappointingly). When I mentioned what I saw as conflicts and possibly a lack of self-esteem, she understood (though I'm not sure that she readily agreed). She insisted she had nothing to offer a man. Carol felt she might get fired because she thought about men too much to be productive.

"I can't seem to get a grip," she said.

I wondered about her absentee father and the childhood fantasies she might have had about him in relation to her problems with men. (He died in a car crash after her parents' divorce, thereby permanently – irreversibly – removing himself from her life). It seemed likely that he played a part in her leaving men before *they* abandoned *her*. After all, her father hadn't even willfully abandoned her; it just happened because the world had turned its back, first on him and then (as a consequence) on her. How (she might imagine) can you fight blind fate? I could see that she might see herself as preternaturally, inevitably unlucky. Part of our work together, therefore, might involve a decoupling of Carol's fate – that is, her sense of herself in the world – from an ideational pattern that her father's fate seemed to legitimate and her mother's almost certainly reinforced. After a few months of initial sessions, we began a course of psychoanalysis, meeting four times a week.

Settling in

During the initial phase of analysis, Carol was ambivalent about me and psychoanalysis (in the first session, she literally had one foot on and one foot off the couch). She suggested that maybe we could have "a few more days on the chair to get to know each other better."

She tried to establish a minimum of personal contact, commenting on my art, for example, or the upright piano in my office.

Contradicting herself, she spoke in glowing terms about her previous therapist. Although quitting treatment with him had ostensibly been a mutual decision (two years prior to her seeing me), she felt she'd been "forced to give him up." I wasn't so sure. But I could see how the increasing temporal distance had, as with Javier, contributed to turning him into an ideal. Dr. G was the supportive father she'd never had. He gave her "strength and unconditional love." He was "benevolent and understanding." She did acknowledge, however, that she regarded him as "an aristocratic WASP, elegant but cold."

I found it interesting that this last observation was not a criticism. Like Javier, Dr. G was remote. He dwelt in an impenetrable sphere. This was, perhaps, part of his attraction. He fit the pattern of men in Carol's life: connecting with her but only provisionally, then likely to depart or return to where they came from, or be rejected before they could do either.

Did Carol see the pattern or, at least, how Dr. G exemplified it? I thought not.

I was faintly amused when, unlike Dr. G, she found me to be "working class." She meant, I think, that because I was Jewish, I could understand her aspirational background. She needed to see one of us, me or Dr. G, as respectively understanding and remote. She called me *Ahron* because *Dr. Friedberg* seemed "distancing." She hinted in small ways that she wanted to reveal herself – by taking off her glasses or shoes, for example – but it was apparently a struggle because being open with any man left her vulnerable to being hurt.

Would she try to short-circuit our relationship as soon as she felt *too* vulnerable – that is, as soon as we were getting somewhere?

It was ugly

Carol had chronic problems with her teaching jobs and a history of changing employers. She'd taught English in high school (sometimes full-time, sometimes as a substitute), at prep schools, and as both an adjunct and assistant professor at various universities. She was well versed in her field, but typically, after a year or so, she'd manage to get fired.

The reasons were avoidable – being late for meetings, or not submitting grades on time. Currently, she was behind on her grading four sections of composition (admittedly, a superhuman task). The chair of her department was supportive but still frustrated. He'd spoken to her several times. She had received a written warning from the dean.

Carol saw this problematic pattern as something "they" were doing to *her*. It was no different in how she saw her breakups with men. It never occurred to her that she was failing to perform at a level consistent with accepted professional standards. She fantasized about coming before a tribunal and being forgiven because she was poor, suffering, and basically good. A little match girl.

The image defined her exculpating fantasy. While it originated in and animated her relationships with men, it had crept into her professional life.

"Have you noticed," I asked, "that what's happening has as much to do with your behavior as with the dynamics of your workplace?"

Her face hardened. "You don't understand me."

"All right," I answered, "help me."

Her expression softened. Tentatively, she opened up about her passive-aggressive behavior – the little things she did to evade the demands of one job or another. She thought, I was sure, that she would somehow squeak past them. Here was her fantasy at work.

Further, she mentioned having carelessly revealed an abortion to a colleague. "I had one. It was ugly. I'm not even sure who got me pregnant." After a pause she said, "I tend to abort things in my life, don't I? Especially when it comes to relationships and my career."

Yes, she did, but by now it was clear that she also denied the underlying guilt by seeing herself as a good, put-upon person, acting defensively. It was a self-protective narrative that, for the most part, was fiction. Moreover, the fiction (I was sure) signified a lack of self-esteem, traceable to a disappeared father and a mother too wrapped up in herself to sufficiently love her children. So, it would not be enough merely to treat Carol's near-obsession with the little match girl, so much as we had to get to the root of that fantasy in her personal history. If we could not deal effectively with that history, the fantasy would keep getting away from us – as would Carol's capacity to create the basis for a viable sense of herself as a woman who was sexually and professionally successful.

I also felt that her father's act of abandonment (however unwilling) had not just left her feeling like a little orphan but also left her to think that only a man could restore the *status quo ante* – that she needed a man in order to be capable of growth, maturation, and success. This was an unnerving prospect, both for Carol and for our work together, given her acknowledged proclivity to push men away when the relationship started to show promise.

I didn't broach these concerns at this point, and we kept going. However, my objective was to help Carol, ultimately, to realize that she did not need a man merely so that she could feel complete, capable, and mature.

Penis envy

At a staff meeting regarding her performance, Carol proposed a rotating buddy-system to keep herself on track with her grading. Several colleagues agreed to pitch in. Yet after sticking to the system for a few weeks, she found herself resenting it, her colleagues, and her job. By the middle of the term, she was once again behind, satisfying her desire to "get back at" her tormentors but sabotaging herself.

She was issued a second written warning. One more strike and she was out.

"Have you ever considered your rebellious behavior as a kind of test for your colleagues?" I asked. "To see whether or not they like you?"

"No, no really."

"So then, what comes to mind about your work situation?"

"The way my new family excluded me when my mother remarried because I was a Jew in a Catholic house."

We discussed her idea that if only she were the "right stuff" she'd receive unconditional love without having to earn it. Her underlying resentments would evaporate.

I pointed out, however, that academe doesn't work that way. "You *have* to earn your keep. It's got nothing to do with love, and the situations are not parallel." Part of her problem, I thought, was that she made gross generalizations from her childhood to her professional life, failing to recognize that the demands – and the relationships – were so different. "We can expect our parents to love us," I said, "but we have to earn the esteem of our colleagues."

But Carol came back to her childhood. She said that she'd felt supplanted by the birth of her half-sister, which deepened her sense of alienation. I wasn't sure that she'd taken in what I had just said, and said so.

She seemed to be trying to provoke me. It was as if – as the put-upon underdog – she could dismiss the line of inquiry that I had opened up.

"Have you noticed," I asked, "that you tend to create an expectation in someone then frustrate it? You asked for my help, but now you're rejecting it."

She shrugged. "Maybe I create problems as a way of connecting. It's perverse. I behave like a wayward child in need of discipline – the discipline *is* the connection. I would do things to infuriate my mother, who would then hit me and later apologize." She said that sometimes it was the most contact that they'd have for a week.

"It seems to me," I responded, "that this need to provoke punishment is a way of conflating the department chair and me with your mother. You make us angry and frustrated so that we punish you and pay you attention."

"I felt empowered when I angered my mother," she admitted. "Provoking a supervisor gives me the same feeling."

"Do you see the distortion in treating me – and others – like your mother? Do you see how it can impact any relationship?" In the short term, it felt good. But it was a long-term disaster as people peeled away and rejected her (if she didn't anticipate their rejection and act first).

She had articulated a version of the inevitable trajectory, or at least the initial phase where she enjoys being a provocateur.

While she was under the second warning, she tried to constrain herself. But ultimately, she left at the end of the semester, since she didn't like having to watch herself. "It almost feels natural to stick it to the chair," she said. "Maybe if I don't have anyone around in authority, I won't be tempted." She also admitted how exhausting it was to expect to be loved by colleagues who only expected her to perform.

She decided to try working for herself – no chair, or colleagues, or performance metrics. She developed a tutoring practice. But she had difficulty in asking for payment, often accepting whatever was offered, irrespective of a student's family resources. Again, it was the same problem of low self-esteem that dogged her relationships with men. If anyone could reject her just because she was herself, then best to be self-effacing. We still had work to do on her fundamentals if she were to succeed in her new venture, let alone with her eternal pursuit of a guy.

Carol claimed she was new at private tutoring and didn't have the savvy to negotiate a fee. She openly envied me.

"You're a man," she observed, "you know how to do this stuff." She imagined that men had intrinsic knowledge and strength, "a birthright" that allowed for success. "I bet you think it's just penis envy, another male construct to keep women powerless."

"I was thinking along different lines, but go on."

She pointed out how she envied co-workers who had more possessions than she did. (Here comes the little match girl again, I thought). She felt that men and possibly certain women were part of a club to which she could never belong. She wanted me to impart some insight that would make her more powerful and able to assert herself. But it sounded like she didn't want to put in the work of psychotherapy – she just wanted the result.

After we explored her sense of inadequacy in relation to her "captain-father," I realized that she felt entitled, as a disadvantaged child, to an access of power without effort or accomplishment. Her self-image was self-defeating by cutting out the middle term between sources of power and herself as recipient. That term, of course, was effort. Empowerment is a process, not the instant gratification that a child expects. I understood, now more fully, that she hadn't escaped the gravitational pull of childhood. In this sense, she was like her idea of her mother – "infantile." Perhaps, perversely, her mother (whom she didn't much respect) served to justify her resistance to work. I wondered how you undo an idea that was apparently ingrained but, as well, submerged in the unconscious. It required work!

If she feared that she was turning into her mother, it was limited to the idea that neither of them could keep a man; her yen for instant success was her own obsession, a twist on the little match girl type.

"Why don't you get some professional advice about running your tutoring service?" I asked.

She took my suggestion, though I feared she might start yet another non-starter relationship with whomever she contacted. The very fact of needing a man professionally – I was sure it would be a man – might seem to her merely a counterpart of needing one in order to access some level of self-esteem. I feared she would make no distinction between a legitimate, professional need and one that was driven by a disappointing personal history reified in a persistent fantasy. In effect, it was like everything provided an opportunity for her to characterize her circumstances as sorry, bereft, and dependent on some man. In this sense, daily life was a minefield, which she had to navigate without falling back into old patterns.

"My Father Promised to Take Me to Paris"

"The closest I ever came to a committed relationship was with a lunatic," Carol laughed.

Ben was a computer programmer she'd met online. It wasn't until they'd gotten serious that she found out he had "a mild case of psychosis." After weaning himself off antipsychotics, he "got weirder" and attacked her. Carol filed criminal charges and Ben was sentenced to a state penitentiary.

"With that kind of a track record, I doubt that analysis will improve my prospects with men," Carol said.

During this phase of the analysis, Carol related to me as a withholding parent. Because she couldn't see me all the time, I was "away," like her father. My not being constantly available meant I wasn't forthcoming or understanding. She saw analysis as depriving her.

She invoked the many people who'd disappointed her – supervisors, teachers, me. She said the Judy Collins song "My Father Promised to Take Me to Paris" summed up her disillusionment with men. Paris, in effect, was everywhere she would have wanted to be for love and emotional support.

"So you feel that, like your father, I will disappoint you," I said. "That expectation makes it difficult for you to share yourself."

She sighed. "I'm scared that if I get too close to you, you'll leave me the way my father did." I thought to add "and all the other men," since that turn was part of her governing narrative.

In our next session, Carol recounted a dream. The first dream a patient shares with a psychotherapist is often a kind of milestone, and this one marked the transition into the next phase of our work together. It was also interesting as much for the content as the context.

"My daughter's friend was in the kitchen," Carol began. "She was obese. She took up the whole kitchen. Literally. Then someone came to the door with a box of Mexican clothing. A family was moving away. My daughter's friend was saying, 'Oh look, they left you those beautiful things.' I said 'I don't have time. I don't have time.'"

Carol brought up her sister: she was coming to visit with their family but didn't have time for Carol.

"The woman in the dream can't be my sister because my Paula's a string bean, and this woman was fat."

Of course, dreams contain disguises, displacements, and condensations. I just listened.

Carol remembered how 30 years ago, during her adolescence, she'd bought her sister a shawl, "a beautiful hippie thing – Mexican, black silk, embroidered with roses." Paula had left it behind in their house when she moved out, and Carol characterized her leaving as "abandoning the family."

"You felt rejected and deserted by the family when your sister was born," I said. "You say the obese woman in the dream can't be your sister because your sister is thin, but you also said she took up the whole kitchen. Physically she's not Paula, but look at it symbolically. Paula's taking up the family's attention – *again* – leaving no room for you."

Carol began to cry, citing myriad ways that her family rejected her once Paula was born.

But she also complimented me – now I was there "to dissect" her dream, and "open up that can of worms." She was "excited." So, I had apparently touched a nerve. She dispensed with dismissing me as just another patriarch. Okay. I would make the most of her about-face for as long as it lasted.

"What excites you by my teasing out the currents in your dream?" I asked.

"Well, sharing that dream, exposing myself, is frightening," she said. "It gives you power over me. I don't think that you would hurt me, but you *could*." I heard the same fear of men and their capacity to "hurt" that was a constant in her relationships, even as the encounter excited her. Could she even have a relationship that wasn't always fraught? She seemed to relish emotional riskiness. In addressing her dream, was I playing right into her perverse brinksmanship?

This was the real challenge: was treatment itself an extended risk that excited her because of the risk? I didn't want to tie myself up in knots, but she had set the stage for just that. I proceeded ... cautiously.

I finally broached the trust issues that she had with men.

"They're probably coming out now," she said. I thought, however, that they'd been "out" all along, and wondered whether she was suppressing the obvious or, finally, acknowledging what she'd always known.

We wouldn't meet over the summer, and Carol was experiencing a kind of separation anxiety. Trust issues remained a persistent problem, and may have increased with our impending separation.

Obviously, from the perspective of hindsight, she couldn't trust her father. This was a major driver in how she viewed men. That is, if you cannot trust someone you love, who is supposed to love and take care of you, how can you trust *any* guy, who will never have the same level of commitment as a parent does? In Carol's mind, I thought, the desire to trust – and, hence, to rely on someone – was at war with the fear that trust will backfire, leaving her bereft. So, best not to trust in the first place.

Of course, love without trust is fragile, which was probably one reason why Carol understood love as something that (for her) did not have a promising future. She had trouble allowing trust to develop and, as a result, allowing love to develop as otherwise it naturally might.

A lot of sex

Carol was concerned about her tutoring fees. She was charging too little to cover her bills. She also allowed fees to go unpaid for months, then had trouble calling them in. She was afraid that if she charged a reasonable fee or required students to pay on time, they'd drop her. Her feelings toward students and their parents were like those toward her mother: she wanted to be loved and feared rejection.

At the same time, Carol fell behind on paying my fee.

"Please be patient," she pleaded, "and believe in my ability to succeed." Since she was perpetually doubtful of her ability, I wonder if she appreciated the irony.

I tried to explore why she wasn't paying my fee. Predictably, our "romance" surrounding her dream didn't last. She experienced me now as "withholding," and complained that I wasn't flexible, spontaneous, or supportive. Did I fail to deserve payment?

Thus, I was surprised when she described a new dream – especially since I was the hero: "I was in a two-seater car with a guy. He was driving. We came to my garage door, and he drove right through. The sunroof and headlights broke. He was laughing. I went to this young, handsome mechanic to fix it. He started to kiss me. It felt good." She paused. "I think you're the mechanic."

I had seen myself as her co-pilot, so I felt somewhat confused. On the one hand, I'm the guy she turns to to "fix" what's broken, even though I'm also non-supportive and, it would seem, not responsive. I asked how she calibrated what seemed like two contrasting assessments.

"That dream's a warning," she said, "about the danger of intimate involvement with you."

What was the outlook for our work together if she was so conflicted about commitment?

She reflected on herself as deprived and disadvantaged – the little match girl – and joked about me as a "sex toy."

"But you're also the driver of the car," she said.

She was anxious that someone else was in control. Mangling the garage door by speeding through it reminded her that sex was a violent act in which she was being hurt by (or hurting) a man.

"So you feel we're interacting in a potentially harmful way," I commented. Specifically, she felt I was criticizing her for not paying my fee simply by calling her attention to it. "Do you think your resistance to paying me might be a veiled expression of your anger? That is, you experience me as withholding from you, so you express anger by not giving to *me*."

She conceded the point.

We considered how her problems with money had to do with a desire to love and be loved. Money was the currency of love for Carol, implicating how she handled student fees as well as her payment of my bill.

"Sometimes," she recalled, "I took money from my mother's wallet."

It was another instance of her response to the frustrated "mother love" of her childhood which, as we saw, was reflected in her attitude toward student fees and toward mine. I made the connection to her explicitly, and she saw the logic (even if, as I surmised, she did not entirely accept it).

I hoped that as we explored her conflicts around love, she would feel less vulnerable, less guarded in pursuing relationships. But for now, she just assumed that her current boyfriend would hurt her – why wouldn't he? Isn't that what men do? She still viewed men generically, through the lens of childhood trauma, rather than getting to know them – that is, giving them a chance – as individuals. This led to self-fulfilling prophecies when, pre-emptively, she would scuttle a relationship.

So, as she approached her latest boyfriend, David, she had to question her assumptions. Why *not* give him a chance?

To Carol, "chance" is a relative term. It butts up against her obsession with an ideal, elusive love. "He's no Javier," she remarked. That is, while David's challenge to her stereotyping may have provided an opening – may even have encouraged her to become aware of its pitfalls – Javier was still the measure of any man she found herself involved with, *inviting* her to discount them.

She described the effect.

"Since I split up with guys like David before," Carol said, "I've looked for relationships that are mainly just sex. No complications."

I asked whether she might, at least, consider something more with David, provided he was interested. "You'll never know if you *don't* try," I said.

She thought she might, though she could barely allow herself to acknowledge the thought. It seemed frightening. Also, in a lopsided way, she felt a loyalty to Javier that even she must have realized was pointless. "Sometimes, it's like I feel he knows, like he's sad that I am with someone else."

I asked that she listen to how that sounded and, she agreed, it sounded self-deluding. "When you have these thoughts," I said, "stand back, and think about how they would sound to a disinterested observer." She said she would.

The relationship with David did not develop along predictable lines. At first, she said there had been three people in bed (presumably, I was the third) but then that changed.

She and David actually seemed to enjoy each other. They liked to cook. David followed recipes exactly, but he was charmed by Carol's improvisations. "We made a chili once," she said, "and when I substituted garbanzos for kidney beans, I thought he'd have a fit – but he liked it!" I wished she could carry that same, spontaneous spirit into the rest of their relationship.

Periodically, she would report some apparent breakthrough. I thought, perhaps, she was making progress. Nonetheless, the growing intimacy with David just highlighted Carol's conflicted feelings toward me – the other man in her life. I had the power to support but also to disappoint her, to wreak havoc in her life by abandoning her.

If I had a scheduling problem, it boded a catastrophe.

"You experience my missing an appointment as being left," I observed, "which reflects how you felt abandoned by your father."

She sighed. "That's why I feel so vulnerable with men. If David and I get close, he'll probably leave me too." Here she was again, generalizing outward from her father to every man she knew.

Would we ever get past this sense that men always abandoned her? Or her inclination to strike back pre-emptively, abandoning them first? Carol had always felt that she was acting defensively. But that was the easy explanation. Beneath it was this gnawing lack of self-esteem, which justified the defensiveness on grounds that a man would always leave her when he discovered that she was a loser. It was a vicious circle, the life-cycle of a little match girl.

A sadomasochistic struggle

Carol's prophecy came true. After a few months, David dumped her, intensifying her anger and self-doubt while confirming her sense of inevitability: if she became sexually and emotionally involved with a man, she was bound to be hurt.

David's rejection, she claimed, resulted from how I had rejected her, and how I had set her up for a fall. "You told me to give him a chance," she said, "and look what happened. You're just playing with my feelings." But she would regain the upper hand! Prior to a long weekend, she dreamed she'd gone to my office in a bathing suit and couldn't find her purse. "Purse," in this instance, had a double meaning: she would withhold both money and her vagina from me. She elaborated on her sense that while men subjugate women (presumably, as how I had just done), she did not want to surrender herself.

"When have you surrendered yourself?" I asked. She was clearly hardening the connection between David and me.

She was eager to respond. "I used to have fantasies of being raped by men," she said. "Women too. I was a prisoner of some king and did his sexual bidding."

She associated these fantasies with a porn film of a black man sodomizing a woman.

A sexual fantasy of punishment – being beaten by a man – also came up.

"Punishment?" I asked.

She blushed while recalling how her stepfather would come to her room at night, pull down the covers, and spank her when she had disobeyed him.

Around this time, Carol was arriving late for her sessions and was again behind on her payments. In the psychoanalytic situation, conflicts between patient and analyst often play out in terms of treatment parameters that involve time, and money.

"What's happening here," I said, "is that you're trying to provoke me into administering those 'stimulating punishments' you got from your stepfather."

In effect, she was trying to engage me in her erotic, sadomasochistic struggle. "I feel like I'm being submissive to you," she complained.

Actually, she was trying to get her analysis to conform to her erotic desires. She wanted to put me in the position of forcing her to show up to her appointments and pay against her will.

She talked about feeling powerless over me. She saw herself as an innocent victim. She denied her own culpability.

I asked her to describe the Hans Christian Andersen story – which she did, until she wobbled on the ending.

"I think she was adopted by a rich, kindly family ... no, I think she dies ... no, I'm pretty sure she was adopted ..."

I commented on the tug-of-war between her wish and her fear: "Are you going to be taken care of or are you going to be poor and homeless? Are you going to be loved or abandoned?"

"I guess I have this fantasy that if I make myself helpless, someone will take care of me."

It wasn't the first time a patient had presented this wish to me. Carol, however, had unwittingly tied her own identity to a character in a work of fiction, which in turn became a myth at the center of her life. The match girl freezes to death.

Deepening treatment

As another summer break approached, we considered meeting five times a week on resuming. This decision triggered a dream in which an evil scientist was planting microchips in people's brains.

"I think you're the scientist," she said.

When I asked what she associated with "getting something implanted," she said, "The idea of coming five times a week." She wanted to see the increased frequency as my idea rather than as a choice on her part.

"Coming more often makes me feel vulnerable," she explained. "That means a closer relationship, and leaving myself open to getting hurt."

It was hard for Carol to acknowledge a desire to get closer to me. Instead, she needed to see any such initiative as having been forced onto her. (In her sexual fantasies, dominant men forced her to do things that she could not admit, even to herself, that she wanted to do). Nonetheless, the limits of the analytic situation frustrated her, since we could touch only through words. Her relationship to me was infused with feelings from her fantasy life, in which she's submissive to a dominant taskmaster.

In exploring this aspect of her fantasy life, she began speaking more openly about "wanting" me, wanting to be close to me, as well as her sense of vulnerability connected to those desires. It was her basic conflict over wanting/rejecting love.

Still, after returning from summer break, Carol came five times a week. She wanted me to know how much she was giving up to keep her commitment to therapy, and was counting on her "sacrifice" to make her special to me.

She was disappointed that I wasn't more taken with her efforts.

"I did something that you wanted," she said (meaning coming five times per week), "and yet I don't get what I want from you."

Her sense of an unfair exchange applied to all the men in her life.

My intimate man

Toward the end of fall, I was to give a presentation at a psychoanalytic meeting. Carol wanted to attend, and spoke about a series of related fantasies. In one, a beautiful woman congratulates me with a sensual kiss. Carol looks on feeling hurt and left out. In another, I give an excellent presentation to the applause of colleagues. She is proud of my achievement but envies the praise and attention I get. In still another, I make a mess of my lecture, and she looks on gleefully.

These fantasies were portals into her own experiences and how they shaped her perception of relationships.

Shortly after my presentation, she had a revealing dream: "The two of us were at a party. I'm not sure whether we wore clothes. We come together in some way. I don't think it was sexual." Her initial thought was of seeing me go off with some colleagues after giving the presentation. She felt excluded.

"Can you recall how we were together in the dream?" I asked.

"After the reception we get a room at the hotel together. We make love."

After this confession, we recognized that the source of her discomfort and of her desire to attend my presentation was connected to forbidden sexual desires that she had toward me. As with her father, Carol wanted what she couldn't have.

For months, she made only the feeblest efforts to go out with men. She became more involved and invested in fantasies about me. In one bit of acting out, she developed a flirtatious relationship with a colleague around my age.

"If you don't want to be my sex object," she sniped, "I'll get it elsewhere."

She elaborated on a series of relationships with younger men she'd had over the years, especially while in treatment with her previous therapist.

"Do you think you have to leave me to have a meaningful relationship with a man?" I asked.

Riffing on a line from Groucho Marx, she replied, "I wouldn't belong to a man who would have me."

Carol was projecting her self-loathing onto men who showed an interest in her.

Kicked in the stomach

Shortly after the start of the New Year, Carol's stepfather was hospitalized for congestive heart failure. Initially, she wanted someone else to take responsibility for his care (her mother had been dead for a decade), but when a neighbor stepped forward, Carol felt excluded.

"My position was usurped," she told me.

She recalled her stepfather's previous hospitalization, when he introduced her and her sister to another patient. "This is my daughter Carol," he said, "and this is my real daughter, Paula." The remark confirmed the hurt that Carol had carried around from childhood. "He acknowledged that I wasn't part of the family." She was angry but, perversely, she felt vindicated, as if her defensiveness with regard to men had been justified.

Soon after her father's hospitalization, she brought her miniature poodle into my office. It was dying of cancer. She made an excuse about not wanting it to wait in the car on the way to the vet.

"I feel like this is a child rather than a dog," she said.

Carol acknowledged that she wanted us to be together as a family, and saw me as the father of her "baby."

"Letting go of Poo," as she called him, "feels like my child is dying. It's like getting kicked in the stomach."

She further associated the pain and the death with having an abortion, and admitted to having had a second one.

I reminded her that previously she had only told me about one.

She nodded. "The one I forgot to mention was the worst. I didn't know who the father was. I was sleeping with two different men at the time. Abortions were illegal, so I had to hide it."

She recognized that the lengths she was going to for her dying poodle – an expensive course of chemotherapy that even the vet said had little chance of success – was an attempt to allay the guilt she felt over her aborted pregnancies.

As the doctor predicted, the dog's condition worsened and Carol decided to put it to sleep. Over the next several sessions, she observed that her mother had "aborted" her finances.

"What do you mean?" I asked.

While Carol was saving money as a teenager to pay for college, her mother forced her to pay rent then to move out.

"I was thrown out prematurely, killed for wanting to better myself," she said. After a pause, she supplied her own interpretation: "It was like doing to my unborn child what I felt had been done to me."

Carol realized she'd been burdened with guilt over her sexuality, and she'd looked for ways of depriving herself of pleasures. Her relationships had to be freighted, on the edge of disappointment – a set-up for inevitable hurt.

Her own parent

Carol's stepfather developed pneumonia, which landed him in the ICU. He recovered but was physically weakened. Certain abilities, such as memory and perception, were impaired. Carol still wanted to be the special daughter who cared for her father, but she deflected thoughts about his impending death.

"It seems you're not allowing yourself to feel sad about your stepfather's condition." Her father's condition gave rise to thoughts about her own.

My comment elicited tears. She whimpered, "I'm afraid that with him gone, no one will really love me!" Of course, she had recently complained that her father only faintly cared for her. Did she realize that? She continued to live with contradictions, swinging from one point of view to the opposite. She inhabited simplified moments of her own design, not in the complex (often ambiguous) reality that most of us inhabit.

"And you want me to take care of you the way a loving parent would." But from my perspective, "care" was not all that she needed. I hoped she would come to rely on herself.

She couldn't remain the little match girl. The myth was disabling.

Displaced again

I mentioned that I'd be moving offices in the spring, but hadn't given her my new address. This left her free to imagine I'd be moving into her building, which had an office available, and that I'd be the boy toy upstairs.

After complaining for years about the clutter and my cramped waiting room, now Carol raved about my office which, she said, felt like an old-fashioned library. But behind her sudden attachment to the space that I was vacating was a fear that I'd throw her out of analysis and cut her out of my life.

As the day of the move approached, Carol claimed to be surprised, as though she were being evicted from her own home. "It's unfair," she insisted, "and unsettling."

"You're taking my move like an injury," I remarked.

She recalled her mother's remarriage. "I was displaced from my home," she said. She'd also had to give up her friends. "I was alone, and there was nothing I could do about it."

It got worse. After relocating, Carol spent the summer at sleep-away camp. On returning home, she found her mother, who had been pregnant, bedridden and weak.

"Isn't it wonderful?" her stepfather said. "You have a sister!"

She pretended to be excited, but mostly she was afraid for her mother and herself. She knew things would never be the same, and no one would have time for her anymore. My move revived old fears that she'd be left and forgotten, displaced and replaced.

She recalled a childhood daydream: "My house was burning down and a fireman would rush in and save me. I used to get excited about that." This was tied to memories of her stepfather, who would sometimes carry her over a shoulder to bed.

The idea of being rescued by a powerful man – Roy Rogers, a man in uniform, the president of the United States – was central to Carol's fantasy life as a child. And now she wanted me to save her by moving upstairs. I could cancel out the move that her stepfather had enforced. But still, she acted in ways that undermined my position, like coming late for sessions. This self-sabotage, reflecting hostility toward her father, was then directed toward me.

Transference, in which feelings for a significant person from the past are projected onto another in the present, is an integral aspect of psychoanalysis. Carol often projected feelings for and fantasies about her father onto me. At times she also conflated me with her mother, such as when she took pleasure in frustrating me, just as she'd thwarted her mother. Far more often, however, I was a stand-in for her father. Imagining her father as a playboy taking up with nymphets in Paris, she leveled these accusations against *me* (was I keeping someone in the back room of my office?). She was constantly anxious that I would abandon her. Though her father had deprived her of his love and attention, she insisted that I was the one depriving her of love and attention.

"I want to be the most important woman in your life," she asserted.

But now that she was no longer being treated in my home office, she felt shut out of my private life.

With my old office, a live–work situation, Carol could fantasize that I was her man-in-waiting. With the new office, she could no longer maintain that fiction. Instead, she needed to see me as her "playboy, fuck-around father" – once again pinning his imagined behavior on me. She was also once again the pitiable match girl, a helpless victim of circumstance.

Her fears and anxieties were exacerbated because we wouldn't be meeting in August. Our vacations did not overlap.

"You're blowing me off for a whole month," she said.

Of course, I wasn't.

However, our not meeting during August resonated with her father's going overseas. She thought I'd forget about her. Moreover, her sense of losing my love meant that she was unlovable. She felt as helpless and worthless as when her father had abandoned the family.

We had rehearsed this many times, but to Carol it was an obsession. She could never let it go, just the way she could not let go her memories of Javier. She created personal truths and then stuck with them, irrespective of whether – as in the case of Javier – they were tantamount to fantasies.

I couldn't help but be frustrated, even as I wanted to help. I often suspected that she understood what I said, but could not accept it and could only discount it.

As the summer break approached, a dream reflected Carol's sense of being wounded and maltreated: "I was with a doctor in a white coat, a periodontist who was sexy but sadistic. I was afraid he was going to hurt me. We shared the same room at first, but then he went into a different one and started doing other stuff. I was pissed off. I took off in his car and didn't pay him, but I knew I'd be charged anyway."

Carol had had dental work recently and said that the dentist was someone who, like me, could help or hurt her. She saw stealing my "car" (i.e., the couch in my office) and not paying me as a way of taking revenge. Withholding my fee was a way of "torturing" me, but it also represented the flip side of her fantasy of being tortured by a man. By not paying, she hoped to provoke me into hurting her. She also imagined that if she owed me money, I wouldn't disappear on her.

Yet, in spite of these conflicts, Carol said she would try to overcome her separation anxiety. She now viewed our impending August break as a chance to see how well she managed on her own. I wasn't sure how she'd do, and was prepared for a torrent of complaint when we met up again. But still, I was encouraged by her willingness to try. I thought perhaps she was setting me up for subsequent blame, but I saw no reason to blame *her* in advance.

An adopted myth

Carol began the first session after our hiatus by putting on her glasses and scrutinizing me. "Is it really you? I kind of forgot about you over the break, and … I guess I just wanted to make sure you're there and haven't changed."

"Still here." I smiled. "Still me."

The problem was actually with *Carol's* position. While developing her tutoring business, she had taken up graduate studies in English literature. She worked diligently on her thesis about George Eliot and the social context of her writing. Carol had only occasionally discussed her research and dissertation in analysis, though she was now at the point of completing her Ph.D. Her program was eager to graduate her by the end of the year, but Carol was procrastinating. She wasn't sure why.

"I'm putting myself in the position of a victim," she concluded. "I'm the little match girl, wandering around with no one to help me."

We had worked on the issue over time, and she had made considerable progress. It would take time to more fully resolve this lifelong alter ego, but we wanted to help her do better with relationships (including with herself). That flimsy (but unshakable) little fiction was blocking Carol's progress.

"Was the little match girl working toward a Ph.D.?" I asked.

Carol looked taken aback. "Of course not."

"Did she run her own business?"

"I see your point," Carol said. "The match girl is helpless. I'm not."

"Exactly."

She covered her face with her hands. "I think I've so adjusted to my sense of deprivation that I've given up dealing with it."

Actually, as mentioned, a few years after her father left, the little match girl persona was reinforced by Carol's move to a new house, where she felt like "an outcast in the family," a stranger (a Jew) in her own home. Then her half-sister was born. Carol identified with the little match girl because it strengthened her belief that she had nothing going for her.

My questions had put a chink in the match-girl façade, but we had a way to go. At some point, we'd have to further dismantle the fantasy. It stood in the way of her developing better self-esteem, without which she would continually obstruct herself romantically and professionally.

Just do the work

At a Christmas party, the chairman of the department complimented Carol on her dissertation. Her response was to eat six brownies.

A short time later, a group of fellow Ph.D. candidates asked her to give a seminar on George Eliot. Carol first complained that they'd only want to hear about *Middlemarch*, Eliot's magnum opus, but that she'd rather talk about the much less complex *Silas Marner*.

"That's my favorite Eliot novel," she said. "I don't care what anyone thinks."

She then proceeded to create a scheduling conflict. Nor had she completed all of the requirements to graduate.

"Just do the work," her thesis advisor told her, "and you can finish in a couple of months."

Instead of taking this advice, Carol involved herself in a number of professional activities.

I continued to frame her intransigence in context with the match girl, and her sense of herself as a victim, but nothing changed. Carol talked for hours about not doing what she had to.

I felt ineffectual. At the end of one session, I snapped, "Just do the work," echoing her advisor.

The next session I asked, "Is there anything I said that stood out for you last time we talked?"

"When you told me, 'Just do the work,'" Carol answered. "That felt more real than your psychoanalytic interpretations. You know what else? I'm glad I got you to do something that isn't in your job description."

Even though my command (since that it was) was delivered somewhat harshly, Carol experienced it as evidence of my concern and immediately set out to complete the requirements. I reminded her, however, that my "job description" was to help her become self-aware which, obviously, I had. I thought it useful to pursue her reaction.

"We spent weeks trying to understand your resistance to getting your Ph.D., and you did next to nothing. But when out of frustration I snapped, you suddenly responded. Why?"

"Well, there were times when I'd gotten supervisors to spur me on. Funny, that word reminds me of horseback riding at sleep-away camp. The spurs hurt the horse but also tickled it to go faster."

"What comes to mind about being tickled?" I asked.

"Being spanked by my stepfather. I wonder, does that mean he cared about me?"

"I'm not sure that's the conclusion I'd draw, but you got me to spur you on, didn't you?"

She smiled. "I sure did."

Spankings

Weeks later, Carol was talking about the semi-erotic punishments she wanted to get from men. She experienced these as pleasurable and a form of love. Referring back to my command ("Just do the work"), which had been a counter-transference reaction or slip of sorts, she said, "I *want* you on my back."

She followed this with the way she would provoke her stepfather into spanking her. Talking on the phone after hours, for example, would earn her a punishment.

"He'd come in my room," she recalled gleefully, "pull down the covers, and whack me on the behind. It was exciting."

"You provoke me too," I observed, "but what you're looking for is a *verbal* spanking."

Carol sighed. "It's not my better self that wants these things," she protested. "But I guess that's the self that sometimes gets the better of me. Paying your bill late and waiting till my rent is overdue – not to mention my tuition payment – are things I do to provoke authority figures."

"Even more than wanting to be in a real relationship with a man," I commented, "you want me to spank you." Where was a commitment to reality in this? It was a type of fantasy.

At first, she denied my assertion and pointed to things she'd done to please me. Then she acknowledged the fantasy of being dominated by a powerful man.

"Looking back at my childhood, I think I took my stepfather's spankings as an act of love, even though I wasn't his favorite. At least he recognized that I was there, that we had to connect. Putting off my dissertation was probably a way of asking to be punished."

The stimulation provided by the quasi-erotic encounter tended to override the pleasure of constructive work. It was trading immediate gratification for a hard-won, solid performance – much as a child would do. Letting go of the little match girl (with a very non-Andersen inclination toward erotic punishment) continued to be mission-critical.

Dating redux

Carol yearned for an intimate, loving relationship, but she didn't think she had the necessary social skills.

Nonetheless, she began to make efforts at finding a relationship. She looked at profiles on the dating sites. She queried friends and colleagues. She treated dating like any important project, and set aside several hours a week to concentrate on it. She composed a profile of herself and uploaded her most flattering pictures to Match.

Eventually, a businessman replied. She made a date and found Roger as charming as she'd hoped. He wined and dined her over the course of a couple of months. She was elated and anxious at the same time – elated to be in a promising relationship with a successful man but anxious because the idea that she might find real-life comfort rubbed against her sense of herself as the match girl.

It was time – once again – to disarm that fantasy.

"*The Little Match Girl* was your favorite story as a child, wasn't it?" I asked.

"Yes."

"Are there any other stories that really stuck with you from childhood?"

"*A Christmas Carol*." She smiled. "My name's in the title, after all."

"But that's not the real reason, is it?" I didn't have to point out that it was written by Charles Dickens, whose novels she taught. "And what about your antiques? Don't you have a roll-top desk?"

She looked puzzled. "Yes, a Cutler. From 1860."

"You took on that whole setting," I observed, "that whole ambience. A simpler time when people read by candlelight or hearth fires. Horses clopping through the streets instead of cars. It's not uncommon, romanticizing a bygone era. But as the match girl becomes central to your identity, studying Victorian literature is a way of keeping her world alive."

"Are you saying that my specialization in Victorian literature has just been a support system for an illusion?"

I'd been afraid she might go there. "Not at all," I reassured her. "I'm just trying to help you understand at least one of your motivations. Remember you told me you didn't want to give a talk on *Middlemarch*?"

"Yes. My favorite George Eliot novel is *Silas Marner*."

"And doesn't Silas adopt a little girl who's been orphaned?" (I'd gone online and read a summary of the book). "He tracks her down in a snowstorm, I believe."

"It's the little match girl all over again," Carol commented.

"Pretty much."

"*A Christmas Carol* is a story of rescue too," she added, "but it's the Cratchit family, not a young girl."

"You've spent your life seeing yourself as a deprived little girl unable to obtain the love she so desires from her father – and looking for that love in other men. Is it time you let the helpless orphan go? She's not you, just your fantasy"

"It's not that easy."

"No, of course not. It will take more time."

Carol nodded.

"There's one other thing – the match girl isn't rescued at the end. She freezes to death."

"She does, doesn't she?" Carol wasn't surprised at all.

"You remembered the story the way you wanted or needed to, even though you knew how it actually ended."

It was a testament to the power of wishful thinking.

"Well, it seems I have a lot to mull over for our next session."

Carol's relationship with Roger didn't pan out, but she didn't wallow in self-pity. Instead, she considered what had happened, learned what she could, and moved on. She'd enjoyed their time together and viewed it as a positive experience. What I had hoped, and perhaps even caught a glimpse of, was that Carol could construct an identity that included self-esteem but that did not require a man to make it credible. If this identity was beginning to take shape, then we were making progress.

After all, Carol's reaction was entirely different from the way she'd dealt with breakups in the past, when for *years* she'd dwell on – or perhaps *in* – her sense of loss and longing. Could she keep up the good work?

Dream vs. reality

Although Carol had thought of Javier often during their decades-long hiatus – and frequently brought him up in therapy – they hadn't spoken in all that time. So, it was a shock when, out of the blue, Javier called.

"I'm in New York," he told her. "Why don't we meet for dinner?"

Carol had dreamed of such a meeting for years, imagining that Javier would fall hopelessly back in love with her and they would go out and build a life together, almost as if no time had elapsed. Her fantasy and the real world were about to meet … in a total anti-climax. The rebel–poet–lover had become a paunchy, low-level bureaucrat. His "writing" consisted mostly of filling out government forms. Carol, in contrast, had become a professional with her own business.

In fact, the whole experience was disappointing, and she berated herself for having kept the fantasy alive all these years.

"It's not just Javier," I pointed out. "Longing to be with a man in a fairytale has been almost forever."

But now, seeing Javier shook her out of her fantasy. It demonstrated the value of reality. She wasn't "cured," but she realized that she had invested in a mirage, a projection of her own fantasy that became ever more fantastical the further she drifted from reality. If the process worked with respect to Javier, could it work with regard to the match girl and all her other self-defeating fantasies?

The answer was a tentative yes. Because she recognized the importance of getting past her fantasies about love, Carol began to speculate on whether she might *deserve* a fulfilling relationship. That is, perhaps a man's interest in her was more than just a one-way street to abandonment. At least, she said, she would try not anticipate *how* he would abandon her, and *when*, and then reject him first. She also acknowledged that *without* a man, she was still okay. "I'm near getting a Ph.D. – that has to count for something."

Of course, it took a shake-up like seeing Javier to shake her out of her intransigence, rather than some revelation in the course of analysis. But analysis predisposed her to reassessing her fantasy life so honestly and directly.

In the past, Carol had been drawn to men who were, like her father, unattainable. She imagined that over time she could persuade them to change, to be different from the way they were – to be more giving, loving, trustworthy. Now the fantasy of being rescued by a man was fading. She focused less on the mechanics of "dating skills" and more on how she felt about the man she was dating.

The dating game

While Carol's attitude toward men and relationships had improved, it was still not what I'd call healthy. Around this time, she began discussing masturbation as a soothing "replacement" for men. She also mentioned various defensive maneuvers. "I usually think of the men I'm seeing as frogs," she said, "and don't get my hopes up that any of them will turn into princes."

I wondered what the men might have thought had they known what was going through her head.

Still, her stories about the various men she was dating were engaging, even entertaining. As if to make light of these guys, she claimed she was only going out with them to please me. But her claim also reflected the illusion that I was *making* her go out. In other words, it was part of a cycle of sadomasochistic fantasies in which she submitted to me. She also still felt vulnerable about opening up to a man other than me.

During one session, she confided that she loved the interracial relationships, younger men with older women, and other unlikely matches featured in the *Sunday Times*.

They populated a corner of her fantasy life – primarily, her desire for me (a younger man), including fantasies of our having sex in a bar, in my bedroom, and on a secluded beach. While Carol felt safe enough with me to explore these aspects of her psychic life, she also felt exposed and susceptible.

She acknowledged that indulging in fantasy got her nowhere. That is, while she *liked* evoking her secret desires, she *realized* they were unfulfilling.

"Fantasies about you aren't enough anymore," she observed. "I want something real. I want something of my *own*. You can't be a replacement for having a man my life."

I sensed an opening.

"Well, think of how far you've come in your professional life."

She smiled, remembering how just a few months earlier it seemed impossible that she'd graduate, but now it was virtually certain. She took heart from the possibility that her professional progress might segue into her personal life.

But still, there was a hitch (as there always is with Carol).

Becoming a full-fledged professor meant giving up a sense of herself as deprived, a little match girl. She resisted. She observed that her dissertation was still incomplete. She brought up a childhood bicycle accident.

"My mother had just taken the training wheels off, and I was riding downhill. I swerved to avoid an oncoming car and fell into a hedge. I wasn't hurt, but I was terrified."

She made the obvious connection between the fulfillment of a desire – having her professional training wheels taken off – and fear of the consequences.

We had something else to work on. Or, rather, it was the same problem, just posed at a slightly different angle.

The desire for punishment

At the beginning of one session, Carol lay down on my couch and pulled her coat over her like a blanket. Eventually, she began to tell me how she'd come home one night smelling of cigarettes. Her stepfather hadn't done anything right away but, an hour later, he rushed up the stairs to her bedroom, tore off her covers, and spanked her.

"It was scary but exciting at the same time to be woken up by a spanking," Carol recalled.

"You seem to be replaying the spanking scene, covering and all, with me," I commented.

"Am I? I guess this need to provoke you is based on the weird disciplinary relationship I had with my stepfather."

"You're trying to turn anyone you see as having authority over you into your warden," I said.

The next day Carol accused me of "verbally spanking" her and complained that the way I'd handled her had been "rough and mean." She segued into a dream in which "these little people who are learning a dance, a jig, are being stepped on." She had her own interpretation: "I think the little people are parts of myself trying to learn to take proper steps, but those big feet of yours keep coming down on me."

She also brought up a diary she'd found while rummaging through some old papers the previous day. One entry, tellingly enough, began, "Today Dickey Lewis slapped me, but at least I'm getting some attention from him." She also recalled playing cards with schoolboys, who punished her when she lost by rapping her knuckles with the deck until they bled.

"You're convinced you can't have the love and attention of a man except through provocation and the resulting pain," I commented. We had been through all of this before. I thought that perhaps she was provoking me through sheer repetition – inciting me to lose my cool like when I issued that famous command. I wondered whether she was playing a game, as she had with the schoolboys, or actually engaging in the work of therapy.

"Being reprimanded," she admitted, "feels like a way of telling me I'm cared about."

After this discussion, I suggested that instead of aggressively undermining her efforts with unrealistic expectations, she set a reasonable goal to write for four hours over the weekend and two hours during the week. I still hoped that if she made professional progress – and could see that she had – the feeling of self-worth would spill over into her personal life. But I was taking a chance. Her game-playing – if that's what it was – was discouraging. Carol was hard to read sometimes, and I expect that she felt that way about herself.

The last obstacle

Carol's tutoring practice was full and her fees more commensurate with her experience and abilities. Men were showing interest. Yet despite these tangible gains, she was becoming demoralized.

Part of the problem was that Carol's quality of life was better than her mother's had been. This sense of moving past her mother left Carol feeling conflicted. On the one hand, she'd worked hard to improve herself and her life. On the other, she felt undeserving.

She began to sabotage her romantic life by not returning phone calls and e-mails, but then complained she felt lonely. She accused me of having "forced" her to attain goals that, nonetheless, she wanted. This was a dodge, so that she wouldn't have to deal with guilt over attaining them.

She compounded this guilt by revisiting her abortions. She equated herself, as a baby-killer, with the Nazis and felt full of remorse. She berated herself for her "impulsive, misguided, and irresponsible" behavior.

"Do you think you're doing any good by punishing yourself for what happened decades ago?" I asked.

She answered with a dream from the previous night: "I was in a house that belonged to other people. A black lady was lying outside in the snow. She'd been badly bitten by a dog. They said, 'She's going to die. Let's leave her.'

I said, 'Either way she'll be more comfortable inside.' I brought her in myself and she recovered."

Carol saw herself as the black woman – wounded, dark, abandoned. She recalled a talk show from the night before in which abortion had come up, and she realized she'd felt "bitten" by the abortions she'd had. She concluded that they stood in for me, and I was giving up on her.

"Did you notice in the dream that you saved yourself?" I asked. "Of course it's hard to feel you deserve being rescued when you feel like a murderer."

Carol conceded the point and said she wanted to put this part of her past behind her.

"I know better now the value of human life, especially after raising a child."

She said she would return to serious dating again, instead of just hooking up.

While I took this as a healthy development, Carol's dating life served several conflicting functions. Of course, she was pursuing a reality-based relationship. But this also guarded against her feelings for me – that is, it protected against possible rejection by me even as it meant that her settling into a monogamous relationship would require that she give me up. Which way would she jump?

"You know," she said, "I still remember a diary entry from 20 years ago. I wrote: 'I can't see loving a man and being in treatment at the same time.'"

Generally, she was involved with two men: a man she loved and another she used for sex.

"The last real issue for me," she announced, "is finding a man to replace you."

Saying it out loud led her to draw an analogy between having to give up the love of her absentee father to gain the love and attention of her stepfather. The reluctance to give up the past sometimes led her to put off men who had a genuine interest in her (and, hence, represented the future).

Addressing this pattern, I said a little playfully, "A man's expressing genuine interest in you is the kiss of death for the relationship."

"That's hurtful," she replied.

After a moment's introspection, however, she admitted that she *did* tend to reject men who seemed sincerely attracted. Beneath it all was her paltry self-esteem, where she imagined that a man worth sharing her life with would be uninterested.

She generally assumed that men were primarily motivated by sex. If a man held her hand, she'd say, "He just wanted to fuck me." Of course, this finessed the fact that she had used *men* for sex. But despite her forays into "love," that pretty much summed up her approach. About one man, she joked, "The real problem is he likes me." What she failed to see was that the "real problem" was that she didn't like herself.

She relaxed her standards a little, calibrating them with the real world. But she was no less determined to find a man who would complete her – that is, fill in all the gaps in an imagined persona far beneath her actual worth.

I commented that while we had been working through specific problems, not least her proclivity to short-circuit relationships, we had been reaching toward restoring her self-esteem. "Look," I said, "when we try to put the little match girl fantasy back where she belongs – in the 19th century – we are actually talking about making your own self-esteem equivalent to who you are. That's the best way to insure that your relationships have a long-term prospect of success, and perhaps the only way that you can get along without a man to rescue you while you are still looking."

Carol seemed to understand, however grudgingly. She acknowledged feeling love for me but insisted that the emotion was not entirely due to transference.

"For me to be able to feel love for you *and* for another man is practically revolutionary."

Giving "birth"

Carol imagined that after working through her issues she'd "give birth" to herself as a complete and independent person. She would, in effect, re-create herself. I would be the catalyst, a sort of father.

She recalled how once, when making love with Javier, she'd called him by her father's name.

"I didn't get it then," she remarked, "but now I see the similarity between them. Both were absent, but both stayed in my head – kind of like you, too."

I waited while she caught up with her train of thought. She narrowed her focus to her father.

"I guess the important thing," she continued, "is to figure out whether I'm doing things because I truly want to or because I'm still trying to win over a man who's barely a memory."

This question helped Carol think about her dating life, but her dissertation was still stalled. As she began to write, she became insecure about her ideas. She'd also become hesitant about putting her thoughts on display. She cited a need to write something that would distinguish her in her field – though this was not a requirement. It undermined the task at hand, which was to finish the thesis she'd been writing for years.

I saw a kind of corollary here to her dating life. I suggested we might help to separate out the practical issues from the emotional ones.

The offer of a practical option helped her to adopt a "just do it" attitude, and she was able to be more open about her ideas. When she spoke to me about writing in abstract terms, I reminded her that writing is a form of work that had to be done regularly. "Put your head down and keep going," I said.

Summer love

As the summer approached, Carol floated the idea that she'd gotten what she needed from our work, and that her analysis would end with being "cured of disease." She had a hermaphroditic fantasy: formerly, she had used a boyfriend to get pregnant, but now she was both mother and father of the child (herself). Being both male and female was defensive: she would not have to suffer the pain inflicted by men.

She also felt that we'd make something together, a baby that would complete her and join us, as she imagined her mother was made whole by her sister's birth. Conversely, Carol believed she would make *me* whole in the process. In effect, all this talk about wholeness and completion was reifying a metaphor, as if she could slip between linguistic constructions and actual, flesh-and-blood life. It was still participating in fantasy, even if it was grounded in personal experience. It warped that experience, turning it into a substrate for obsession. While I was sure that we had weakened the hold of her childhood pain on her imagination, this latest statement was a startling turn. I hoped that she would move past it as more tempting – reality-based – opportunities presented, and she formed more realistic connections.

She continued to describe her dreams. In one, I was a crippled man struggling to climb a ladder. She wanted to mother me back to health, but at the same time keep me going in the direction of my own success (*up* the ladder). In another dream she was driving a bus while traveling with a younger passenger (me) toward TIME, Inc. Though she was nervous at the wheel, she felt that the trip benefited both of us.

What I heard was a continued psychic involvement with me. She was caring for *me*, reversing our ostensible roles. It was not presumptuous or self-indulgent but wishful, and even (in the dreams) she meant well. It expressed a kind of loving care she had come to have for me.

But along with what was perhaps presumption – she was literally in the driver's seat – albeit taking more responsibility, I could still see signs that she was anxious about leaving therapy – that is, about my not being able to take care of *her*. The bus dream occurred the day before a long weekend; she'd been thinking about our time being up for the week. She was also anxious about taking a longer break this summer, and saw it as foreshadowing our ultimate break. After all, she was uncomfortable driving the bus by herself.

Nor did she feel that on her own she could see things for what they were, and we began to explore some of her fantasies about the end of treatment. She observed that she'd leave me for a "real relationship." This motivated some of her efforts to date more often.

But her adopted myth cropped up again: she was afraid she might make a mistake that turned her into "a charred little match girl" (the very matches that the girl carried causing her demise). Thus, by remaining symptomatic, she'd never have to leave analysis. Not finishing her dissertation was another way to stay in treatment. She even offered to pay me more the following year to discourage me from ending her treatment.

In her mind, ending treatment meant terminating our creation – her – and a death or abortion of sorts. She became increasingly upset about our dwindling time together (even as she was the one who had announced it). She fretted that I'd forget her after she was gone.

Perhaps to convince herself that she could bear the pain, she claimed that she would resume dating more seriously (even though dating was, in her mind, on the trajectory to inevitable pain). She kept creating vicious circles, justifying constant withdrawal into her little match girl myth – not to mention pre-emptive strikes against her own success with men or with her dissertation.

A greater capacity to love

When Carol returned from summer break, she found her sense of being separated from me to have been different from what she had expected: she had missed me, but she didn't dwell on it. Nor did she experience our time apart as having been abandoned.

We returned to the subject of her termination. She pointed out that not only had her tutoring practice become successful, but she had good relationships with former colleagues. She was enjoying a social life. She was aware of her inner conflicts and wanted to control them. She returned to the idea that this period would be like a "birth" and, in fact, she saw it as taking about nine months. She saw herself as a child she was bearing. I thought that if she could proceed under this governing metaphor *without* its accompanying, delusional components, then she was making progress. But, of course, you never knew with Carol. Sometimes a fantasy, or a metaphor based on a fantasy, would overwhelm her. I held my breath.

We agreed to end her treatment, and she suggested a final date in the spring.

"Why spring?" I asked.

"It's the season of birth and freedom," she replied.

Apparently, judging from her metaphor, the jury was still out.

She also felt that spring would give us time to discuss some lingering issues – although Carol always seemed to find new versions of old issues.

Moreover, she still feared being psychically on her own, and had a background sadness about giving me up. But this was tempered by efforts to see her failure to find a committed relationship more as a practical matter than as an outgrowth of her internal conflicts. She also felt that even though she had not reached the ultimate goal of that mature relationship, she had still achieved "a greater capacity to love and share in life with other people in healthier ways." I felt that, to a degree, she had talked herself into this feeling, though I hoped that she would try to make it her reality. Sometimes patients announce goals as if they were already achievements, and I had to hope that this was true for Carol.

Coming into her own

"You," Carol said one session, "you're the problem."

Behind this belief was the feeling that Carol needed me if she were to live her life. Similarly, she linked graduating to giving me up.

"Do you think I'm ready for that?" she would ask. Then she'd bring up situations in which she needed someone to rescue her.

One such situation involved Carol's stepfather. His health was continuing to deteriorate. She talked about how helpful he'd been in encouraging her aspirations to grow as a person. She worried that without him (or me), she might lack the wherewithal to live independently.

I said that "your anxiety about moving ahead is tied into fantasies related to hurting or losing your stepfather." This was a reversal of how she'd claimed that he'd hurt her as a child because she was not her sister. Carol's fantasies, and the motivations that she drew from them, often shifted, depending on her circumstances. Here, she was afraid of terminating analysis, so her father became the crutch that she had relied on and would still need. She lived inside a constantly revolving kaleidoscope of fantasies. Nothing was fully stable.

Her discussion shifted again – from her father, to her experience of *me* as a father she was giving up, to us as siblings trying to help each other. She wanted to see me as "a real person" with my own difficulties, able to turn to her when I had a problem. It was hard to get a purchase on any of this. I wondered about her claim that she was adjusting to "life with other people."

She did finally hand in her dissertation, and was cleared for graduation. But was she relieved? Not really. She saw graduation as a *loss* and even a kind of death: she was giving up her candidate status, which meant a loss of dependency and safety. By examining this and similarly themed fantasies, we tried to realign her vision so that she came to see her achievement as part of a new phase of adulthood, and of individuation as a literature professor. She said she would try to accept that view, but continued to fret over what she believed was also a loss. But, to a degree, she saw the end of therapy as a kind of giving birth to a new self with higher self-esteem.

Unfortunately, her stepfather's dire medical condition reinforced Carol's fear that her achievements involved loss and separation. To her credit, she handled the situation by being a caring and attentive daughter while continuing to focus on her own personal and professional growth. She understood the impending end of her treatment as "like a weaning." It was that old baby metaphor again but, I hoped, with less fantastical implications.

It interested me that Carol employed two related, governing metaphors during her treatment: the little match girl, and what might have been her predecessor, the self-as-baby. Yet while the match girl was needy and dependent, the baby was somehow independent – certainly a reversal of the natural order. Together, the metaphors suggested a fantasy that defied the natural (as fantasies often do). If, by means of the baby metaphor, she ultimately did let go of her fantasies, then that would be a real accomplishment – akin to graduation with a Ph.D.

Over the course of several weeks, I noticed that I did not need to talk as much. Carol had acquired some tools of self-analysis. She still saw me as a man she was losing. But she also saw me as an actual person who cared about her and wanted to help. To a degree, we shared a sense of working together that was more reality- than fantasy-based. This was a shift in emphasis rather than an outright change, but we both sensed it. The question was whether Carol could sustain that sense, or whether some event would precipitate her falling back into fantasy, anger, and dependence (on me, and on her fantasies as a justification for self-defeating behavior).

Time would tell.

A wake-up call

Over the next several weeks, Carol began a review of her treatment. Her professional life had never been better – she was earning three times her previous salary. At the beginning of one session, she insisted I step outside to look at her new, red sports car. She was participating in more date-related activities – going to cultural events, charity benefits, and Jewish singles affairs. Finally, she thanked me for her treatment and said she had "nothing but good will toward" me.

"Nothing?" I asked. I was waiting for her to qualify her assertion.

"Well, I can't help feeling I'm not worth your time anymore," she said.

But still, if I was a few minutes late starting a session, she would accuse me of being on the phone with another woman. She imagined I was replacing her with someone "hotter and younger." In effect, she wanted to minimize the time we had spent together, and whatever progress we had made, as a way of minimizing the possibility of loss. It was also a way of protecting herself against a possible reversion to an earlier, obsessional self that, perhaps, she had not entirely left behind. In terms of transference, it was a way of casting blame on me for the pain that other men had caused her.

"I guess I'm wondering whether there's a way to separate from you without destroying our relationship," Carol said.

She was wary of provoking my anger, as she'd done with others in the past, particularly her stepfather. Still, she blamed me some as a surrogate for him, as well as for her real father and, *ad infinitum*, for all the pain-inflicting men in her life.

I wanted to query her on this logic.

"The way you go on seeing your stepfather as caring for you," I observed, "is a way of remaining a child – the little match girl – who needs to be looked after and can't handle responsibility. Are you doing that with me as well?"

My question was a wake-up call. She assumed a larger role in her stepfather's welfare (i.e., making his home safer and getting him a home health aide). She resolved to be more self-determining, and to try to believe that her decision to end treatment was, in fact, correct.

She pointed out how much more direct she was in meeting men, and in pursuing what she wanted in a relationship. She also felt that she'd become a good catch, a far cry from the little match girl.

"You *have* come a long way," I said, "but I'm still wondering whether your emotional connection to me is an impediment to making continued progress in your love life."

"I think I'm over the hurdle of loving more than one man at the same time," she said. "Maybe," she teased, "it would be better if I came less often to see whether you still need your quotidian dose of me."

It was encouraging to see that she was confident enough to be playful about testing my limits.

A final fantasy

Carol offered to help with my phone system, my social life, decorating my office. She felt I needed mothering. This gave her a sense of turning the tables: I was supposed to submit myself to her as she'd done with me.

Her desire was a defense: she didn't want to feel that she was losing anything by letting me go. It was a way of saying "I don't need you anymore," and now "You're the needy one and I'll take care of you."

But a few sessions before her analysis ended, Carol misplaced her wallet. Perhaps she was still anxious, however unconsciously, about her treatment ending.

She remained concerned about how she would do on her own, without a man "to protect" her. Her association was to her recent birthday, the date of which, as she pointed out, was the same as that of the woman who'd been the sole survivor of the Triangle Shirtwaist Factory Fire of 1911.

"Remember your childhood fantasy?" I prompted. "That a fireman would rescue you and carry you off?"

"Oh yes," she replied. "That didn't occur to me."

"On a conscious level," I added.

"Right. Still, it makes me feel reassured somehow. And ending treatment doesn't seem so much like rejection." She closed her eyes and thought for a moment. "I find it difficult sometimes to reconcile my love life with my professional obligations, and I guess it would help to know that you're stuck with the same balancing act, you know? I don't want to feel alone in this, like I'm the only one with a complicated life."

"You're not," I assured her.

That we were in the same proverbial boat may have been soothing, but it didn't change the fact that our professional interactions were ending. Fantasies about various men she was involved with helped lessen her sense of losing me, although they did not portend a swift, painless transition to post-therapy attempts to establish mature relationships. With Carol's fantasies, it was often a choice between lesser and greater evils.

We worked on her fantasies right up to the end of analysis. We never dispatched her conflicts completely. But a shift among them probably produced a new, healthier constellation of compromise formations.

She tended to be more satisfied with what she had – rather than lamenting what she didn't – and worked toward what she wanted without cutting herself off at the pass just to satisfy some self-defeating fantasy. She had a higher opinion of herself and was less fearful concerning her future.

Just as in the Hans Christian Andersen story, the little match girl had had to die. But in separating herself from that metaphor – or, at least, trying to more fully – Carol had made and was continuing to make progress.

References

Andersen, Hans Christian. *The Complete Fairy Tales*, trans. J.H. Stickney (indep. pub., 2020), p.50 ff., story orig. published in Danish, 1815.

Kohut, Heinz. *The Analysis of the Self: A Systematic Approach to the Psychoanalytic Treatment of Narcissistic Personality Disorder*. (New York: International Universities Press, 1971)

Orenstein, Paul, ed. *The Search for the Self: Selected Writings of Heinz Kohut, 1950–1978*, Vols. 1 & 2. (New York: International Universities Press, 1978)

Chapter 3

Gatsby

This study is named "Gatsby" after the eponymous hero of the great American novel The Great Gatsby *(Fitzgerald, 1925) who, like my patient, organizes his life around a false, inflated image of himself that he displays in public, while in private he lacks self-esteem.*

Also as in Gatsby, my patient is obsessed with the forbidden pursuit of an unattainable woman. For my patient, the consequences of his obsession are dramatic, and contribute to the disparity between his public persona and his reality: he represses his desire, uses other women as placeholders, and constructs a persona based primarily on appearance because he cannot face his true, indeed illicit, motivations. It takes years for him even to acknowledge his feelings, much less deal with them. This study examines the power of desire to take hold of us, and our resistance to letting go of fantasies that support our ability to sustain such desire.

But the desire that my patient feels is complicated. It emanates from a love/ hate relationship that began in childhood. It becomes the paradigm for how he conducts his life, which proceeds by on/off decision making that constantly doubles back on itself and renders him unable to act. He loses self-esteem, which only further prevents him from functioning effectively. He becomes prone to severe panic attacks, and worries obsessively that people are watching him, measuring his inadequacy. It is only as he finally acknowledges the depth of his illicit desire that the pall it created begins to recede. But the journey is hard, and he suffers relapses – repeating, even in therapy, his on/off, ingrained modus operandi.

So, this study is about the intersection of two faces of love: sexual obsession and our regard for ourselves. We have all experienced the trauma of loving someone who will not, cannot, love us. We wonder whether there was something about us that brought on their lack of response. It's normal. But for my patient, the obsession remains in his psyche, buried but still potent. How does he learn to face it? How does he learn, finally, to keep it from infecting the rest of his life?

Well, he never really learns completely, but he comes a long way. Intense, obsessive love is hard to get over – when it is illicit, it is even hard to acknowledge at all. But my patient, in his own best interest, at least reaches a still point where

DOI: 10.4324/9781003352624-4

he can make adjustments and feel better about himself. When love is concerned, sometimes that's all we can ask.

If we are not comfortable with ourselves, it is difficult to share our life with someone else – who, after all, are we even sharing? In this sense, there is a continuum between self-love, the stability of self-acceptance, and a romantic attachment. Of course, self-love does not have to entail narcissism, but only a healthy regard for our own worth. It involves acknowledging the complexity of our desires, and living with them despite themselves, even when they cannot be realized.

The psychoanalyst and pediatrician Donald Winnicott (1896–1971) proposed a distinction between a true and false self. As opposed to the true self – who we know that we are – its false counterpart refers to how we present ourselves to others so that we can get along in the world. To be successful, the individual has to find the right balance between the two. In this patient, however, the false self was dominant, so that he felt more fragile and, hence, vulnerable. He tended to compensate with perfectionist tendencies and outsize ambitions that would (he thought) prove his manhood.

These tendencies were traceable, in part, to another element of Winnicott's theories, the "good enough" mother. In this patient's case, his mother tended to coddle him and shield him from embarrassment over his childhood bed-wetting. Thus, while she was caring and warm, she curtailed his developing any sense of himself as a capable young man. This sense of incapacity persisted into adulthood, and we had to work towards resolving it.

The patient's stunted development also calls up a third theory proposed by Winnicott, involving the importance of a play space and the transitional object. The transitional object helps to mediate between play and reality (think of a child playing with a doll). Unfortunately, this patient became too playful with a forbidden object – his sibling – retreating from other objects that might have made hm feel better and more confident. The patient had to work on acknowledging his feelings so that he could finally redirect them, exiting the play space into the reality of mature relationships.

None of this work came easily. The structure of this study, which is characterized by repeated attempts to withdraw from analysis, demonstrates that the process of analysis becomes an image of a patient's neuroses and conflicts. If the patient is obsessive or conflicted (as this one was), then the analysis will follow the course of their obsessions and conflicts as these emerge into consciousness. Free association bears with it sometimes sudden encounters with some conflict that may precipitate an equally sudden effort to leave therapy … only to be overridden, often in the same session, by a renewed commitment (however shaky) to continue. Psychoanalysts expect this type of churn, and I have tried to render it in this study. It can impart a sense of whiplash but, as will become apparent, each on/off incident of departure and return leads to a new insight as the patient explores the motivations behind such incidents.

Finally, I should note that while the resistance demonstrated by this patient may seem extreme, patients in analysis necessarily have at least some resistance – in the beginning (when they are not really sure if they are committed), in the middle (when difficult challenges arise), or toward the end (when they think they are further along than they really are). One way to understand the process of analysis, in large measure, is to see it as helping clear away patients' resistance to analysis – that is, to facilitate a patient's unencumbered free association, so that they can actually open up about their neuroses and conflicts (an essential step toward insight and understanding). In this study, the patient struggles with resistance until, finally, he becomes relatively capable of free association. It takes six years.

Jock walked into my office just after New Year's. The city was typically cold, and sooty piles of snow melted and froze again on impassable icy streets. Everyone looked like unisex Michelin-people and tried not to skid into anyone else.

So, Jock looked like an anomaly. He wore no coat, just a sweater. He had no hat or gloves. I thought maybe he'd been a Navy SEAL. In that case, what's a little frostbite?

But then he appeared to be sweating. He wiped his face and neck repeatedly. This seemed even more anomalous. My thermostat was set at 70 degrees.

I looked down at my notes. Jock's sweating was not related to temperature. It was, rather, his Chief Complaint – a chronic condition, the reason he was here. Apparently, he'd sweated on the way to my office.

"I have sweat attacks," he said.

By then, it was obvious.

"If I think someone is watching me – or if I think they will – I get anxious and sweat. Then I imagine that other people are watching, or that they might. I get *more* anxious, and then I *really* sweat. Pretty soon my shirt is soaked and it feels like a cascade is running down my back."

I imagined Albert Brooks' character in *Broadcast News*, who sweats in front of a national audience (then quickly loses his job).

But I stayed cool. "Any other symptoms besides sweating?" I asked. There had to be underlying reasons, but first I wanted to understand the physical manifestations.

"My heart pounds," he said, and "I get short of breath. The attack comes on suddenly, and then peaks. Then it's over."

He closed his eyes, and recounted his condition's painful origins. It began in high school, when he was making a class presentation. He'd mangled what he'd planned to say, and started sweating. "I felt humiliated," he told me. "Not just because I looked stupid, but because I was dripping – it was like I'd wet my pants." In Jock's mind, there was an apparent connection between sweat and uncontrolled peeing, or at least feeling infantilized. It would turn out to be significant.

But in any case, after this incident he avoided situations where he might have an attack. "In college, I skipped seminars. I only took lecture courses." The problem was that now he worked as a quick-response data analyst and had to give daily presentations. "I'm terrified I'll sweat in front of everyone," he said, "and they'll think I don't know my stuff."

Jock was 23 years old, but his voice cracked as if he were 12. He seemed nervous just telling me what he just had. I thought he generated anxiety or pressure internally, and carried it around. Hence the sweats when he felt exposed. His grooming was a giveaway. His hair was in a buzz-cut just so the sweat couldn't run down his scalp and plaster his hair to his face.

He claimed that the sweats were unstoppable. "They plow through deodorants like kamikazes," he said. "They're out of my control." If at work he was terrified, then on dates he chose dark, noisy, gyrating places where it seemed natural to sweat. "I take women clubbing," he said. "But a lot of times, they turn me down when I suggest those places again."

He seemed at his wits' end. He'd consulted and struck out with several physicians.

An internist, an endocrinologist, and a dermatologist had found nothing wrong. I was not surprised. What was "wrong" was likely, at least in part, a psychological problem that had remained unaddressed.

As we spoke, the sweating segued into a larger, psychological issue. Jock complained of "thinking about thinking." He was indecisive, plagued by self-doubt. He'd make a decision, then ask why he'd made it. Then he'd ask why he was asking. It was an infinite regress toward inaction – that is, toward a self-induced incompetence or at least inhibition that, when he caught himself, could provoke a sweat attack.

His sweat attacks were actually panic attacks, sometimes self-induced, sometimes situational. He was his own adversary. Right away, I sensed that he disliked himself, so he'd bicker internally until he was exhausted. He'd create an endless vicious circle of doubt, disdain, inaction, and more doubt. I pictured a snake swallowing its tail. I thought, perhaps, the first line of treatment might be to work on raising his self-estimation – but how do you do that when someone is compelled to question every move that they make (even, presumably, ones that are in their own self-interest)? So, I wondered how I might help.

Jock's on/off behavior unmistakably reflected obsessive-compulsive traits, rather than careful thought. He told me, for example, that he'd buy a shirt and find the stitching "wrong." He'd exchange it for another, only to find a flaw in the new one. Then he'd wonder if he needed a new shirt at all, and finally feel compelled to return it for a refund.

He'd exchange shirts and socks and ties over and over before finding ones he could live with.

He also obsessed at work, and had trouble completing assignments. The circularity of his thought process distressed him. He dreaded the fallout ("I could go biking, but why should I?"). He knew his self-questioning was excessive, but (like his sweats) it came on seemingly out of the blue. He couldn't identify any preceding thoughts.

Previously, a psychopharmacologist had prescribed a beta-blocker, but the attacks continued. An anti-anxiety medication had some effect, but it slowed him down. "It takes six rings before I decide to answer the phone," he said. "By then, the person's hung up." He was losing confidence by obsessing, and the medications just set him back even further.

He'd also tried cognitive and behavioral therapy, and practiced relaxation and breathing. He rehearsed his behavior with role-playing and feedback. But still, he had performance anxiety, social phobia, and those sweat attacks. "I want a treatment," he said, "to take care of the problem once and for all."

Was I his last resort?

Patients often want me to advise or at times rescue them, even as they imply that they'd never have approached me if they thought someone else offered better, quicker, cheaper solutions. It comes with being a psychotherapist in a world of pills and evidence-based medicine.

Obviously, none of Jock's previous treatments had sought to help him understand the psychological processes underlying his sweat attacks. They hadn't explored issues around self-esteem. So, that job now fell to me.

Jock's father had undergone psychodynamic psychiatric treatment for major depression following a bout with cancer, and had found it helpful. He continued to work through his problems, including occasional panic attacks. Because he had benefited, he would support Jock's attempt at psychotherapy.

Jock, however, seemed reluctant.

"Do you know cognitive and behavioral techniques?" he asked.

But he had already told me that these had failed.

"Maybe you don't want psychodynamic psychotherapy," I said. "You seem to have other ideas."

He smiled sheepishly. "Okay, your turn."

"Look," I said. We can work on your symptoms, but that will finally require addressing your underlying issues." That's how insight-oriented psychotherapy works.

"I'm not sure," he responded. "I really don't think I need some journey into myself. And even if I tried it, I doubt it would fix my problem."

He seemed to have no idea that a glaring part of his "problem" was a lack of self-esteem, leading to a destructive back-and-forth that short-circuited his taking any positive actions. It was on display as we spoke but, to Jock, it was just business as usual. He had a limited perspective on himself, and didn't seem to want anything more. He just wanted to fix an embarrassing, uncomfortable physical reaction to being around other people. He would have taken a pill if he could.

In line with his resistance to any searching inquiry, he claimed things were "stable" at work, and that his personal relationships were "progressing."

But then (typically) he back-tracked. "I'm still exploring my options," he admitted, as if a certain amount of disorientation was to be expected. What I heard was his chronic uncertainty, his lack of self-awareness, his doubts about how well he was handling anything.

In fact, though he was dating someone, he planned to break things off before the woman got hurt. This was just more of the same. So, I asked, "Isn't this more about you than her – aren't you scared you'll think and rethink the relationship until it's destroyed?"

I saw that sheepish look again.

"And what about friendships?" I asked.

"Well, I might be closer with some of my buddies. But I guess in the back of my mind, I'm worried that if I expose myself, people won't like what they see."

"Can you give me an example?"

He shook his head. "We're not going to get into that. I mean what does that have to do with sweat attacks?"

So, there was that standoffishness again, separating him from everyone else, including me. Not wanting to "get into" things would likely be his primary form of resistance to treatment. He lacked the self-confidence to expose himself enough to be treated for lacking self-confidence. Ultimately, he lacked sufficient self-esteem to think that what he revealed would not also be to his detriment.

Maybe he wasn't even sure that what he said today would hold true tomorrow, so why bother?

The black sheep

Jock described his family as "normal." His parents were "caring, loving, and supportive." According to him, they hadn't pressured him in any way since childhood. "They just wanted me to do my best," he said.

His father had his own business, and was a deacon at church. Jock looked to him for advice.

His mother was "a housewife, a good mom." After his father's bout with cancer, the family set up a research foundation which his mother ran.

"So, any childhood experiences that stand out for you?" I asked.

Jock shook his head. "Nothing comes to mind."

"Nothing?"

"No."

"How about your earliest memory?"

"I can't recall."

"It's a little odd, this childhood amnesia," I ventured.

"Maybe to a shrink. Not to me."

I didn't want to make him uncomfortable, so I let the subject drop.

Jock's sister, Jenny, was the proverbial black sheep.

"She doesn't have much to do with our family," Jock said, "and she has nothing to do with my symptoms. We hardly speak." Surely, *that* disconnect had an origin story, so I pressed him.

Jenny began experimenting with drugs in high school. She dropped out of college, then announced she was "gender neutral." When she turned up in flamboyant men's attire, the family called in a psychiatrist – but she was already over the age limit where she *had* to cooperate.

Jock just felt she was lost. He avoided her phone calls ("There's always weird music in the background"). Crucially, he felt their relationship had no bearing on his sweat attacks ("She's nuts, and there's no point discussing her").

I backed off. We could revisit his relationship with Jenny at another time.

What concerned me, however, was how Jock ignored whatever was distasteful – including whatever he disliked in himself. How could I uncover the underlying issues which I'd told him we needed to address?

In this regard, I saw a disjunction between Jock's careful grooming (that buzz-cut was very recent) and the way he tried to disengage from people (including himself). That is, while he was socially guarded, he tried to seem typical and normal by means of a studied self-presentation. What mattered was on the surface – how he appeared. In the back of his mind there was always the mantra, *Don't sweat, don't let people see who you are and force you to sweat.*

In a word, he was self-conscious, not self-aware. He didn't see self-esteem as an issue involving him.

He'd graduated Phi Beta Kappa from a good college, but was intellectually insecure ("I'm surrounded by quants," he sighed). His grooming was a form of over-compensation.

Within the context of his family, he was still "a good boy," especially in contrast to his sister. So, he finally acquiesced in the therapy, though he couldn't hide his resentment.

He insisted that all he needed was weekly sessions with a behavioral focus.

I thought he needed deeper, exploratory therapy, and pressed him to consider the alternatives. He agreed, begrudgingly, to meet twice a week ("But maybe I'll buck it down to only once," he asserted, unaware that this instant rethinking was *why* he needed the therapy).

Exposed

Our sessions were filled with the week's events. Jock wanted to use me as a coach. He worked hard, but found himself becoming more unfulfilled. Nor was there any change in the frequency or duration of his panic attacks.

The better he did at work, the more his boss – whom he found controlling – told him to do.

I suggested he talk to her about scaling back her requests, but he was reluctant because of how that could "appear."

"If I ask her to ease up, then it looks like I'm not dedicated," he said. "Like I can't handle the work." I thought that *he* was afraid he couldn't handle it, and endured the demands just to prove to himself that he could. He seemed caught in a vicious circle – the more demands, the more he'd be afraid of falling short ... so, the more demands.

In the same way, he resisted the woman he was dating. The closer she got, the more closed-off he was.

"She wants me to meet her parents. But why?" He knew perfectly well "why." He was just scared. He was second-guessing himself, again. Even when he followed through with decisions, like when he did what his boss requested, it was out of fear – which returned full-throttle when she asked again.

I said that he found intimacy "scary." He was afraid that by opening up, he might reveal something shameful. It was the moral equivalent of sweating in public.

"There's probably some truth to that," he acknowledged.

I followed up. "Your fear of being exposed may be connected to how you feel when you're making a presentation, which puts you at risk of an attack."

Jock flushed, and recalled how his mother would film him as a child.

"I couldn't escape the lens of her camcorder. I'd cry when people looked at me."

Apparently, that lens was stuck in his mind, pointing at him perpetually. He'd developed counter-moves to elude it, making no distinction between colleagues, bosses, and girlfriends. The lens might catch him sweating. The mere thought of it might make him sweat. It might get inside his head and capture his fears.

His kind, indulgent mother emerged from the sidelines of his personal history to be wielding a menacing instrument, which distorted his self-confidence and sent him running for cover. I wanted to explore this notion, but waited to see if he could breach the fourth wall of his on-screen performance and open up on his own.

Nonetheless, I had the small revelation that, since childhood, Jock sensed he was performing on a stage with no exit. Who *wouldn't* be scared, especially in front of a possibly hostile audience? To be safe, he was *always* afraid of exposure. It was his default position in every situation.

Thus, I was not surprised when, over the next weeks, Jock felt that he didn't have much to say. He refused to say whatever came to mind, wondering what that would get him. "You want an information dump," he asked?

Besides, he said, he had a hard time letting go.

He used the phrase *letting go* repeatedly.

"What comes to mind about letting go?" I asked.

"Nothing."

"Nothing?"

There was a long, awkward pause. Finally, he blurted out, "I used to wet my bed. It didn't mean anything," rethinking his response, covering his tracks as he always did. "It didn't bother me. At camp I had to have a special mattress with plastic around it, and a woman would come every morning to change the sheets. There were other kids like that. Anyway, how does that relate to my panic symptoms?"

Apparently, he was not conscious of the semantic (much less emotional) connection between letting go and bed-wetting. Perhaps exposing himself – exposing what was really inside him, even his thoughts about data analysis – was a form of letting go and, hence, a precursor to sweating or its childhood equivalent, bed-wetting.

I had to follow up, at least insofar as he was reticent with me. "You're embarrassed about telling me too much – about *letting go*."

I had jarred him, slightly. So, he "let go" a little. He described his bed-wetting, which had begun around age 4 and continued until he was 12, occurring several times a week. His family did not discuss it openly, and his parents never criticized him for it. When he asked his mother about it, she said it would stop on its own, that it was okay, and he shouldn't worry.

Part of Jock's problem with reticence, I thought, was that his family encouraged it. He needn't expose himself because no one wanted to know. Problems would go away on their own. But when they didn't go away, reticence just gave way to fear. It was like there was no middle way – no way to manage fear and, thus, limit his unwillingness to confront his problems and engage with people (who were, in effect, just walking-talking problems that he had no choice but to fear). I could see that he'd have to shed some basic early MOs if he was ever to get past his default, extreme reaction to potential problems: sweat attacks.

At this point in treatment, I couldn't count on Jock to make the conscious associations that would lead to opening up during therapy (after all, he hadn't associated his repeated use of "letting go" with his history of bed-wetting). Rather, he rationalized everything to conform to contrived appearances, and denied unconscious meanings.

So, I followed his lead. We began to explore his need to "look good."

He'd had a brief but telling dream: "I'm in a glass house with someone. I have a shotgun. There are bats and buzzing things outside so I can't escape."

Jock saw his character as a glass house: if he looked too carefully at himself, he felt he might shatter. What, he wondered, would be left of him?

"I have no idea who my true self is," he said. "Maybe there's nothing there."

He seemed on the verge of panicking. In effect, he was saying that he had no self to esteem.

"Sometimes, the only way out starts from looking inside," I said. "I think you should consider analysis."

He demurred. If I thought we'd made progress, he had now back-tracked. "I didn't come here for analysis. How will that help? And how long will it take?"

For the next two months, Jock questioned me about analysis. I got a taste of his typical circularity. His questions were unending, and my answers led to more questions. Still uncertain, he began a session by asking for "an ulti-matum ... like be in analysis or nothing." He wanted someone else – me, his father, a mentor – to take responsibility for his choices. In the end, he agreed to analysis, although he said he could only come three times a week.

Shocking news

Despite our agreement, Jock resisted the analytic process. When I asked at various points what came to his mind, I got "nothing," "I don't know," or "my mind's a blank." He wanted *me* to supply his associations; it was a way of avoiding responsibility for expressing his own thoughts and feelings – for which, apparently, he lacked high regard.

Yet when I tried to help by making a suggestion, he'd just reply, "Yeah, but ..."

"Perhaps you might be more curious about what's on your mind," I suggested. "Right now, you don't seem very curious about yourself."

"Curiosity has nothing to do with it," he replied. "I just want to do what I need to and get on with things."

Apparently, he was angry about having agreed to more intense treatment, which was reflected in one of his dreams.

"Someone," he said "was banging at my door. I thought it was my land-lord, who said, in a deep voice, 'Are you there?' His voice and the banging felt very real."

When I asked what might have inspired the dream, he mentioned that he'd deducted $25 from the rent for a smoke alarm. He also recalled that his neighbor had been banging on the door the night before.

"And the voice?" I asked.

"I don't think it's yours. You don't have an especially deep voice."

Silence followed. I was somewhat frustrated by the superficiality of his thinking. So, I asked, "How do you suppose the dream looks to me?"

Jock recalled how he had written out my "rent check" for ten dollars less than the amount billed and resented the insurance company for being slow to reimburse him. But he didn't see – or, at least, didn't acknowledge – that I had been banging on the door of his thoughts, repeatedly wondering why they came up empty. In effect, I was the one, "the voice," wondering if he was "there."

Typically, he knew and didn't know what we were trying to accomplish. Nonetheless, he tried to deny it.

Or, maybe, he wanted to approach the need for "exposure" on his own terms, not mine. He brought up another scenario that succeeded the bed-wetting.

"I was masturbating once – I was 13 or 14 – and my sister walked in the bathroom. It was bad enough that she caught me, but she told our parents. I could've died of embarrassment."

"Well now I think I understand at least part of your resistance," I said. "You see me as a parental figure, and if you show me your thoughts, you won't seem like the 'good child,' which is the image you've tried to keep up for your father."

This observation felt "real" to him. He acknowledged a connection between his current issues, such as panic attacks, and his past experience.

But a few months into the second year of his treatment, what had seemed like discrete experiences from his past – bed-wetting, masturbation – were suddenly just the leading edge of a larger (and heretofore overlooked) conflict that might still be haunting him. Could it be that his perfect parents were not so perfect after all? Was anything what it seemed?

The next session, Jock reported the "shocking news" that his father was not in love with his mother anymore and wanted a divorce. "He said he hadn't loved her for years, and that my mother knew it. They were just putting on a show – once the cancer was beat, they drifted apart irretrievably." Jock had seen his parents' marriage as ideal. "But maybe I just saw what I wanted to see – or what they wanted me to see." I sensed that he had fallen into despair. It took the form of an intense fear that what seemed worthwhile and solid, wasn't.

"How," he asked, "can I stop anticipating the worst when I should have anticipated it all along, and was unable to?" The question was at once profound, touching on the fragility of what calls itself "real," and also pointless, since fear has to be managed so that it doesn't consume us.

But I was afraid that the "shocking news" would set him back. He was already having trouble opening himself up to women, and now here was validation (in his mind) for his reticence. Could I say anything to keep him on track, at least in analysis, until he could overcome his fears more generally? In addition, I realized that reticence ran in the family – everyone seemed unable to acknowledge how they felt except, ironically, Jenny, who outraged everyone with her let-it-all-hang-out behavior. Jock's role models were situated at either extreme of where well-adjusted, forthcoming people might hope to exist.

So, finally, I suggested that we shouldn't measure our lives, or anyone's, by the standards of Camelot. Of course, Camelot (at least the Kennedys' version) wasn't what it seemed to be either. "No one expects that of you, nor should you expect that of anyone."

I don't think I killed her

From early adolescence, Jenny's problems with drugs and gender dysphoria had embarrassed the family. They became a family secret, kept from everyone but their closest friends.

"She went from 'gender neutral' to lesbian," Jock said with obvious distaste, "and then the woman she took up with was old and ugly."

Jock was initially so upset by his sister's relationship that he couldn't speak to her. This time, he felt, she'd gone too far.

"Why is her relationship so upsetting?" I asked.

"Are you kidding?" he shot back. "How does it look to people? What does it say about my family?" Once again, he was focused on appearances.

"Are your sister's sexual activities a reflection on you?" I asked.

"Well, not exactly," he answered. "But when she had to be hospitalized because she totally lost it, it was a huge embarrassment."

He was referring to Jenny's suicide attempt. She took pills, and had to be monitored overnight in the ER. Then she was admitted to a psychiatric hospital for a week. I thought, perhaps, that much as he disdained Jenny, he felt a certain uncomfortable closeness to her that he could only eradicate by avoiding her.

I followed up. "You're in psychiatric treatment, aren't you?" I reminded him. Then I took a leap. "Could some of your discomfort with Jenny relate to your own sexuality?"

He bristled. "I have no homosexual tendencies, period."

I had apparently touched a nerve and, he scolded, "Maybe I should drop out of treatment. You just insulted me." That is, I tried to penetrate his carefully constructed appearance, where his only "problem" was the physical fact of his sweat attacks. But because of his response, I realized just how sensitive he was about his sexuality – that is, how shaky it may have been – and that, if we continued, there would be a lot to explore. In fact, as we got deeper into analysis, he revealed that Jenny *had* influenced his sexuality (though, at this juncture, he was still repressing any thoughts about it).

Over the next several weeks, he still insisted he was ending treatment.

"I've given it a fair chance," he said, "and it hasn't helped."

But we kept talking.

With his sister uppermost in his mind, he had a dream: "I was in a colonial village. Jenny and I were on the run from other villagers. We made it into the neighboring town. Somehow Jenny died. I think she committed suicide. I had to go back and explain to my parents what had happened."

His initial thoughts were to the day before when he'd played a Civil War game with his young cousin. The boy was going to Williamsburg with his parents, and he and Jock had played with toy muskets. Jock also mentioned a business presentation from which he'd "escaped" without having a sweat attack. He said that nothing else came to mind about the dream and moved on to a recent work incident.

"Wait a minute," I said. "Jenny died in the dream. What about that?"

"No, she committed suicide," he said as though suicide never resulted in death. "And I don't remember the details." He grew silent and visibly anxious. "I may have helped her. I don't think I killed her."

Now he associated the dream with Jenny's teenage suicide attempt.

"I remember how I wanted to avoid the whole thing and not know about it," he said.

After a pause, he admitted he still felt guilty that he might have had something to do with her attempt to kill herself, such as consistently siding with their parents against her.

"Let's talk about your guilt," I suggested.

Jock admitted he'd been given opportunities that she'd been denied.

"I think you can add intensive psychotherapy to your list," I said.

He acknowledged feeling guilty that he was receiving the gold standard of psychotherapies with a psychiatrist while she was in a weekly support group with a social worker.

My purpose was to explore whether Jock's low self-esteem resulted, in part, from his indifference to Jenny's problems because (in his mind) they tarnished the family. They also may have reminded him of how, by comparison, he was almost pathologically reticent. In other words, I wanted Jock to consider how Jenny – as his own mirror-image – made him doubt himself *and* how he was viewed by other people. He was so judgmental toward his sister because of the enmity he bore toward himself. Could he let go of it?

He had a series of dreams about being imprisoned.

"Is there something you did that might be loosely interpreted as a crime?" I asked.

Jock evaded the question, and I didn't press him. Nonetheless, what he'd mentioned so far didn't add up to the kind of guilt he seemed to be experiencing. I recalled the uncertainty in his expression when he said, "I don't think I killed her." Something involving his sister disturbed him, deeply, but he wasn't yet ready to talk about it. Most likely, he hadn't even opened up to himself about whatever had happened with his sister.

Whatever his relationship with Jenny, I was unable to determine how – at least so far – it inflected his sense of himself.

Self-knowledge

Ostensibly, Jock had chosen a girlfriend who was like his mother – caring, supportive, and full of compliments. He seemed to appreciate their time together, and thought that she'd be a good partner. He was still unsure, however, about whether Nancy was "the one."

Instead of dealing with his conflicts around intimacy, he obsessed about Nancy's "defects" and his own inexperience in relationships. He described their sex together as satisfactory, but didn't feel comfortable going into detail.

When I asked about his discomfort, he became defensive.

"There's nothing to talk about," he snapped.

I wondered about his sexual inhibitions, and in what way his problems with intimacy played out in his sex life but, once again, I didn't push. I was afraid he'd be embarrassed or feel criticized to the extent that it might impede our work.

So, he stayed in a kind of obsessional holding pattern with Nancy, unsure as to whether he should or shouldn't break up with her. He cited her "blemishes" – her thin hair, her height (she was short), her lack of any professional aspirations. He fantasized about being with women who were more exotic, more self-assured – even while he acknowledged that they might have scared him.

During this phase of treatment, I felt I was in a position similar to Nancy's: Jock could neither leave nor make a full commitment.

At one point, when he was thinking of dropping out of treatment and breaking up with Nancy, he recounted a dream in which two kittens had died. He was hesitant to acknowledge that the kittens might represent his young relationship with Nancy or with me (or both), but he mentioned not wanting to be "trapped" by the analysis. He might want to go to business school in another city and didn't want being in treatment to limit his options.

The idea of being trapped brought to mind situations in which he had to make a presentation. He elaborated on the physical sense of discomfort he experienced – as though he were in a hot, crowded room in uncomfortable clothing.

"What I see here," I said, "is that these situations where you feel trapped are like those from your childhood when you felt anxious about being exposed – as the little boy who wet his bed, for example. When your conflicts come up in treatment, analysis is difficult because you're afraid of losing control of your thoughts or feelings and embarrassing yourself." In his unconscious mind sweat equals urine equals losing control.

Jock winced. "Well," he said, "I guess that's a link between my personal history and my sweat attacks." He was affirming what he'd previously denied.

Although he was finally able to understand the equation between sweat and bed-wetting – between his personal history and now – this had no effect on the panic attacks. His understanding was primarily intellectual. He still lacked the desire to address his past and understand how it affected him.

Thus, he became angry that I had dredged up his past, seemingly to no purpose.

"Problems don't go away instantaneously, Jock. That's not how psychotherapy works," I explained.

He stuck with our work. Slowly, he recognized how the way he experienced making a presentation related to competitive feelings with father figures who made up the audience and to his resentment about needing to please them.

The formula describing one of his neurotic dilemmas now emerged: *I'll be a good boy and please my father so he'll love me (in particular, love me more than my sister). But I'm angry and resentful about having to be obedient and good. If my boss (father) sees how resentful and competitive with him I am, he won't think I'm good, won't love me, and will retaliate.*

Understanding what was going on beneath the surface made him more comfortable in stressful situations and less inclined to panic.

He re-evaluated his relationship with Nancy. She reminded him of his mother, so winning her was a source of anxiety. Because he lacked the self-esteem common to most men, he needed to pursue her as a little boy – as a child to be cared for – rather than as a grown-up in a mature relationship with a woman. But he also had to consider whether Nancy liked this arrangement. If she did, it would continue to infantilize him, and keep him from achieving the self-esteem that, ultimately, would help him stop fretting and sweating.

However long it takes

We explored Jock's resistance to treatment, since it exemplified his resistance to intimacy.

He was ashamed to be lying down on my couch, because he associated his recumbent position with bed-wetting (opening up meant his thoughts would spill out like urine). He couldn't let things spill out and still remain clean and dry. He projected his judgment of himself onto me.

But what kept him from dropping out of analysis was his fear that I'd see him as "bad or rebellious." Some patients flaunt their rebellion and love to one-up me, but Jock was just the opposite.

"The idea that you're a good or a bad boy reflects on how your mind categorizes situations. This good boy/bad boy characterization comes up in relation to your father."

He disagreed with my observations and went off on a rant about how analysis hadn't worked.

"You want to fight me," I said, "but you feel constrained. You're compliant on the surface, but underneath you feel angry and resentful. This way you get to remain a child, acquiescing to parental authority, rather than handling things like a man."

A business school interview demonstrated the link between his panic attacks and repressed competitive tendencies. A question about why he was pursuing a business degree threw him. All he'd wanted to say was that he hoped to outdo his father. But, instead, he became self-conscious and felt trapped. He had a sweat attack right there. Humiliated, he apologized and explained he was still recovering from the flu.

Jock's associations to this mini-disaster were to bed-wetting, being videotaped by his mother, and giving a work presentation – other shame-inducing situations.

"You felt that a powerful man was trying to keep you from one of your goals," I suggested. "And you couldn't explain yourself." I added (with a straight face) "You were probably right in the interview not to admit that you resented him and your father and me, and all the powerful men that you want to beat at their own game."

"C'mon, that's not what it is," Jock said. "My father's always been on my side, always wanted what's best for me." But, after a pause, he wondered whether there'd be "breathing room" for him in the family company, or whether his father would stand in the way. Finally, he acknowledged he'd seen the interviewer as a father figure and projected his own competitive feelings onto him. He agreed to consider the role of his own bottled-up aggression in his panic attacks.

Over the next few sessions, he talked about his lack of close male friends. He mentioned a number of incidents where his competitive tendencies had interfered. "I wanted to compete, but I just ended up full of resentment," he said. "It was toxic."

As he became more aware of his negative aggression, he became somewhat more open with the guys about (in his words) "beating the hell out of them." His panic attacks showed signs of decreasing.

Again, he thought that perhaps it was time to quit analysis.

His paradigm, however, was one of competition vs. compliance (now he'd compete) rather than learning how to cultivate a mature sense of himself. Moreover, staying in analysis represented my victory. Most importantly, perhaps, continuing analysis meant continuing to look at himself.

His guilt over being in top-tier treatment resurfaced; he viewed it as "an indulgence" compared to Jenny's retail therapy. He referred to advantages he'd had over Jenny, and wondered whether his mere existence had hurt her progress. "I was my mother's favorite," he said, "and that had to translate into damaging Jenny."

Still, Jock was no longer in acute need of treatment and continued to push against analysis. Rather, he was in a kind of limbo, where I was the expert and I recommended that he continue analysis. I was not convinced that he'd gotten to the core of his problems. He was still sensitive about his sex life and seemed, at times, on the verge of a panic attack whenever the topic of his sister came up.

When I nudged him on resisting further analysis, he cracked.

"I'm afraid, okay?"

"Of what?" I asked, trying to suggest that the topic was nothing extraordinary.

"If I attack the parts of myself that bothered me, if I let you attack them too, my whole sense of myself will be shattered. Don't you get that?"

I did get it, actually. Jock would rather a false sense of himself than face whatever might be disturbing. That is, he'd rather have a shaky sense of himself, and low self-esteem, than risk what seemed to him like a headlong fall into a personal abyss. He liked a pleasing surface which, he thought, he could manage.

But instead of confronting him with this, I focused on his perception of treatment.

"The problem, Jock, is that you see psychotherapy as destructive rather than an opportunity to learn more about yourself," I said, "or as something that can enrich you as a person."

"Well," he said, "that's my right, isn't it?"

He became obsessional, thinking and rethinking his reasoning for rethinking his therapy (bringing us back to his inability to buy a shirt without half a dozen trips to the store).

We explored how obsessional thinking was a way of keeping his problems with aggression under wraps. The doubting, the endless indecision kept the underlying conflicts submerged. I observed that his obsessional nature was more a personality trait than his panic attacks, and indicated the need to deepen rather than end our work together.

I'm not sure how much of this Jock took in, but he agreed to keep talking. Perhaps, I thought, he was just tired of fighting. Moreover, perhaps he realized that every time we examined his resistance to treatment, we uncovered some aspect of his history – some aspect of his recursive personality – that he had not fully acknowledged. It was as if his continued resistance, and then provisional commitment, was all part of the treatment – that is, a necessary concomitant of the process. Now (so it seemed) he was in the commitment phase ... again, for a while, likely to encounter himself from another perspective.

Narcissism

After the summer break, Jock did an about-face and busted treatment down to twice-weekly sessions. He'd been accepted to business school and, with the busy schedule of a first-year student, he thought that four or five times a week would be too much.

I felt that analysis was still the best choice and reminded him that beyond symptoms of panic, he still had issues with intimacy and with obsessive indecision. Fundamentally, he had problems with self-esteem.

But Jock wouldn't budge, which meant (at least to me) resistance was still very much a problem.

During our sessions, he described how his condition had improved. I felt that this was a riposte to me and that, for that reason, he enjoyed it. It was also a way to reassure himself that he didn't have more serious, underlying sources of guilt and anxiety.

Though psychotherapy requires patients to (honestly) look at and address their problems, Jock wanted to see himself as having them under control. It was a form of narcissism ("Hey, maybe I'm not perfect, but I sure can act that way"). The issue came to the fore around the time of his first exams. He had always been an excellent student, but now his grades were unspectacular. He was forced to deal with the reality that he was not at the top of his class, and that no amount of preening would change that.

"It's hard for you to look at your issues," I said, "because self-examination threatens your sense that you can 'appear' your way to success." That is, so long as he didn't sweat, his reality as a human being didn't really matter.

"I know," he said. "I just feel vulnerable in treatment. When you put my problems under a microscope, I can't maintain a sense that anyone will see past them."

Exposure in therapy wasn't just analogous to exposure at a meeting or in a relationship. Rather, it meant that he *would* be exposed in these situations. It was a category mistake, whether willing or unconscious, that cast me as the villain. He was turning therapy into an obstacle to his success which, to him, meant presenting an un-sweaty appearance where he was in control.

A dream in which I was an IRS agent, accusing him of a massive underpayment, bore this out.

"I feel like I don't have enough time to study," he said. As a confiscatory G-man, I was robbing him of resources – that is, time and money. He went on to describe in a remote, intellectualized way how every life is constrained by time.

"What comes to mind about being constrained?"

"It reminds me of being stuck in an elevator with no way out. Or of being trapped in a coffin underground. I think of my death and not breathing, and that makes me anxious. I could just lose it, like Jenny almost did."

His mental connection to "losing it" was to bed-wetting – a loss of bladder control.

Jock's fear of death was related to his symptoms of panic, to painful memories of bed-wetting.

He also talked about feeling "locked into something" with Nancy.

"Intimacy with another person, such as Nancy or me, can carry a sense of being trapped," I observed.

"I feel like a deer caught in the headlights," he replied. "I don't know how much more involved I want to get with either one of you."

Sharing emotions is a more intimate act than sharing thoughts, and Jock would only share his emotions when necessary. Not touching physically or emotionally would keep things nice and neat.

No one upset that sense of order like Jenny. She relapsed several times and needed in-hospital rehab for substance abuse. In addition to drug use, her borderline personality disorder became increasingly evident. Jock could no longer (in good conscience) just ignore her.

Jock had several dreams suggesting that he felt guilty over Jenny. In one dream, she couldn't attend a family party. Jock gloated while their mother announced that she was sorry her daughter was absent. It was as if he'd gotten his wish, and this depressed him.

As the summer break approached, Jock was feeling in crisis, and agreed that when we picked up he would come four times a week. "I'm really not managing my problems," he said. "They're just coming out in other ways."

Dark secrets

Jock began our renewed sessions complaining that his emotional life interfered with his decisions. Having bumped therapy up to four times a week, he was – no surprise -- concerned that more intensity might "open up a can of worms." While he hoped his "true self" would emerge, at the same time he was afraid of what he might find.

We'd been here before.

In his relationship with Nancy, Jock still focused on negatives, particularly on how her emotional dependency was unattractive. However, the real issues had more to do with him. She was working toward independence. He, on the other hand, was afraid of his own feelings, of being in need of her and of how that would leave him powerless. In the abstract, he wanted more intimacy, but he felt anxious about being "trapped" in it.

He also tended to criticize things about Nancy that he saw in himself. For example, his complaints that she didn't have enough self-confidence and assertiveness, reflecting the same shortcomings he perceived in himself.

When I pointed this out, he became defensive.

"My ambivalence about the relationship has to do with *her*," he said, "not me."

He wondered whether exploring his sexual fantasies with other women might help him decide about Nancy. Clearly, he wanted love, but he was apprehensive: how important was it, given the limitations that a relationship imposes? The idea, I gathered, was that the less you loved someone, the less they power they had over you and, therefore, the fewer limitations you would have to endure. He wondered what sacrifices he'd have to make. Nor could he escape feeling that committed relationships had the finality of death. "My parents got divorced, but I don't ever want to go through that. Nor could I do it to somebody" (the assumption, of course, was that he'd be the person who fell out of love).

For months, he obsessed over his relationship with Nancy in terms of pluses and minuses. On the plus side, he loved Nancy. He liked their familiarity and felt comfortable enough to be more himself with her. On the negative side were his familiar complaints about her hair and lack of professional ambition.

But instead of dealing with his resistance to making a commitment, he blamed me: I was the father who'd failed to provide him with direction. This constellation of feelings coalesced one morning at a bagel shop where I go to get my coffee. Once inside, I noticed Jock and Nancy at a table. Jock and I made eye contact while I waited in line. But the line was so slow that I left before placing an order.

The next morning, he began the session by describing the incident from his perspective. Whereas in the past he would have ignored our chance meeting, he now saw it as "two worlds colliding" – his intrapsychic and real life had met head on. He interpreted my leaving without coffee as following the psycho-analytic protocol to minimize contact between analyst and patient.

"You know I felt sorry for you because you couldn't stay although, at the same time, I was uncomfortable running into you there. I don't really like the idea that someone out there knows my darkest secrets." He was also frustrated with "the one-way street of psychoanalysis," where he had to tell me every-thing about himself, but I shared nothing about myself.

Another troubling aspect of the encounter was that I'd seen Nancy.

"All my friends tell me she's very pretty," he remarked. "One of them asked whether she's a model."

"You seem to be trying to ask what I thought about her without asking," I said.

"Well, I don't want our relationship to become too personal. Now that you've seen Nancy, you might be biased when you're supposed to be objective."

I didn't reply.

Then, unable to resist, he asked, "Well, do you think she's pretty?"

He recalled a number of situations in which he'd sought his father's approval, such as in certain professional choices.

"You're looking for my approval of Nancy," I said.

"I suppose I am," he acknowledged.

With their three-year anniversary approaching, Jock wanted Nancy to give him an ultimatum: "Marry me or not."

I reminded him of how at one time he'd wanted me to give him a similar ultimatum: "Be in analysis or not." This made it clear to him that he was doing with Nancy what he'd done in his treatment as well as with other people throughout his life – that is, he had shifted his responsibility elsewhere. He did not feel competent to make large decisions and, moreover, didn't want to put in the work so that he would be.

"I need to let this sink in," he said. "Maybe then I can decide." I heard a possible cop-out – he'd split the difference between himself and me.

What about your sister?

Despite Jock's progress in some areas, we appeared to be making little headway in resolving his relationship. Jock reiterated, in different words, his conviction that there was, to borrow a phrase, "a brave, new world" of women he was missing out on.

Again, somewhat frustrated (as well as curious), I asked, "If you were listening to yourself, how would you respond?"

"I'd recommend I give Nancy up and look elsewhere."

"Maybe that's what you were hoping I'd say."

Jock needed my permission to act, like a son who wanted to be a good boy.

He fantasized about being with women who were sexier than Nancy and made an association to a *Playboy* magazine he'd pilfered from his father and looked at in secret. "The women on those pages," he sighed, "were unattainable goddesses."

He was reluctant, however, to explore his childhood sexual fantasies, remarking sarcastically, "No, the women didn't look anything like my *mother*."

He was in conflict about being a good boy versus acting out his desires.

"I'm not aware of wanting to be with my mother or a woman like her," he added.

I asked, "What about Jenny?"

He tugged at the collar and wiped his forehead – he was having a panic attack. I gave him a few minutes to collect himself.

"Jock ...? What about Jenny?" I repeated.

"Okay," he said. "I'm going to tell you. Remember that time she came into the bathroom when I was masturbating? She ran to my parents, but it's not the whole story. This part nobody knows, especially Jenny – I was fantasizing about her when she caught me."

This was a revelation.

Suddenly, I understood at least some of his reticence. He couldn't recall early childhood memories because they had been *mixed up with* illicit fantasies about Jenny. This helped explain his discomfort talking about his sex life. Perhaps most importantly, whatever else Jock feared would come out in analysis, this was likely what he'd feared most.

"It never went beyond fantasies," Jock insisted, "and it's not something I've fantasized about since I was a kid. But I still feel guilty about it. It's even worse because when she walked in on me, it was like she *knew* what was going on in my head."

"Maybe your animosity toward Jenny stems from how, subconsciously, she is the source of your guilt – sort of like a temptress, though she never intended to be," I suggested.

He returned to his reticent mode. "But that was a long time ago. I'm done with it." Clearly, he wasn't.

"Sure, you are – consciously," I said. "But there's still a lot of suppression going on."

"Well in case you're wondering, Nancy doesn't look like Jenny," Jock said, "and they're nothing alike."

But Jock didn't want to go any deeper into his Jenny-based guilt. I tried to reassure him that sexual attraction between siblings wasn't uncommon but, at the same time, I suggested not leaving any related issues unexplored.

"The problem right now," he insisted, "is Nancy."

Jock had all but decided to break up with her even though he knew how painful it would be for them both.

He described a dream in which two young children, both 3 years old and related, died. One was beautiful and innocent, the other aggressive and hyperactive. His associations were to Nancy and me (he'd been in a relationship with both of us for three years).

Despite his having dismissed any continuing attraction to Jenny, Jock felt he had issues to work on, so he couldn't let "our baby" die. With Nancy, however, he felt he'd gone as far as he could. So, after struggling with his commitment for several months, he finally ended it.

In effect, he hadn't really gotten over his panic attacks so much as he had turned them into how he dealt with commitment. That is, commitment frightened him. It meant somebody would be looking at him, now and forever. Instead of sweating, however, he would run and hide. In front of an audience, that was impossible. But he could leave a woman whenever he felt her presence was too close.

Predictably, Jock felt depressed after he'd ended things with Nancy, and kept bringing up his sense of loss. He was reluctant to let her go completely, and seemed to secretly hope that they'd get back together.

Conversely, he experienced the relief of a prisoner released after a long period of confinement – the freedom to pursue other women.

He was thinking and rethinking, going around in circles.

So, during this time, I suggested that we look more closely at why he resisted committed relationships, including self-esteem issues. I thought I'd circle back to unfinished business regarding his panic attacks.

But he dismissed the idea, saying "I'd rather have a woman to chase after."

He emphasized the excitement of the pursuit.

Beneath it, however, I heard a need for continual self-affirmation. He was, I felt, unconvinced that he was worth someone's abiding love. In short, he felt unlovable.

Consequently, he saw Nancy's love as making her less desirable.

Moreover, he had worked out a whole rationale as to why he should move on. In effect, he projected his insecurities onto her. From his descriptions, Nancy was quite independent and assured, and had a decent job. She was not emotionally dependent on him. Rather, his dislike of her emotional displays reflected his embarrassment at how Jenny never controlled her emotions.

His girlfriend and his sister became a blur. He never apologized, never explained. For a guy with such low self-esteem, he could act with unstinting self-interest.

Still, he was conflicted: he wanted to be a bad boy with women, but he also cultivated guilt.

"Look," I said, "these reality-based concerns of yours are relevant, but your deeper issues involve sexual taboos from your childhood."

He demurred, however, determined to focus on the practical.

He had a series of dreams that opened a window into his underlying sexual feelings. As we discussed their implications, it became clear that his sexual desires – and fear of being punished for them – took shape over the years with reference to his desire for his sister. Since she was unavailable (except by breaking a taboo), other women took her place ... but never quite came up to his original, primal fantasy. After a while, he'd reject them, as he rejected Nancy.

His relationship with Jenny involved love and disdain, each roiling around in a mix that he could not sort through. He brought the same confusion to other relationships. This was, simply, how he related to women. The question was whether it would ever change – that is, whether therapy could help change it.

Trapped again

Jock felt "trapped" in his relationship with me as he had with Nancy. Analysis had not been his preference, he insisted, and he complained about feeling "constrained." In reality, he was staring down that part of him that was fraught with forbidden desires – and that I wanted him to reflect on.

Jock also objected that while he had to open up to me, the relationship was "asymmetrical."

"You're too distant," he said.

When I tried to point out that our sessions were about him, he reverted to that instance in the bagel shop. "You didn't even stop to say hello," he said, conveniently forgetting that, just a while ago, he seemed nonplussed that I'd been there at all.

Jock was the elusive one, changing facts to suit himself, trying to score points so that I'd stop asking him to face his own conflicts. Patients do that and, I suppose, it reflects human nature. But, in order to help him face uncomfortable aspects of himself, I changed things up a bit.

He was about to graduate from business school, and I asked whether Jenny was planning to come. "This might be good time to patch things up," I offered.

But as it turned out, she relapsed just before the ceremony. Her girlfriend had phoned, tearful and apologetic. Jock was disgusted. At the same time, however, he felt guilty, reminded that *his* accomplishment probably came at her expense – at least as he saw it.

"Do you want to talk about you and Jenny?" I asked.

No, he did not. "Maybe I feel guilty, but whatever happened is in the past. Now I'm looking ahead." He brought up his salary and benefits package, and wanted to know how it compared to what I earn.

"You see us as competitive," I said. "There's some of that with Jenny too."

"How many times do I have to tell you?" he shouted. "Jenny's over and done, and I'm moving on." Except with all that guilt, he really wasn't.

Nonetheless, he wanted to move on, whether or not Jenny loomed in the background. I saw it in a dream he had, where a skier tosses away his ski poles on a treacherous slope. His associations to several new women he was plowing through suggested that the slope represented more about his dating life than anything to do with his profession. I thought that what really mattered to him now was being able to navigate around his inhibitions – the guilt over Jenny, the guilt over his fantasies – and experience his sexuality more freely. Putting Jenny "in the past" meant moving beyond the feelings of guilt that she still could precipitate.

In another dream, one woman led another in a dance. This inspired him to recount a fantasy he'd had involving two women. In describing it, he meant to say that *he* wanted to *be with* the women, but instead he said he wanted *Jenny* to be *like* other women (i.e., heterosexual). The implication, of course, was that then he could be leading Jenny in a dance.

He corrected himself at once, knowing I'd call out his Freudian slip (slips reveal underlying unconscious processes).

"I was just thinking of my sister and her girlfriend" he said. "I wish she had a boyfriend. I don't want to *be* her boyfriend." He looked uncomfortable, and turned the tables. "Do I really have to be under a spotlight like this?"

Demurring about his last remark, I said, "I don't mean to be critical, but it's your slip."

He started sweating heavily, then tried to pass if off by saying, "Once it starts, it's inevitable." But still, *some*thing had triggered the attack, and it was connected to whatever he'd been thinking about Jenny.

After the episode, he steered the conversation back toward his new job.

"You're deflecting from having had a sweat attack," I said.

"No, I'm not," he insisted, and brought the conversation back to disputing how I'd interpreted his slip of the tongue. In effect, he felt more secure in his battling me than in treating me as an ally in understanding his sexuality. I wondered how, from his perspective, we'd finally get on the same side – and, if doing so, perhaps suggested to him homoerotic implications.

Acceptance

Not long after, analysis of another dream opened up Jock's awareness of his sexuality.

"I'd left the door to my apartment slightly open," he began. "My crazy next-door neighbor stepped in. I thanked her. This happened with my eyes closed. When I opened my eyes, she was standing over me, like a witch."

His initial association was to Jenny's announcement that now, after a period of rehab, she was moving back to New York. The crazy neighbor in the dream represented Jenny, whom he felt was encroaching on him.

"I really don't want her just showing up at my place without warning," he said.

"What about your eyes being closed and then open?" I asked.

He shrugged. "I don't want to see her, but now she's going to be in my face every day."

"So, you want to shut your eyes to her and her problems," I prompted.

"Bingo."

"You know you generally keep your eyes closed while you're on the couch too," I observed. The implication, of course, was that he didn't want his own problems "in his face."

Jock mumbled something about "decreasing external stimulation" but, after reflecting a moment, he acknowledged, "There are things I don't want to look at with you." And he went on to speak obsessionally about work-related matters.

I cited the flow of his thoughts turning away from an uncomfortable subject. He acknowledged this.

"Look," he said, "I'm not the one whose homosexual."

I thought that was true, given his history with and desires for woman as well as his sexual fantasy life. But I observed that sexuality can be complicated, adding that plenty of heterosexual men have all kinds of fantasies.

Returning to Jenny, he said, "Look, I'm embarrassed by my sister, but I'm also ashamed of the role she plays in my sexuality." I thought that was an insight. Not wanting to face this fact – that is, to "look at" it – was allied with not feeling comfortable when people were looking at *him*. They were two sides of the same coin, mediated by a desire to remain uninvolved, detached, a person of appearances that could not be penetrated. I also thought that if he could further understand his relationship with Jenny, he could see how it reflected his larger issues with fear and low self-esteem which, of course, were a catalyst for his sweat attacks. But so long as he continued to shut his eyes, so to speak, it would be hard to help him see what I was getting at.

As we spoke, I broached the idea that his sexual feelings toward Jenny were related, in part, to his childhood bed-wetting. At least both were forbidden and developed around the same time. The connection seemed kind of obvious, albeit uncomfortable. Still, it was present for us and perhaps he'd consider it. I thought he might accept unflattering ideas about himself when presented with them in clear and limited increments. In other words, perhaps he'd come out of hiding inch by inch, even if he was afraid of the big picture.

However, Jock still harbored the fear that if he led us down the path we were on, I might become like his sister (who was prone to act impulsively, unpredictably, and somewhat uncontrollably) or his father (who was so critical). We'd have to strike a balance, feeling our way so that he wouldn't revert to his default MO of undoing whatever he'd just accomplished.

A friendly takeover

After boasting about his compensation, Jock had difficulty with his decision to work for his father. He disliked being dependent, and considered his assignments beneath his abilities. At times, he felt that his father was keeping him from expanding the business. He felt infantilized, not like an independent adult who was in training. "My dad never went to business school," he complained. "He's so out of touch."

He was also uncomfortable because everyone knew he was the boss' son ("It's like I'm back in my family as the favored child – history is repeating itself. I don't need another load of guilt.") This was heavier than his problem with a bruised ego and a father who was out of touch. I was concerned that if this additional source of guilt became more significant, it could lead to greater anxiety, derail our progress, and cause Jock to hide from himself even more.

He was beginning to feel insecure. "People are looking at me, evaluating my performance. I know they talk behind my back – 'Who's this guy, anyway?'" Here we go again, I thought. Grounds for another panic attack.

Still, rather than evading these challenges, as he would have in the past, Jock tried to deal with them. He consulted management experts, including a former professor. He adopted a business development strategy and expanded the marketing plan. He built a team. The point was to inspire confidence, so that when people did look at him, he wouldn't assume the worst. "I've got to earn their respect," he said. Exactly right.

Nonetheless, I realized that he remained intensely self-conscious, always anticipating that people would find one fault or another in his performance. He was still on the stage.

When I brought this up, he agreed, but it was as if I were finding fault in him. His association was to how, as a child, he hated performing. "Jenny was this drama queen, always seeking attention, but I never liked to stand out. That's why I dreaded giving presentations at business school." In his mind, I had replaced all these old, unforgiving audiences with my own insistent scrutiny.

He wanted me to be as accepting of his less attractive aspects as his mother had been of his bed-wetting. He outright told me so. But all I could say was that I wasn't judging him, only trying to help him better understand conflicts he was struggling with – a distinction that, in his present state of agitation, he had trouble accepting.

Jock himself suspected that his bed-wetting was related to his libidinal attachment to Jenny. Exactly how was less clear. There was a lot about his relationship with her that remained opaque to him, not least because he wanted to repress it and, as he said, "move on."

Love's executioner

Shortly after returning from our seasonal hiatus, Jock reported a dream that was a harbinger of the year's underlying theme.

"I was trying to get into a parking space and kept hitting the car behind me. The other driver was laughing at me, mocking my efforts."

His initial association was to a charity event from the previous night, where he'd felt uncomfortable and out of place. Then he began to complain about being back in analysis.

"It's a pain in the ass, all the time I spend here. And I keep bumping up against all your demands."

"So you feel negative about being back and exploring your feelings," I said.

Jock sighed. "I guess I'm just frustrated with myself. We're touching on important stuff and should keep going, just because I'm anxious talking about it." That was progress.

He was also frustrated because whatever self-understanding he'd achieved had not produced much evidence of change. He still felt unwilling to commit to a serious relationship. He still had sweat attacks on occasion (albeit less frequently) when he made video presentations to clients. "I told myself it was the lights," he said. "But I knew it wasn't."

I wanted to focus on his issues with love and relationships, but knew that my role was to wait and see what came to *his* mind. "Well," he said after a long pause, "it's scary to love someone and have to relinquish a certain amount of control over my life."

Logically, he understood this. He also accepted that his problems with intimacy went beyond any particular relationship. But still, he wasn't trying to be intimate with anyone. He'd go to bars, pick up someone, and invite them back to his apartment. He was making up for lost time. He didn't feel guilty about these liaisons because, he claimed, "everyone knows what's going on."

Yet of all the women who might be interested in him, he started an affair with a colleague.

"Why would you pick someone you work with?" I asked.

First, he argued that Claudette did not really work with him. "She's only sharing office space," he said and, technically, this was true. But then he revealed that he liked the need to hide from everyone. "I guess it's sort of illicit," he admitted. There was an obvious association with his sister. It was like he was reviving the relationship in another key, which seemed to whet his desire.

"You're playing out a family romance," I said. "It's Jenny 2.0."

He got angry, calling me "love's executioner," launching a barrage of criticism that was aimed at me but actually reflected how he felt about himself.

After several minutes, he conceded that his feelings toward Jenny were complex. He'd been aroused by how they tussled as children, even as he dreaded being caught. His dread of being seen with Claudette recapitulated the excitement/dread that defined his relationship with Jenny. He was drawn to this new affair for the same reasons – it excited and panicked him. Case in point: the one time that Jock saw Claudette in public, he had a sweat attack.

He went to the event anyway, of course, but later admitted that "I'm anxious someone will find out what's going on." It was the pattern – excitement/dread – that he craved and that, it seemed, he didn't want to break.

"Your illicit relationship is a stand-in for you and your sister," I said.

"Yeah. It's upsetting enough as it is, without the whole *world* finding out."

He fell silent for a moment then recalled an incident from childhood that involved Jenny.

"We used to fight all the time. I resented her taking stuff from me, like the remote. Once, I clobbered her with it. She had to get stitches. We weren't close."

"Not close?" I inquired ironically.

My question forced him to confront the fable he'd been telling himself – all his life perhaps – and was now telling me. In an effort to be more honest, he admitted how uncomfortable and anxiety-provoking his closeness to his sister really was.

"Your hostility toward Jenny keeps her at a safe distance," I observed. "Maybe you don't resent her behavior as much as you resent *her*. She reminds you of what you would rather repress."

His dislike of Jenny was a defense against intense, sexual desire.

"Guilt," he said. "I'm full of guilt for the way I feel about my sister."

In this context, he had an odd dream: "I had my teeth redone. The dentist filed them down so they were too short. No one else noticed, but when I looked in the mirror, they were horrible. He'd gone too far. The damage was irreparable."

Initially, he had no associations to the dream. He did, however, comment that his teeth seemed to represent strength and power. He elaborated on a memory he'd previously mentioned only in passing – a Little League baseball game in which he was pitching. He threw a fastball down the pike, and the batter drove it back up the middle, a line drive that slammed into Jock's mouth. He needed 56 stitches and dental reconstruction. His jaw was wired shut for several weeks, he drank only liquid food, and his braces had to be refitted. After this traumatic accident, he could not get back on the mound.

"Tell me more about the dentist in your dream," I said.

"He was out of sight and behind me," Jock replied. "He also butchered the procedure."

"Do you ever think of me as being like that dentist?"

"Sometimes; I think your comments go too far," he said.

He also felt like our work together rendered him less powerful. After the reconstructive surgery, he said, he looked deformed – a little too good, with all those artificial implants and veneers. "Now, that's what you're doing," he insisted, "making me into something I'm not."

Obviously, he felt threatened by our work together. He told me that since the accident occurred just around his entering puberty, he later saw it as punishment for his sexual development and desires. "I can't help seeing you that way," he said, "dragging up stuff about Jenny, tying it to Claudette. Why should any of this matter?"

I assumed that he was asking a rhetorical question, and that it was my prerogative to finesse it and just listen.

Well, at least this *was* a rhetorical question, rather than an outright challenge coupled with a threat to quit. We had, at least, made *some* progress.

Another Gatsby?

Throughout his relationship with Claudette, Jock emphasized that most of what he wanted was sex. He remained anxious, however, because much of her appeal was as a stand-in for Jenny. Their physicality was never, therefore, guilt-free.

He dated other women as well, and was apprehensive about settling down.

He had a dream that crystallized some of these issues: "Nancy and I cross paths on the street. Then she starts crying."

He was angry at Nancy even though *he'd* broken up with *her*, and he speculated – correctly – that his anger protected him from a sense of loss. He admitted feeling lonely; there were several women in his life, but none was "special." This kind of introspection showed some further progress, even though he was still acting in ways that harked back to adolescence. At least he *knew* he was acting that way.

Moreover, his panic attacks were becoming rarer. He used behavioral, cognitive, and emotional strategies to stave off the anxiety that typically precipitated them. In effect, he was doing what he'd wanted me to do all along – treat his symptoms.

Over the next several weeks, he focused on what he saw as improvement. He felt more in touch with himself, at least insofar as he understood the basis for some of his anxieties (even if he still resisted the hard work to fully analyze them). He felt he'd made steady gains in terms of becoming more comfortable with himself, even confident (and hence less likely to sweat).

His frustration with analysis was that it had not been more transformational in terms of helping him professionally. He still wanted to build a team like the 1978 Yankees, and maybe have "Great" attached to his name like Jay Gatsby. These fantasies translated into building up his family business and eventually selling it for a newsworthy sum. He envied his friends, whom he perceived as building their net worth – like Gatsby's.

Jock reminded me of Gatsby in other ways as well. Like Gatsby, he cared desperately about appearances and the image that he projected (while fending off anyone who would peer underneath). They were both strivers, captured by a fantasy (Gatsby's Daisy; Jock's Jenny).

Jock was serious about building a small business empire, and I began to see him as a Gatsby, guarding another set of secrets. One was his childhood bed-wetting, which, psychologically, he'd never outgrown and which still defined him, epitomizing his lack of self-confidence. How could he be a titan if, underneath, he was just a little boy without bladder control – a little pisher? Nor would any woman be attracted if she knew his true nature. He harbored at least one other secret – his lingering, if metamorphosed obsession with Jenny. How would that play?

So, I was surprised when, once again, he announced it was time to leave treatment.

"I'm better now," he said. "I don't think I need it anymore."

He had, in fact, grown considerably, but that was not the real reason he was talking about dropping treatment. We'd reached a point where Jenny was the main topic, and he felt unsafe exploring his sexual attraction to her. We both knew it.

Either he'd dive in now, or there was good reason to stop. So, shortly after his announcement, he missed a session and neglected my bill.

But then he returned and paid up. Was he testing me or himself? Probably the latter, and I guess he decided that passive-aggressive acting out was not in his interest. The subject of Jenny's rebelliousness came up again, and he saw parallels to himself: both had struggled with issues of authority, control, and sexuality. We talked for a while, and at times he sounded almost empathetic. Was there a brewing rapprochement?

No. Despite my suggestions, he did not want to go any deeper. He said he was leaving treatment within six months. "I feel more confident just saying it," he said.

But we were still talking.

During this phase of analysis, he assumed more responsibility for the family business. I think, in part, the rush of power he experienced translated into a sense that he could *tell* me how his treatment would go, and I would have to acquiesce. I saw no point in challenging him since, of course, I already had and he'd made the decision on his own.

In fact, he continued to voice frustration with analysis, which focused on his inner life rather than on tangible results (he was still downplaying, if not ignoring, the near-certainty that they were intimately connected).

"Is more self-understanding really going to help me reach my business goals?" he asked, as if his measure of himself was premised on how he performed at work.

He tended to see anything that inhibited his ambitions located somewhere outside himself. In effect, he was saying "Don't look at me" to anyone who might literally look and cause him to panic or at least get anxious. He was also, figuratively, denying responsibility even as he claimed to be assuming more. I thought he was being disingenuous – with himself, me, and everyone. This was not a good time to leave analysis, but he couldn't be dissuaded. He saw making up his mind as an expression of self-confidence.

"You have made a lot of good progress," I acknowledged. "But you still have a way to go with being more fully confident, and comfortable in your own skin. Most of us do." Power does not automatically segue into confidence, and perhaps he was starting to realize that.

He conceded the point. He also admitted that it was hard to contemplate actually leading the company when his father retired.

"I'm afraid," he said, "that I might not succeed. I might even embarrass myself."

"Well then," I said, "perhaps there is work to do." Tentatively, he agreed.

Sturm und Drang

I began renovations on my offices in the spring. Jock had been silent when, earlier that year, I changed my address. But now he was vocal. He was glad, he said, that I'd "traded-up." The new office had "a prestigious address" and an "Old World air" that he liked. So, was I, in his mind, becoming more like him, obsessed with surfaces? As if to say *yes*, he opined that the office now prompted him to reevaluate our relationship. It had become "integral" to his life, a marker of how we had *both* worked our way up. He felt justified, from his perch, in complimenting me.

Was this a type of egocentrism, or a rather awkward expression of self-confidence, even the emergence of self-esteem?

Whatever it was, his expansiveness didn't last.

A deal that fell through at work demonstrated how vulnerable he was. Referring to a painting on my wall of a cabin in the woods, he said, "I'd rather be there." He seemed visibly discouraged, but he didn't quit. He tried, instead, to manage.

He acknowledged that analysis was helping. "Without it," he said, "I would have been bucked down to accounting." That is, he would have disappointed everyone, including his father, with his utter lack of self-confidence and indecisiveness.

Now he reserved that indecisiveness for me, with on-again/off-again commitments to remain in analysis. So, if our relationship was "integral" to his life, it was integral to that part of him still hung up on fear of being exposed.

"Maybe I *do* have sexual feelings for Jenny," he blurted out.

He mentioned being bathed by his sister as a boy, but that was as far as he allowed his recollection to go. His self-protective amnesia was on display in a dream he had.

"I was being held captive by a random adult. I don't know why. There wasn't much food or water. I asked to use the restroom and locked the door. I escaped through a window, and then I ran naked across the roofs of townhouses."

The townhouses, apparently, reminded him of my old office, where he had complained of feeling trapped. The nakedness symbolized his fear of exposure. Moreover, he explained, "It's not just analysis I want to escape. I want to run away from my sexual anxieties." About Jenny? About commitment? He was moving toward greater honesty, but was still being opaque.

Whatever the case, he understood that he still had some therapeutic work to do. He decided to continue in treatment.

It really is over

As we entered the sixth and final year of Jock's treatment, his sense of himself had clearly altered. He didn't *want* to engage in the sort of strategic repression that allowed him to think that everything seemed fine. He knew that appearances were insufficient, if for no other reason than that they could not – over a lifetime – allay his anxieties. He wanted a more permanent solution to toxic guilt and fear and, for that, he knew that he'd have to confront himself. With honesty. So, he had begun to cultivate self-reflection. He recognized that his core fantasies were, for the most part, traceable to his relationship with Jenny, even as he began to understand their continuing ramifications.

As he became more comfortable with his own feelings, he felt less need to fight me. Correspondingly, his relationships with his colleagues improved. He felt less exposed – or, rather, he became less afraid of the inevitable exposure. "I know they're watching," he said, "but I'm watching them so we're even." As the soon-to-be boss, that little bit of cockiness was justifiable, especially if it kept him from panicking. He reported that he expressed his opinions more freely. "I think being funny helps," he said – it took his mind off the serious business of real-time decision making.

But he experienced a setback when Nancy got engaged. He was angry and hurt.

"She told me she was seeing someone, but she never said it was *real*," he admitted. I was struck by how he attributed the same sort of fantasizing to Nancy as he had engaged in, and once again sold her short with regard to her personal independence

He saw her action as a reflection on him, rather than her simply moving on with her life. It reminded him that he still had work to do.

Moreover, he was envious. So, now *he* wanted to get married – though I feared this was mainly as a riposte to Nancy, as well as to bolster his bruised ego. In fact, he reported meeting one "sub-par" woman after another. So, I asked, "Do you really want to get married, or is it just that you don't want to feel like a loser?" He knew what I was driving at, but he demurred. Now Nancy had – ironically – become the gold standard, to which no one measured up.

The progress he had made, at least in part, was unraveling. He couldn't commit.

"Your sense of vulnerability, your fear," I observed, "are based in underlying conflicts about intimacy and trust."

He was silent, just like he used to be when the likelihood of exposure seemed imminent.

"I'm starting to wonder," he said, "whether my aggressiveness in relationships is pushing women away." He closed his eyes. "I think I did something to hurt my sister." He was repeating himself. I worried whether he had repressed what, months earlier, he had acknowledged.

In any case, he was actively reflecting on that crucial relationship.

"I remember now," he said. "I used to spy on Jenny when she was in the bathroom, especially if I knew she was taking a shower. I wanted to see her getting undressed. Once, when I was 7 or 8, she caught me. The door was open just a crack, and I was peeking in. When Jenny opened it, I jumped back, but she knew what I was doing. She walked to her room in a towel and slammed the door. She must have known there were other times – she probably even caught me those other times. So, I disoriented her. I have some guilt about that."

"There are also mitigating factors," I suggested. "You were a boy. Children are curious about the opposite sex, and a parent or sibling is more available than anyone else." He felt good about sharing that with me, like we finally broke through more of his resistance. So, I added "You recalled something you had every reason to repress – every reason not to tell me – and yet you related the whole thing without panicking."

"This *is* a pretty big deal," he said, "like, I mean, not just remembering what I did but opening up about it."

"Yes. And now that you know more about yourself and what happened with Jenny, you better understand your actions rather than condemning yourself for them." Perhaps Jock's self-esteem would increase further if he jettisoned some of his guilt.

He was, in fact, becoming less closeted, and was even able to acknowledge intermittent homosexual desires (allowing him to see that his distaste for Jenny's lesbianism was, partly, a reflection of his own fears). He tried to be more understanding of Jenny's sexual preferences. He talked about her now with a certain objectivity – rather than visceral dislike – and he didn't just shut down when I mentioned her.

He was back on track – more or less.

Exit strategy

As Jock felt freer to reflect on himself, the notion that *other* people might get closer continued to become less frightening. "I guess I'm just sort of out there," he said. "I can't stay bunkered forever." Did he mean it literally? Well, I was glad that he had, at least, formulated the idea. Before, he just would have brooded.

In fact, he rarely talked about sweating. In addition to his cognitive and behavioral strategies, he'd imagine what other people might be thinking. "It was usually so weird, that I'd always feel they had nothing on *me*." It was a way of externalizing his anxieties. It was fine. His obsessiveness had also faded. He made decisions and stuck to them (no more "thinking about thinking"). The trick, he said, was to get things right the first time by slowing

down. "I'm not always running," he said, "and I'm definitely more careful."
You'd have thought they taught this in business school ... but, fair enough.

"So what's your exit strategy?" I asked.

My question reminded him of a dream he'd had the previous night: "I was
moving downtown. My parents looked at the apartment, and they liked it.
I didn't think my chances of getting it were great. My dad had on a chunky
gold ring with four diamonds that seemed to be a talisman for luck."

One line of association to the dream was his leaving analysis for better
circumstances, but he wanted my approval.

"In the past, you've seen me as curtailing your improvement," I said. But he
disagreed (finessing what he once said). He did say, however, that he'd gone as
far as he wanted to go at this point in his life – notwithstanding that he could
still make more progress.

In the time remaining, therefore, I continued to use his resistances to analysis to help him better understand his intrapsychic conflicts. For example,
about two months before his treatment ended, he had a dream: "I was para-
chuting to earth. Floating. I was concerned about my safety. I don't remember
the plane or the ground."

His association was to a sculpture that his mother had brought back from a
trip to France. It depicted a man inside a man. He imagined that it represented
a person who looked large on the outside but felt small on the inside.

"I see this as a projection of how I felt about myself in the past," he
explained. "Even now, when I think about some of my experiences – bed-
wetting, losing my teeth, how I couldn't keep a relationship – it leaves me
feeling small."

Even though Jock was now acting out a type of greater self-esteem –
giving more presentations, visiting clients – it was as if he *knew* it was an act.
The point was to bring his sense of self, internal and external, into greater
alignment. I didn't think they would be perfectly aligned.

He described another airborne dream: "I was in Donald Trump's heli-
copter. He wasn't with us, and I felt scared. Then I was watching a musical,
but got bored and walked out. I ended up in a shopping mall, but there was
no exit. Finally, I landed back in the seat I started from."

In the context of Jock's analysis, which was ending, it seemed he felt insecure about venturing out on his own. He wanted to leave the theater of his
mind, but saw himself ending up back in treatment (the seat where he started).
He wasn't fully where he wanted to be. Perhaps at some point he would seek
further treatment.

But still, his panic attacks were all but gone. So, although he claimed to have
landed in the wrong place, the landing had been soft. Moreover, he had done
Gatsby one better – unlike that icon of the Jazz Age, Jock had mostly come
to terms with his obsessions. He knew that chasing a fantasy was pointless,
and that he wanted to live the best version of his life in the real world. In that
sense, he'd come a long way.

References

Fitzgerald, F. Scott. *The Great Gatsby* (New York: Charles Scribner's Sons, 1925)

Winnicott, Donald W. *Playing & Reality* (London: Tavistock, 1971)

Winnicott, Donald W. "Ego distortion in terms of true and fake self." In *The Person Who Is Me*, pp. 7–22 (New York: Routledge, 2018)

Chapter 4

Reluctance

This study concerns a young man who loves his father (ambivalently), but is conflicted over versions of aggressive masculinity that his father demands. He struggles to define his own sense of maleness, complicated by what he feels are his feminizing, homoerotic tendencies. In his more "feminine" mode, he disdains his father, especially with regard to his father's indifference to his mother's sensibilities. The family dynamic remains a source of self-doubt, as well as anger at patriarchal figures whose swagger he nonetheless tries to emulate. He finally seeks my help – though I too am a "patriarch" – with how to manage maleness on his own terms.

The problem is that, as therapy proceeds, he needs to compete with me, to prove me ineffectual and unable to help. Thus, he falls into a contradiction from which it is hard to escape. The more he feels the need to compete, the less likely his therapy is to succeed. Yet he still cannot do without the competition, and fantasizes my defeat at his hands. In the fantasy world that he inhabits, he emerges as dominant, even while forcing his treatment toward abrupt reversals and failures. We make some progress, but a negative transference emerges where I become a stand-in for his father, a homosexual partner, and even the professors whose grading he resents.

I try to help him to accept his homoerotic tendencies so that he can construct a sense of his masculinity that is not subject to constant self-doubt. If he can resolve or at least manage his conflicts over aggressive masculinity, he will be less likely to compensate through fantasies of dominance. But our progress is slow. He clings to his father's notions, continuing to find new challengers whom he feels the need to vanquish.

His relationship with a woman, a major player in this story, is fraught. He has not told her about his fantasies – either the cartoonishly violent, where women are subjugated, or the homoerotic, which he regards as feminizing. He worries about their compatibility, mainly because she does not satisfy some of his sexual desires and because he feels intimidated by her intellectual success. We talk about how this relationship may or may not work out, and he remains conflicted over how firmly to commit to it.

DOI: 10.4324/9781003352624-5

So, this becomes a study where the patient is intensely reluctant to declare himself – for or against one form of love or another, for or against his father, or me, or his girlfriend. He is even troubled for a time to commit himself to graduate school, though he has already enrolled. By the time he fully embraces the profession, he sees it as a way to compete with me. He never fully shakes his obsessions.

Yet, toward the end of his analysis – a treatment of almost four years – he experiences a significant moment of clarity when, all of a sudden, he is able to diagnose the factors that, in collision, are responsible for his conflicts. Whether he will deal with them effectively remains uncertain, but he has nonetheless made progress. He has learned how to think about himself with a degree of insight and understanding. He likes himself more because he does not feel guilty over who he is – that is, he is himself, his own version of "male," and he will likely keep working on refining it. He takes significant steps toward resolving issues with his relationship based, in part, on a conviction that he will be able to see them through to success. But will he succeed?

Because all forms of love – sexual, familial, self-love – are so complex, they challenge the treatment to sort through them to some more definitive version of what is feasible, much less desirable. Moreover, the patient needs to help. In this case and not uncommonly, the patient's conflicts interfered, and so we were caught in a bind: the more the patient resisted, the less progress we made, and the more his conflicts kept asserting themselves in new, disconcerting ways. We had to settle into treatment, and wait for the conflicts to emerge in the transference, so that the patient could finally clarify how he would untangle the various strands of love that made up his complex existence. We could not out-wait his conflicts but, because of what he learned in analysis, he may go the rest of the way on his own.

As this treatment unfolded, I began to understand the patient in terms of "attachment theory," developed by John Bowlby in the 1950s. The "attachment" is the bond that an infant develops with its parents or primary care-giver, which can affect the person's relationships going forward. There are three types of attachment styles, one of which is anxious-preoccupied, in which a person seeks intimacy but needs constant reassurance and readiness from the partner. It applies to the patient in this study: he sought closeness with his fiancée, but then needed reassurance that she cared and would be there. He'd seek to embrace her more fully, and then would pull away – an attitude that was on display when he addressed me, and not without homoerotic implications. From Bowlby's perspective, the patient's behavior reflects a frustrated yearning for closeness with his mother who, for the most part, was passive and remote.

The patient dwells on his mother, in fact, who was so beaten down by his father that she rarely had time to provide him with a refuge. While he repeatedly sought his mother's love and attention, he was shunted off into his schoolwork. Excelling at school – and especially in sports – became his way of gaining *her attention, though it left him as an anxious-avoidant participant in future relationships.*

Andy swaggered into his initial visit in ripped jeans and a *Save the Whales* T-shirt. He wore a gold stud in his ear. A ring in an eyebrow. "This guy's cocky," I thought. At 5'6", he was likely over-compensating. So, I was not surprised when – first thing, before we shook hands – he said he'd wrestled in college. "I competed in the nationals," he added. Translation: "Hey doc, I can handle myself."

Which raised the question: why then was be here? I thought we could start with the obvious. "Why *are* you here?" I asked.

As if on cue, the bravado gave way to defense mode (which you'd expect from a wrestler who sensed a long bout). Andy craved my respect, apparently, but felt vulnerable. "I'm scared," he admitted. He had moved to New York to start graduate school in clinical psychology, and had been accepted into a prestigious program. He had considered becoming a doctor like his fiancée, but just couldn't face the workload she had endured. So, since he still wanted to be involved with healing, he settled on a Psy.D.

But then the conflicts started. "I'm not even sure I want to be a psychologist," he sighed. "Maybe I'm putting myself through this for nothing." The wrestler was hesitant, which made him uncomfortable, which upended the image he liked to project.

Yet, even as he winced, we seemed to be getting somewhere. Andy needed to think of himself as a fighter, but wasn't sure that he could. His sense of himself was shaky.

I tried to reassure him. "It's okay to pursue something tentatively as you learn more about it."

Andy winced again, and acknowledged that his problem was not just about pursuing a doctorate. I wasn't surprised. Things are rarely "about" the first issue that a patient raises. Usually, these initial complaints – what finally pushes them over the edge of walking in through my door – are the culmination of issues that have been troubling them for years, whether or not they know it.

Actually, Andy was also anxious about being distant from Diane, his fiancée, who was in Los Angeles finishing med school. In other words, he was anxious about work and love, Freud's two pillars of happiness. It doesn't get much broader.

"So," I asked, "what are your symptoms?"

Andy complained of restlessness, irritability, fatigue, trouble concentrating, and difficulty falling asleep. This had gone on for about two months. Over the past several weeks, he'd felt depressed.

"I'm worried about the work, of course, but I'm more concerned about how my state of mind will affect my relationship. This could be the last straw, given the distance between us." His expression suddenly sank. "Or maybe I want it to be. I mean, I love her, but I don't know if I'm ready to get married."

He picked at himself while he talked, usually at his arms but sometimes at his face. At one point he examined a forearm. "I'm starting to leave marks." I could see them.

He segued into observing that when he felt especially anxious, like when he and Diane fought, he might "pick on" his cat, Motor. If Motor broke the rules (no scratching, no avoiding the litter box), he might spank her or even toss her against a wall (she always landed unharmed on her feet).

"Something must be roiling around if I take out my frustration on a cat," he said. At least he had some capacity to observe and assess his behavior.

"Have you ever hurt a person because you couldn't control your temper?" I asked.

Exhaling, he answered "Yes."

"What happened?"

"Well, Diane and I were arguing, and we were in the kitchen. I slapped a coffee cup – really *whacked* it – and I still don't know how it hit her, but it did. Under her eye, which swelled up and started to bleed. I rushed her to the hospital, and everyone looked at me, as if to say '*He* did that to her.' I can't let something like that happen again."

I added rage to his mix of symptoms. But in his first sessions we focused on depression. He'd first struggled with it during adolescence, when he'd had severe acne – a constant source of distress. He'd spend hours "picking at" himself in front of a mirror, making a wreck of his face. His father would say, "You look like shit," and Andy was hurt by his insensitivity. But his mother pretended not to notice. He felt that she was too passive and never tried to support him.

The onset of his current mix of anxiety and depression occurred during another major change in his life: starting college.

"I had trouble adjusting to being a small fish in a big, prestigious pond."

He had also been upset that his father left his mother and moved in with another woman. He returned after a while, claiming that it had all been a "misadventure," but Andy had become distraught. "Maybe I just absorbed it from my mother. She never spoke about it, but I'd hear her crying." He couldn't sleep, lost his appetite, and lost interest in sports. His picking at himself grew worse.

"I lost faith in what had seemed permanent," he said. "This was an existential crisis for me – it was like my world fell apart." As we spoke, he admitted that his crisis had become *crises* – he'd felt guilty over not defending his mother. "I should have told that fucker off," he said. "I had fantasies of rescuing my mother, like some knight in shining armor, but I never acted on them. Then I worried that I was a pussy."

The wrestler as weakling. Here was another, apparent conflict in Andy's sense of self. Was this the reason for his bravado, an attempt to convince himself that he was *no* pussy? But there were other possibilities. I wondered whether, perhaps, he might finesse his apparent weakness by seeking strong, competent women – unlike his mother – who could make their way on their own. Is this what Diane represented?

Yes, actually.

After the crisis, he quickly "bonded" with his supervisor at a program where he worked with troubled kids. They defied professional decorum, and became romantically involved. The supervisor – Diane – eventually became his fiancée. In effect, she was the older, high-achieving woman who was attractive precisely because she didn't need him, except insofar as he could provide sex and other forms of life-enhancement that didn't call into question his nerve or strength of character. This would-be M.D. was the hard-science counterpart to his less consistently rigorous persona, the guy who couldn't come up to his own high standards, who might be a "pussy."

But he got a boost when he graduated college in three years with honors. So, when Diane started her M.D. work, he followed her without having much sense of what he wanted. He supported himself as a fitness coach and then as a teacher.

Through Diane he became interested in psychology and fulfilled his pre-doctoral requirements. She was in therapy and, after they both attended a pop psychology lecture on "healing the inner child," he entered therapy as well. His father dismissed it as quackery and refused to pay. So, Andy arranged to be seen at a reduced fee, working overtime to finance it.

"What was it about your 'inner child' that needed healing?" I asked, trying not to sound facetious.

Andy answered obliquely, talking about his father as "a rugged dude with red-neck morality."

He was trying to be funny, but his father was obviously a flashpoint. Andy called him out as chronically dissatisfied – with everyone and with himself. He was a bank administrator, but hated it. "It was too orderly. He took out his frustration on the family," he said.

His mother, he observed, was the opposite, "vulnerable, quiet – she just watched." She taught first grade.

Andy was the middle son of three boys. His older brother had married and also gone into banking. His other brother was "still searching."

"But I'm the favorite," Andy said, "especially when it comes to my mom. I'm the smart one and the athlete."

To Andy, wrestling may have been a way of remaining his mother's favorite. It marked him as strong, which she wasn't. It was rule-bound, which his father did everything to escape. It was a major component of his self-presentation, and he didn't want to risk the appearance of strength associated with it – it would be risking his mother's love.

Of course, the flip side of this logic was that Andy wanted the strength – of character – to protect his mother from his father's behavior.

"She never defended herself," he said. "She just stood there and took it."

His father seemed to find himself funny, but Andy saw how he hurt his wife. "Sometimes, I'd try to tell him. But he'd call me 'pimple face' and my mother would cry." The pattern never changed, though Andy felt that his mother understood his moral support for her. "Maybe it would have been worse without me," he sighed.

I felt that Andy wanted his mother's love – and to be the knight in shining armor who earned it – without putting in the emotional, morally demanding work required to confront his father. It was the same attitude with which he pursued the Psy.D. instead of an M.D. I wondered whether, in ultimate terms, he was afraid that he lacked the personal resources to undertake such work. I felt that he understood the role of fear in constricting his initiatives, even as he did not want to deal with it head-on. As I would discover, this pattern of perceiving a problem, but not being able to fully address it, would become his defining trait as he proceeded through treatment. It all came back to a sense that he could get along by reaching for external compensation, rather than by trying to be whole in himself, with his own personal integrity.

But never mind whether Andy felt (albeit tepidly) that he was supporting his mother. When his father left pornography lying around, the tables were turned. Andy took the stuff to his room. "I told myself I was protecting my mother," he admitted, "but that wasn't so." He'd gaze at the pictures and masturbate, and he saw the women as objects to conquer. He said that because of the "impossible fantasies" that the porn still made him crave, his sexual relationship with Diane was "miserable."

"I dissociate," he said. "Passionate sex is like rape. The woman gets hurt." With Diane, he'd often fail to get an erection. So, despite the contempt that he bore toward his father, he nonetheless identified with him. He objectified women, reducing them to providers of brute sex on the one hand or sexless, delicate creatures on the other. There was no room for mutuality, where a woman took pleasure along with a loving man. The view was primitive, adolescent, debasing. Thus, even though Diane represented the kind of strong woman that he craved, still, she was fundamentally a woman, subject to the categories that he imposed and, in that sense, unable to offer the kind of porn-inspired sex that he craved. It rarely occurred to him that he was hurting himself, limiting a relationship that might have satisfied them both.

Andy saw Diane as sexually repressed. "She can't pick up on what I need," he said. Clearly, this was his father and the pornography talking.

How had they agreed to get married? Was it some fantasy that marriage would solve their sexual limitations? I thought that if we could explore this issue, and if Andy stopped feeling that he had to get married so soon, his sense of himself would be clearer. He'd also have a better idea if he *wanted* a career in psychology.

However, I was concerned about pursuing an intensive course of psychoanalytic treatment during his Psy.D. work and training (assuming that he stayed on that trajectory), so we agreed to meet three times a week. As a preliminary, he asked what he should call me.

"Dr. Friedberg seems too distant," he said, "too impersonal. I was on a first-name basis with my last shrink, but calling you by your first name might be a little too friendly. Do you have a preference?"

I didn't reply.

After a pause he recalled how, at the end of his previous treatment, he'd asked for a hug. His therapist reluctantly complied and when they "analyzed" the incident, Andy felt they had crossed a line. He wondered whether he'd "seduced" the therapist.

The thought prompted him to recall a rabbi, who had been an early mentor. Andy hinted at boundary violations again, but didn't elaborate. But given that he'd brought up both these unlikely incidents, I thought that the common thread – a veiled homoeroticism – might be involved in Andy's anxieties. Was he repressing such homoeroticism, diving into other desires while fumbling with a real woman? It remained to be seen.

It could be, I thought, that Andy was drawn to pornography – at least, in part – because he feared giving way to a homoeroticism that he found troubling, and that his father would have deplored. Pornography, in this sense, would have been correlative to a conventional masculinity consistent with the wrestler, and other forms of undeniable gender identity that made him feel potent, strong, able to be somebody equal to women like Diane. These first dim indicia of an unstable gender identity interested me, therefore, because I thought that they could illuminate his fears, and his need to compete with Diane more or less on her own terms.

On the other hand, if he actually exploited this instability – after all, it opened up more sexual options – then I'd want to watch for that too. It was not inconceivable that he might selectively reveal a certain homoeroticism if he thought it might attract powerful men, or at least those who might help him when he felt inadequate. This might include the rabbi whom, he said, had been a mentor. It might extend to any man, since who knows which of them might harbor similar feelings? He might resent these men-in-power even as he sought to win their favor, using his own sexuality as a type of currency. I had seen this before and, given all of Andy's other conflicts around sex, I would not have been surprised if, as his treatment proceeded, he both bemoaned a conflicted sexuality and also chose not to deal with it. For sure, it might come out in relation to me.

Moving to New York to start his doctorate, as with entering college, seemed like the catalyst for depression and anxiety. While Andy hoped to get past his symptoms, he was still curious to understand their origins. "I can't deal with them," he said, "if I don't know the etiology" (he grinned at the fancy diagnostic term about the origin of a pathology, and we both laughed).

But I found his attitude encouraging. Since psychotherapy is based in self-understanding, it helps to be curious about a symptom's origin.

I was also pleased that Andy requested help controlling his temper, though all his chronic symptoms were subordinate to two immediate, pressing issues: whether to commit to a doctorate, and whether to back out of marriage. The challenge was that these concerns intersected. As we began to broach one of them, the other would, necessarily, become involved.

Of course, we had to start somewhere. So, my approach was to ask Andy what came to mind, or what was he thinking.

I thought this might involve Andy's alignment (through pornography and aggression) with his domineering, sexually unabashed father; how this affected his relations with women; and in what ways pornography and his parents' relationship may have influenced the development and expression of his sexuality. I struggled with what to call Andy's mediated relationship with his father ("alignment" seemed imperfect, though it did capture Andy's willingness to follow his father's example without openly sharing his interest). Andy, who wasn't close with his father and even resented him, still displayed many of his least likable traits, however unwillingly. It all felt somewhat paradoxical – though if you dig deep enough in any relationship (based in an unconscious identification or "alignment") it is usually fraught with contradiction.

I was also not clear about his relationship with his mother during childhood. I considered him an anxious-avoidant type, and wondered if this reflected a lack of maternal care and attention earlier in his life. In a sense, his regret at not having protected his mother (and his feeling that she knew that he'd wanted to) was a way of repairing their relationship. It replayed their relationship in the key of fantasy, where Andy and his mother had been effective allies. They had been unified, almost like they were when she was pregnant. It mollified his sense that his mother was passive, unable to encourage him with emotion when he'd been available to support her (he just needed some sign). It was a kind of "but for" rationale that made his beaten-down, readily shrinking mother into his tacit ally. It made him feel better when he felt that, objectively speaking, he had not done enough.

Regarding Andy's relationship with his father, I also wondered how potential homosexual tendencies might play out in terms of transference. I suspected that the pornography may have been a refuge from these tendencies, even a way of denying them as Andy skirted any firm commitment to Diane. At some level, he may have been unsure that he wanted her sexually, irrespective of whether she was or wasn't conventionally attractive. Her academic success just made her more formidable, on top of what may have been Andy's issues with sexual orientation.

Golden boy no longer

Andy worked at his graduate studies but was frustrated by the results. He'd always done well in school without working *too* hard, so the first year was humiliating. Unlike Diane, who had excelled throughout her graduate program, he got average grades and, again, doubted that psychology was the right career. "Maybe I just felt that I had to keep up with Diane," he said. "Maybe I had to compete with and try to dominate her." He seemed dismayed to hear himself talk about a career in such charged terms. "I should be able to think about psychology without having to *beat* someone – especially someone I love." He finessed his apparent interest in women who satisfied his need to dominate.

But, at the very least, Andy's reaction reflected a sense of narcissistic entitlement – he *should* excel. It implied that being mother's "golden boy" should be enough.

Andy continued to struggle with his commitment to Diane. They'd been involved for six years and lived together for three. Though the wedding was set for the following year, he still obsessed about the relationship.

In the "pro" column: they had developed shared interests, liked each other, and had similar values. Their chemistry wasn't great, but Andy thought it was "sufficient." Still, he focused on the "cons" (and picked at his forearm while he did). These included what he considered her physical flaws and sexual shortcomings. She had thin hair and small breasts, for example, and disliked oral sex. Then there was Diane's religion. Andy was Jewish, and though Diane had agreed to convert, he was hung up on her not having been Jewish by birth. He worried that, in the eyes of the State of Israel, she would never be Jewish without an Orthodox conversion. He himself was not Orthodox but wanted, ostensibly, to ensure that she and their children would be considered Jewish.

Yet, while I could appreciate his concerns, I saw this religious hair-splitting as a dodge, a delaying tactic, and ultimately a potential way to back out.

So, we began to assess how Andy used Diane's alleged physical flaws, and her religious background to distance himself from her, motivated by his *own* problems with intimacy and commitment. "Think about it," I said, "aren't you really looking in the mirror?" He reluctantly acknowledged that I might have a point. He was, at least, willing to pursue the possibility.

So, we discussed the way he deflected his own problems with commitment, giving them an ostensibly rational basis in Diane's perceived shortcomings. It was slow going, since no one likes to admit that they are playing mind games with themselves, especially when the effect is to blame someone else. But, after a while, Andy spoke more candidly about his relationship with Diane. "Okay, I'm worried whether I'm up to her intellectually, at least if I stay in psychology. I'm worried she'll leave me behind." I noted that if she was inclined to compete on those terms, she would have shown some indication already. "Has she?" I asked. "No," he admitted.

He spoke about women as though he were in the ring with them (old wrestlers never die), and as if he had to dominate them as in some porn-inspired fantasy. I pointed this out. He said he felt "exposed." But I said that he should remember that he was only looking at himself, as in a mirror – no one else, at this point, was privy to his thoughts (except me). He said his father came to mind, who didn't value the choices Andy made and was critical of his being in treatment. I suggested that he didn't have to feel ashamed based on a parent's narrow view but, rather, that he could use what he understood about himself to weigh his options more realistically. If he loved Diane and they *could* work through their differences – provided both were honest – then it might be worth trying.

He decided, on balance, that it was worth remaining engaged, at least for now. "Let's see how I do in a couple of months. We can always push the wedding date back." I wasn't going to argue. He still seemed open to the *idea* of marriage but, apparently, had to reassure himself that he was *entitled* to back out if his doubts remained. "It's only fair to Diane," he said, shifting (once again) the onus for their success onto her. We discussed sharing his feelings more openly with her, and that they speak openly about sexual hang-ups and intellectual competition. He said that he would, and we agreed to keep discussing it.

A few weeks later, when I asked whether the wedding was still on, he broke into a grin. I expected that everything was all set, right down to the caterer … but, not quite. Diane had been offered a prestigious two-year fellowship in Boston, which would open up other academic opportunities. She *couldn't* turn it down. So, she didn't. They'd still be within commuting distance (sort of), and by the time Diane finished they'd have a much better idea of how to calibrate their careers (at least that was the plan). I was sure that Andy had been *very* encouraging. He seemed *very* relieved.

Displaying emotion

Andy experienced his grandfather's death as a profound loss. His voice quavered as he spoke about it. Yet, despite his grief, he held back any tears. "I don't want to come off as emotional. That's my mother's department," he said. While Andy valued emotion, he found it hard to communicate feeling, even in my office. He didn't want anyone to see him as emotional, irrespective of how he felt.

I commented, "You see expressing loss as a weakness."

Furtively, he wiped away a few tears. He acted out the idea that boys don't cry.

His reaction to the death was internalized. He said it raised the specter of his own father's coming death – and his role in it. He thought that his educational accomplishments diminished his father and brought his death closer. "I may not be sure about psychology," he said, "but I'm just smarter than my father, and he knows it." I added guilt to the list of Andy's conflicts. Actually, it might have contributed to his reluctance to pursue psychology, whether or not he credited Diane's competence.

Obviously, Andy's assertion demonstrated how his issues – not least with sexual and filial love – all tended to animate each other.

I was interested in the competitive aspect of Andy's father–son conflict, but didn't bring it up because he needed space to mourn his grandfather (albeit without tears).

We moved on, talking about his anger, leaving his family dynamic aside for a while.

Andy found it difficult to articulate his anger (as when he flung the cat at the wall). For example, when he had to accommodate a change in my schedule, he'd agree without complaint. But then he'd oversleep and arrive late – a form of tacit protest.

Likewise, in graduate school, he was angry at the professors, although they were just doing their jobs, and he criticized their lectures. He resented having to study, memorize, and recite reams of technical information and theory. "Why should I?" he once asked me, as if this were a direct and not a rhetorical question. This pattern reflected a neurotic dilemma: *I have to be good* (i.e., be obedient, study, do psychotherapy, love my fiancée), *but I'm angry and resentful because it's hard work and it's restrictive. I feel guilty about my anger, torture myself to purge the guilt, then take another shot at being good ...* and so on. It was a long way around not saying anything. It was an internalization of anger, much as he internalized grief.

"You see the vicious circle?" I asked. "How you created your life (and treatment) in the image of your neurosis?"

Andy experienced treatment as something he *had* to do, without room for choice. If he wanted to manage his issues, he *had* to see me. Period, end-of-story. He was frustrated with how treatment works, and angry that he had to work if he wanted to see progress. Furthermore, even if he followed the "rules," there was no assurance that the outcome would be satisfactory. "It's a crapshoot," he said, "and yet I have to play." I reminded him that the house doesn't always win, and that if he did make the effort his odds were actually pretty good. "Part of your problem," I suggested, "is a sense of entitlement. It won't work in psychotherapy, it won't work with sexual pleasure, it won't work in grad school." He said I had a point.

Andy's anger was ignited by anything he experienced as a disruption in our sessions. The phone, for example, was an intrusion on our time ("they're stealing my time, they're scattering my focus"). He was disturbed by my keeping him waiting a few minutes ("I can tell you're disengaged"), and he'd comfort himself by recounting childhood indignities. That is, he took refuge by playing the victim.

His older brother, for example, used to pin him down during wrestling matches and tickle him until he peed. A bully in elementary school put his head in the toilet and flushed. Another bully broke his nose.

"I get the feeling," I said, "that you'd be more comfortable talking about war stories from the past than any difficulties that you have now."

"Oh bullshit," he snapped. "You just couldn't care less what I went through as a kid."

"Are you sure that's what's going on here?" I asked. "That there's nothing you're avoiding in terms of what's going on in your life now?"

He picked at a scab near his elbow, a sure sign that he was tensing up.

But he finally spoke.

"Okay," he admitted, "I'm having problems with Diane that I'd rather not discuss. I guess I don't like it that parts of her body are 'off limits.'" He winced. "I'm pissed that she likes sex the most when I'm not even hard."

He repeated his notion that passionate sex is like rape. "You know what my big fear is here?" he asked. "I'm afraid I might enjoy being abusive." His impulse to hurt Motor occurred to me.

In effect, he wanted Diane to want to be raped, but he was afraid of hurting her if he followed through. It was not an uncommon conflict, grounded in the collision of a fantasy and the reality of an actual woman – you could do anything to a fantasy woman, but you had to respect and be careful with a real one. His problem was that he could not even postulate some resolution, where two people discuss their needs and come to some legitimate understanding of how to meet them.

After grousing about me and the obstacles posed by his porn-induced convictions, he avoided any talk about sex. Over the next few sessions, therefore, we focused on how he controlled his cat the way his father had controlled him. I observed it was hard for him to express anger directly toward me. He countered with his abiding fear that if he expressed his anger openly, he'd hurt me or someone else like how he'd hurt Diane with the coffee cup. It felt as though we were in a repetitive cycle, mainly because as a patient he didn't want to get into things too deeply – but therapy often feels that way, and you go with the flow.

Andy remembered playing football with his father in the front yard, where his father dashed up the sideline, Andy tackled him, and his father came down with a thud on his shoulder.

"Stop stalling, old man!" Andy yelled.

His father's fractured collarbone took a year to heal. That was the last time they played football together. Andy had a sense that he had tried to beat his father, and had hurt him. He might try to dominate Diane, and hurt her too. He never said so explicitly, but he didn't have to. We had talked about her, and their relationship, without even mentioning her name.

Toe to toe in the office

A dream toward the end of the first year of treatment helped us clarify an aspect of our relationship: "I'd been given a job digging ditches," he began. "People were teasing me. I didn't have any shoes. I was talking to my older brother, saying what a hard time I was having with wrestling."

While discussing the dream, he mentioned feeling exposed during our sessions.

"It reminds me of one of my biggest losses in high school," he said. "I was going up against a wrestler I'd faced the year before. Won one, lost one. We were the same weight, but he was a head taller. He cradled me with those long arms and pinned me in front of a home crowd. It was humiliating."

I was at least a head taller than Andy and pointed this out. "You and your brother used to wrestle," I added. He demurred. "So, sometimes you experience me as like your brother. We compete. Treatment is like wrestling for you. The dream suggests you'd rather wrestle than do the hard work – like ditch-digging."

"Yeah," Andy replied, "could be."

Talking about the dream brought back more of it.

"We were outside," he said, "doing analysis informally. It's odd but you brought out a duffel bag. Baggage. 'It's not really mine,' you said. 'Yes, it is. Take it.'"

Baggage became a word we applied to something that expressed both inner conflict and a seductive gift. If he "unpacked" or accepted his own baggage, he'd be vulnerable to getting hurt (by me).

"That would make you vulnerable," I observed.

He brought up his rabbi again: "I placed my trust in him, and he abused it."

Andy was still short on specifics, but in essence he claimed his rabbi had taken advantage of him by seducing him. He was uncomfortable with the topic, but even more uncomfortable articulating his homosexual feelings. I thought that eventually he'd relate the full story of what had happened, but for now it was clear that homoeroticism had entered our relationship by means of transference – as I had suspected that it would. I'm not sure that Andy fully appreciated the connection but, to the extent that he did, it must have contributed to his reticence.

He was also agitated because, while he believed he'd made substantial gains in therapy, he wasn't yet in classical psychoanalysis, which generally required four to five visits a week, at least at some American institutes. He referred to analysis as the "alpha and omega" of psychotherapeutic treatment, and blamed me for putting it off.

"Is it possible you're using your anger at me to deflect other emotions?" I asked. "Feelings of disappointment, maybe?"

"Isn't it possible I just don't like you?" he retorted. "If I weren't your patient, would I be your friend?" He looked at my furniture. "You're more mahogany. I'm more beech."

He was referring to his impression that mahogany was a colder, more formal, more pretentious wood.

Expressing distaste for me was unusual for Andy. Generally, he was afraid that if he displayed anger or *any* feelings, I'd send him elsewhere for treatment (in part because I'd agreed to see him for a reduced fee). In other words, I was mercenary, uncaring, insensitive – like his father, at least as Andy saw him. Except for the occasional outburst, he felt "impotent" to show anger toward me.

The following day, he apologized for being rude.

"Well," I said, "maybe there's something in your dislike of me to explore."

He laughed. "I never said 'I don't like you' to anyone. That's not part of being angry. It's mean and judgmental." He got specific. "Look," he said, "I don't want to turn into my father. I don't want to put you down the way my father put down my mother, or abuse you the way I sometimes lose my temper and take it out on Motor."

He wanted to be the good, compliant son/patient, but he was also resentful about feeling he had to be obedient. Rather than experiencing his anger and exploring the emotion, he tended to shut down and withdraw or be passively provocative.

"So how about formal psychoanalysis?" he asked. "Don't you think I might do better with that?" We had discussed increasing the frequency of our work before and both thought it might facilitate the treatment.

"How about we increase analysis to four times a week after the summer break?"

"Deal."

He said he'd hoped all along to be in classical psychoanalysis, but that he was becoming anxious about some of the more "complex" feelings he had developed toward me. I saw these as anger, but also a certain, incompletely repressed homoeroticism. When I offered a fuller analytic experience, there-fore, I braced myself for another patient who might identify me with an overbearing father and an imagined lover. I was willing to deal with these responses, but hoped that understanding them might be useful in treating Andy's overweening problems – his difficulty deciding on a career and whether to go through with marriage.

Playing doctor

Once we resumed our work, Andy started right in on career issues.

His grad school curriculum included a yearlong course in developmental psychology, which had a component in human sexual anatomy. He imagined himself doing a physical exam. While examining a female patient (in his mind), he got an erection and was then racked by fear that he might lose con-trol of his impulses. He connected this fear with the ways he sometimes lost his temper with Motor.

Previously, one evening during his fiancée's physical exam course, he had in fact asked "to play doctor." He suggested Diane pretend she was the mock patient and turned it into sex play. "Playing doctor" meant crossing a forbidden boundary, breaking a taboo. He mentioned a doctor game he'd played with a childhood friend when he was 5: "We ate colored sprinkles – we pretended they were medication – and touched each other's penises. Now

I can't help but wonder if I had become an M.D. like you whether I'd want to rape a good-looking teen during her pelvic exam. Would I fondle the breasts of a maternal woman while checking for lumps? Would inspecting a man's genitals stir up homosexual feelings? I probably made a good choice with psychology."

He felt anxious and guilty about his pondering these questions. They kept him up at night. The urges behind them might have stayed relatively dormant had it not been for his studies.

He saw examining patients even *psychologically* as a sexual experience, which undermined the professional endeavor. He said my being an actual "doctor" might authorize giving in to temptation; he imagined himself in my shoes during training, performing "forbidden" acts and the patients having to comply. Even though the prospect frightened him, he said it felt empowering. He found the aggressive, sexualized possibilities exciting – toward women, but also with regard to a "rough trade" model of homoeroticism. "Am I regressing?" he asked. "If I became an M.D., would I have become a sex offender?" He wasn't joking. His studies had brought home to him that sex fantasies and non-binary attraction might run deep in his psyche, and that suppression or repression (which had been his main MOs) is insufficient when real opportunity presents. "I'm sort of scared," he acknowledged, "and I certainly can't tell Diane."

We discussed how he eroticized clinical situations with patients, like a single woman coming to see him, "opening up" about her problems. "It gets intimate," he commented. Not surprisingly, his early masturbatory experience was based on playing out pornographic scenes from magazines and movies. He'd fantasize that a woman would reveal every part of herself to him, and he wouldn't share anything. Like a doctor, he'd be the one in control. Now, as an adult, he got aroused while watching nipple-piercing on TV. A scene from a pornographic film in which a man performs sexual acts on a woman lying prone on a table captured his imagination.

Andy himself had had a physical exam recently. The woman doctor had done a rectal exam, which was now a particular preoccupation. He told me how his anus had been a "battleground" during his early childhood. When he was sick, his mother took his temperature rectally. "I'd resist," he said. "She'd say she had to do it. She'd have me pull down my pants, put me on her lap, and stick in the thermometer. It felt kind of good going in, cool and smooth. It didn't hurt as I expected." He interpreted these occasions as actually having beaten his mother at her own game. "I wasn't supposed to like it, but the sensation actually stimulated me."

Over several sessions, he talked more about his mother and their connection. He thought she was "there" and "loving and caring" to the extent possible. But he found that she was "encumbered and put upon" by his father. "One day when I was around 5, I found her crying after a fight with my father. She said, 'I can't take this anymore.'" But she didn't leave or even do anything about it. Andy vowed to himself to be her protector. He talked more about often feeling anxious as a child about where she actually was, since she was often preoccupied with her marriage. This left Andy feeling anxious about their connection, and the feeling stayed with him into adulthood. He felt he couldn't do anything about it.

Now, Andy wanted to be the one in control, and became angry when he wasn't. The problem was that he did not differentiate between controlling others – mainly women, in sexualized situations – and himself, which he interpreted as exercising legitimate autonomy as an adult. Part of our work would be to help him make this differentiation, so that while he exercised control over himself, and perhaps shed his anger at others whom he thought were controlling him, he could still cease to regard women as potential objects over whom he could exercise sexual sway. This would not be easy.

Andy's struggle as a psychologist in training laid bare, so to speak, his undifferentiated needs for control. On the one hand, every consultation was a potential sexual temptation, where he might exercise control over the patient and, in effect, lose control of his own (very unprofessional) impulses. But, on the other, he also wanted to be in charge of his career, and not have me or anyone else directing him.

His struggle for autonomy as a budding psychologist reminded him of his earlier struggles. He recalled an incident from around age 4: he was angry because his parents had left him with a babysitter. She told him to ride his tricycle though he'd already learned to ride a bike. He stomped off and shat in his pants as if to say, *I'll show you what a baby I can be*. But then he felt humiliated when the babysitter put him in his younger brother's diapers for the day.

"You seem to express conflicts about control through your body," I commented.

A second memory he'd "forgotten" came to mind: "My parents went away for the week. I was *so* angry I didn't have a bowel movement the whole time. When they came back, I was impacted. They had to take me to the emergency room, where a nurse gave me an enema. My shit came out all over, and I felt that I had managed the whole incident."

As a child exerting power over adults, he'd gotten attention and expressed his anger – and someone else cleaned up the mess.

"So, again," I observed, "your conflicts are expressed through your body. The conflict arose from your feelings around separation, and your reaction was to restrict your bowel movements."

He then described dressing up as a cheerleader in high school, playing Queen Esther for the Jewish holiday of Purim, and trying on his mother's jewelry and high heels. He also recalled an image from a recent dream in which he had breasts and was getting something shoved into him from behind. In this context he mentioned that he enjoyed having a woman put a finger in his anus during sex. So, for Andy, love was always erotic, sex aggressive or controlling, and sexuality fluid.

Still, Andy had a tendency to identify with the feminine – the very opposite of his male-identified competitive self. The point was that he could retreat into the feminine as a sort of private indulgence, almost a game, whereas in his public, "real" life he wanted to be the dominant, alpha male, controlling women and his emotions. Neither pose – for that is what they were – was entirely, exclusively him. He had elements of the masculine and feminine, repressing or displaying one or the other as it suited him. So, if he could accept that his personality had potential in both directions, he might not be so obsessed with being assertively male, intent on controlling women and striving for such strict autonomy that he felt put upon by his professors and me. We discussed the possibility.

"You're hardly androgynous," I said, "but you might consider recognizing your own complexity. Perhaps don't worry so much about asserting control. Your personal integrity is in your complexity (which is true of everyone, actually)."

Andy said that he was afraid of becoming more like his father, who could be mean and condescending, but also didn't want to end up like his passive and ineffectual mother. He thought to practice and try, for example, to be less resentful of his psychology studies and routine. He spoke less grudgingly of one professor who always got under his skin. In family matters, he spoke honestly to his father about one of his father's "girlfriends" – he wasn't confrontational, but tried to tell his father how much his mother suffered because of his infidelity. It was a start.

He remained anxious, however, about having initial consultations, in particular taking a sexual history of a gay man. During a teaching exercise, he'd volunteered to be the patient for a consultation in front of his group. He'd pretend to be gay. "I almost got a date with the instructor," he told me. "He was known to be gay." The whole idea of physical intimacy with a man disturbed him – just because he might like it.

The flip side of his erotic conflict around being a psychotherapist also turned up in analysis. He had already felt that he might seduce me. Now he felt that he had. My looking at him became, in his mind, the classic male gaze, which made him feel like an object of my desire. He imagined me sitting behind him and masturbating in response to what he was revealing – that is, to what I *saw* in him. He finally got so uncomfortable that he could barely tolerate being on the couch. The irony, of course, was that where he had first fantasized about a homoerotic relationship with me, the fantasy that I was now reciprocating totally scared him.

"It seems that you experience analysis the way you would a homosexual encounter," I commented.

"I feel sexually vulnerable lying here," he replied. "And the threat of your examining me feels real."

"Why do you think that is?" I asked.

He hesitated. "Maybe it's time I told you about the rabbi."

Andy had met the rabbi in his junior year of high school, and was initially filled with admiration. He was touched and flattered by his offer of friendship, and enjoyed their long walks and discussions.

Handshakes gradually turned into friendly hugs.

The rabbi wrote him a glowing letter of recommendation for college, and when Andy was wait-listed by his first choice, the rabbi picked up the phone. Andy was in.

The hugs turned into "innocent kisses," but their increasing intimacy was always couched in terms of friendship. The rabbi was helping him evaluate his courses. It was exciting.

Once, they spent the day in Manhattan, palling around and sightseeing. When they returned to the hotel room after dinner, the rabbi took his shirt off to get ready for bed. His intentions were unmistakable. But Andy felt uncomfortable. He pulled the covers over his head and slept on the couch. The next morning, he left without a word.

He now needed to understand what he'd been repressing for years: his own role in what had happened. Yes, the rabbi had acted unethically, but Andy had been complicit, following the rabbi's leads and in some ways offering encouragement. He finally began to realize what I had seen already – that is, that behind his concern that I might seduce him was his desire to seduce *me* into crossing a sexual boundary. He knew enough, by now, to speculate on whether he was exercising power over me, such that I couldn't resist. Perversely, he'd have the upper hand and could then pull out. It was like his attitude toward the engagement – go right up to the edge, then retreat into safety. Here, he'd also have it both ways, indulging a homoerotic fantasy (to which I'd succumb), then exercising control in reverse by calling me out. He was playing power games rather than being honest and forthcoming. Could we even proceed with analysis if he planned to go on like this? I made an observation about his conflict.

Though Andy had initially demanded analysis, maybe now he thought he didn't want to pursue it after all. Or maybe he did, in his way, though he liked (or couldn't resist) playing games with our time. I thought we were getting somewhere, but he kept acting in spite of his own interests.

Not surprisingly, Andy once again brought up the end of his previous treatment, when he'd gotten his psychiatrist to give him a hug.

"I lured him into an unprofessional act," he said. "That's really what happened. Maybe because you're older and more experienced, you couldn't be tempted into doing more."

He was almost flaunting his attempt to subvert the process – perhaps out of vanity? Was he daring himself? I felt it was about his underlying attachments, and I was like an instrument for their expression. Maybe he felt potent if he could imagine seducing me – that is, imposing his will on me – rather than actually trying to seduce a woman with her own sexual preferences.

He remembered a dream from the previous night where he was playing with a cousin whose first name sounded like mine.

"The dream becomes violent. He bites my finger and won't let go. He's strong and I can't push him away. He convulses and no one understands what's going on."

Andy realized that the cousin was a stand-in for me. He now recalled seeing a patient with epilepsy the previous day (suggesting the convulsion in his dream).

After listening further to his associations to the dream, which included various uncomfortable experiences with men, I said, "You fear losing control with a man, and that's represented by the seizure in the dream." I added that his general anger toward me was a defense, distancing him from feelings that frighten him more than anger – being close to a man. "You make war, so to speak, rather than love, fighting your cousin in the dream, and you use fantasies of homosexual submission to confess your desire for closeness to men." It was a mouthful and perhaps too much to say.

At the time, I was treating Andy at a reduced fee, part of a professional commitment to serve the community. So, in Andy's eyes I was "using" him to fulfill this commitment. His notion of being "used" was a fantasy and, as he admitted, it was "like a woman in a porn magazine." Never mind that we had just discussed his dominating *me*. Andy's fantasy world seemed topsy-turvy. Nonetheless, it pivoted around a latent homoeroticism that was progressively becoming less latent as he turned his examining eye on himself. The question was how this emerging realization would affect his life choices. No one survives on repression forever. I recalled that classic Dirk Bogarde film, *Victim* (1961), where a repressed homoeroticism ineluctably resurfaces notwithstanding one's best efforts to avoid it.

"I wanted," Andy said, following up on his dream, "to have an orgasm, so my cousin would be proud of me," he added, "like I was his student."

Andy knew that, at the medical center, I might at times discuss his case (and others) with colleagues. I lead a case conference group for which he'd seen an e-mail.

"So," he asserted, "maybe those notes about me are like a porn mag you and your colleagues get off on."

A short time later, when Andy was studying for a psychopharmacology exam, a drug called Cisapride that his father took for reflux stuck in his head. I repeated the name to him, pronouncing each syllable, slowly and distinctly.

At first nothing came to mind, but then he described feeling weak, "like a sissy ... incompetent ... not much to take pride in." He recalled being kicked in the genitals by one of the neighborhood boys as a child and how he'd been humiliated.

Over the next several weeks, *Cisapride* became a catchword for his fears and shameful feelings of losing control. As a boy, he'd taught himself to pee just a little in his pants, so no one would notice – a practice that required exceptional control. He worried that if he free-associated without any inhibition, he'd lose control of his thoughts.

He was angry about having to be a "mamma's boy" in analysis and having to tell me things he was embarrassed to talk about. He described, for example, hanging out as a boy with older children and the way they made fun of him. The leader of the gang would call him "sissy boy." Andy didn't resist, he told me, because he wanted to be accepted. Still, the verbal abuse left its mark.

"What's the difference between that and hazing pledges in a frat house?" he asked defensively.

The source of Andy's rage, I thought, was connected to his conflicts about masculinity and individuality – in other words, to his conflicts about what it means to be a man and his own man.

Lined up and shot

Andy began talking more about his sexual fantasies and use of pornography. He was aroused by a tape of two women undressing each other and playing with a dildo. This led to reflections on his homosexual yearnings and, even, his hazy identification with the feminine. To him, both were two sides of the same coin – departures from a cis-male orientation.

"It's really hard," he said "talking about my gay feelings. I mean, am I a pervert? That's what my dad would say."

When I suggested that discussing homoeroticism with me was, for him, like a sexual experience, he missed the next session. Apparently, he wanted to define that area of his life as a medical condition – to be diagnosed and managed – rather than as part of how he lived and related to men in an array of settings. He was still resisting his homoeroticism, and trying to restrict it to fantasy so that it wouldn't obtrude into (and distort) his relationships with women. I had reminded him that his sexual orientation was not as subject to his control as he would have liked, and that it emerged into situations where he would have preferred that it didn't.

In the session that followed, he told me that he had become somewhat distant toward Diane. "I'm getting tired," he said, "of asking for sexual 'favors' from her that I know she won't bestow." I thought that perhaps what he really wanted was another man, and that subconsciously he resented Diane for not fulfilling his real needs.

I asked about that, though I was concerned that he might bridle at the suggestion. Instead, however, he just tried to change the subject – unaware, I think, that all of his issues were related insofar as they all affected the course he would choose for the rest of his life.

So, we returned to his struggles to become a psychologist. The sessions began to drag – an expression of his hostility toward me as some sort of medical competitor. Essentially, he preferred struggling with me in therapy to competing directly in the field.

Andy experienced this phase of treatment as a wrestling match. Our back-and-forth had a physical quality just because there was (from his perspective) an undercurrent of sexuality. Under the guise of "understanding," we were getting naked together. The analytic situation was like a homosexual encounter, even as we competed. For that reason, it was both thrilling and a threat. I challenged his equanimity, such that he felt he had to address aspects of himself, including his sexuality, that he wanted the prerogative to repress. I threatened the way that he thought about women and, specifically, Diane. He had submitted to my authority by seeking help, but he felt I was also making his life harder.

"Maybe," he said at one point, "I just want some guidance in how to navigate psychology. Nothing more searching than that." But I wasn't buying it. "You're here with a lot more on your mind, and it won't just go away by burying it," I said. Of course, he knew. At the very least, he understood that he couldn't get away with such a feint – it was against the rules of legitimate wrestling.

So, we kept talking.

"Homosexual feelings threaten you because if you feel that way, you *are* that way," I said. "Or at least you think you are. 'Gay' conflicts with your father's idea of manliness, and you've internalized some of his views."

I asked whether he had spoken with Diane openly about his fantasies, and he said that he was scared of what she might think. But I said that sharing stuff about yourself was often a way to more intensely connect. "If you are always hiding, you'll tend to feel you can't be yourself." It's true that being "closeted" tends to limit or even interfere with relationships. Often, by taking the risk in revealing an aspect of yourself, especially in intimate relationships, you won't suffer continually for not having taken it. I thought that, deep down, Andy didn't trust himself. Perhaps he thought he might tell Diane only part of the story, or that he might make promises in the moment that he couldn't keep.

He said he'd think about it. "Is Diane worth getting to know yourself better?" I asked. "Do you really love her?" He thought he did, but he also said that marriage had always just seemed like the natural progression – until he started questioning his sexuality, and even his commitment to a career (which he thought, in part, was motivated by competition with Diane and, hence, by his need to dominate women). We agreed, at least, that no marriage *should* take place until he had sorted through his feelings for Diane and whether he was prepared to be more honest with her.

I still triggered Andy's underlying hostility, in part because he saw me as an angry father, exposing his confused sexuality. I wasn't denigrating it, as his real father would, but I questioned him, disturbing the veil of repression that allowed him his fantasies while he continued in a conventional, if troubled, life as a guy with a fiancée.

Transference, like so many products of the human mind, isn't simple, even if it's a simple concept. Sometimes Andy saw me as his older brother, pinning him down on the floor. At other times I was a sexually stimulating mother giving him a thermometer rectally. Lately I was his powerful father. But, whoever I was to him in the moment, the transference was primarily erotic.

I picked on him, he said, by analyzing and critiquing his behavior. I was cold and objective like his human sexuality professor, onto whom he displaced many of his negative feelings toward me. I was dissecting him.

The metaphors toggled between wrestling and having sex.

"I'm starting to wonder," he observed, "whether all this picking is going to leave me psychologically scarred." Well, however much patients had complained, they had rarely claimed that analysis might actually be harmful. Andy was challenging me with the Hippocratic oath.

His startling reaction may have been connected to his initial complaint of picking at his arms and face to disfiguring effect. The habit was obviously on his mind, since it had returned after having subsided. He didn't have acne anymore, but I noticed raised welts on a forearm.

"You're going to be critical of my performance with you the same way my father was with how I played baseball," Andy insisted. "I mean, you sit there and stare at me and take notes. How can you say you're not judging me? Writing down all my fuckups and inadequacies."

He saw some of my interpretations as assaults (the sexual equivalent of being anally penetrated by force). But I accepted his homoerotic feelings without rejecting or humiliating him, drawing a stark contrast with his father and eventually leading to another shift in the transference. Andy began to see me as like his college wrestling coach – pushing him to the point of pain, but fairly and in his own interest. He understood that his primary conflict was between notions of "manliness" internalized from his father and his own tilt toward homosexuality and the feminine. Ideally, he thought he could "practice" manliness on his *own* terms, irrespective of inclinations that his father – or anyone – might consider aberrant.

The competition

As he entered his third year of treatment, Andy began to understand more deeply how his experience of childhood was manifest in his present sexual conflicts and conduct. As a consequence, his sexualization of the treatment situation faded. This enabled him to focus on his role as a student psychologist, which he performed professionally.

This was also the third year of Andy's psychology training, and he became openly competitive. He saw becoming a psychologist as surpassing his father, both professionally and, in the long run, financially. He saw becoming a "real doctor" as Diane had, as not necessarily bettering him, since he would (like me) be able to facilitate a healing process without actually touching his patients.

Taking a closer look at such competitive striving, however, led him to become more focused on aspects of psychology in which he had a genuine interest. He began to gravitate toward a career in medical psychology, which he felt would allow him to fulfill his vision of what a psychologist working in a hospital setting should be.

But his father continued to loom large. He was having another affair without even bothering to hide it. This time, Andy's mother filed for divorce. She sought out Andy's advice. "I'm holding my father off and supporting my mother," he said, "and I'm closer to my mother than I've ever been." He saw the rupture as a contest between two males over a woman, where he emerges as the victor. He clearly needed to display his win, though his mother was likely oblivious to the struggle – as his father may also have been. It was a test of his manhood, even better because it was outside the risky space of the bedroom.

Ultimately, he confronted his father, who took the unprecedented step of apologizing. He promised he would never have another affair. While Andy doubted his father's resolve, he reveled in feeling morally superior. "But don't you think," I asked, "that you're still conflicted about your father? His idea of brash masculinity haunts you – you conform to it and you don't." He still wanted to dominate women but sometimes fantasized about men. Andy asked me to give him a break. "Hey, if I do something right, you're on my case because I don't do everything right." Of course, that wasn't so. He was being defensive. His conflicts around sex and gender-identification were deeply upsetting to him, and he knew it. That's why we were talking. "I guess," he said on reflection, "my need to win is so strong, that I'm willing to deny the obvious." Then he went silent and didn't respond, but clearly felt that I had robbed him of even a moment's self-satisfaction.

In subsequent sessions, he described a series of dreams that brought his issues regarding competition into sharp focus. Here is how he described one such dream: "We were all camping – mom, dad, me, my two brothers. Someone was shooting at animals. Someone else decided to put the animals on strings with pulleys and keep shooting at them. I felt like I'd killed someone and I wanted to run away. The animals were strange – an armadillo, an aardvark, a koala bear. Someone was shooting at close range."

I commented that these animals seemed like the new patients he was seeing in his rotations, with their odd names and diagnoses.

These patients' conditions upset him, and he felt that they were locked up "like animals." He wondered whether some might be better off dead. He'd also been scared by a threatening patient and had wanted to run away.

The next day he came late, and looked anxious. I could see he struggled not to pick at his forearms (he kept rubbing them instead).

"I was the 'someone' shooting the animals," he said. "Their helplessness was no protection from my violent impulses." He was competing, I thought, with an idea of himself – the "nice guy" who hated when patients were locked up and who cared about them as represented by the animals. His need to compete was so ingrained that, even when there was no one else around, he'd turn that need inward against himself. Here, to a degree, he was exercising a need to feel morally superior even as he acted out his need to dominate. As it did most of the time, the dream had allowed both these impulses to operate in tandem. I wasn't sure that he realized what he'd done, just because it was so much more of what he always did. The whole exercise may have played out automatically, without his reflecting on it beyond reporting it to me.

Later, he remembered a second part to the dream: "I'm inside a tent in the trailer park. I'm with my mom, lying on a couch. It's a ruse, a friendly ruse to trap this guy outside. He's going to come in and say, 'Who's been killing these animals?' I'm going to say, 'It's me. Now I'll kill you.'"

His associations were to tennis games with his father. Once, after losing a match to Andy, his father told him, "I've become an old man."

"Winning," I said, "isn't a harmless activity for you. It means someone loses, maybe gets hurt and humiliated. You see becoming your own man as diminishing your father – hurting or at least humiliating him."

When Andy got to his rotation through the psychiatry service, he became curious about my choice to go into psychiatry. He wondered whether my professional choices were a reflection of my own problems. But there was more going on – questions of individuation, of becoming his own man.

"Can I feel better about you but still choose another area than psychotherapy?"

I assured him it was fine, although I noted to myself that such concerns suggested early separation and termination issues in the analysis. During one session, he brought up the subject of non-compliant patients and controlling physicians.

"You mean you and me, don't you?" I asked.

He became defensive, saying he didn't want to "go too deep into this topic" and rationalized not talking about us. "I have more pressing issues," he said, though his relationship to me reflected so many of them.

During one of his rotations, Andy documented a correct but impolitic opinion in the chart, knowing that the case supervisor would scold him. Andy then denigrated him, in a blatant breach of hospital decorum. The provocation, I felt, was a way of venting pent-up anger – indiscriminately, against whomever was there. We explored how he'd contrive to provoke just so he could put someone down, be it the supervisor, his father, or me.

In the spotlight

Andy performed well in his rotations. Despite his concerns to the contrary, he was professional in caring for patients, and earned praise for his interpersonal skills. His fears about failing to control his sexual impulses decreased, if only because he felt those impulses less frequently. "Sometimes," he said, "I don't have time to think about sex."

Nonetheless, the school's clinical competence assessment (where Andy was videotaped) resurrected his concerns about being like a pornographic object. He imagined he'd get an erection that would be caught on tape, and he'd be exposed as a pervert.

He brought up a recent incident where a new patient stood outside the door to my office after Andy's session ended. This stirred a childhood memory of his mother standing outside his bedroom door while he masturbated. She literally caught him with his "pants down, dick in hand." She went about her business, putting clean clothes in the closet, and pretended not to notice. Neither of them ever mentioned what had happened. But the fear of getting caught remained.

"You experience being observed as humiliating," I said, "because you feel it throws a spotlight on your inadequacies."

My remark made him think about the way he'd look in my waiting-room mirror, and he convinced himself that I could observe him and see his faults (I'd need some sort of periscope, but never mind). He harbored feelings of guilt going way back and into the present, which he thought that others could observe in his conduct. I said that here was yet another reason for being more open – with me and with Diane. It was as if he knew that he couldn't hide, so what was the need to do so about? Andy needed to work on his conflicts over being (or not being) straight with people.

Unfinished business

Andy passed his competence assessment, and was relieved to know that his treatment would be suspended with summer break. He saw his freedom – finally! – from an array of conflicts that he was tired of contemplating, including those that involved homosexuality, which was intimately tied to his masculine identity.

Yet, even while he anticipated a break from analysis, he was conflicted about any protracted break, and blamed me for what he called "the big separation." We fell back into discussing homosexuality, since he was obviously still attached to me beyond our mere professional relationship.

"You interpret your desire to be close to me as something homosexual," I said, "but you take that to mean you're like a woman."

My comment brought to mind the humiliation of being diapered by the babysitter: "I looked like a girl in a tutu."

We didn't get much further before summer arrived. Andy still tended to handle separation and abandonment by what might be termed erotic redress, that is, like a child who relies on masturbation for comfort when faced with a troubling situation. He could lose himself in himself, turning inwards and nurturing his conflicts.

Less of a man

Entering his fourth year of psychoanalysis (and his training), Andy decided to specialize in medical psychology. In contrast to earlier periods in the analysis, he no longer felt as intense a need to devalue me or himself. Apparently, decisiveness made him feel self-confident – that is, that he was in charge of his life. So, during this final phase he stopped talking about abandonment, and focused on new opportunities for mature connection. He viewed me more as a peer.

But there were still uncertainties. Diane had almost fulfilled her fellowship, and spoke about working for the U.N. Andy wasn't sure what that meant for their relationship – even if *he* was still interested in getting married, was she? He had tried being more honest with her about his conflicted sexuality, but they had never fully faced it together as a committed pair. He imagined her moving to Africa, or some other far-away place where the U.N. has operations, and slowly forgetting about him. Had he tried to head her off? Not really. They had developed a sort of tacit agreement not to talk about the future. Now he wanted to discuss it with her directly.

Partly, this was because he was now focused on his own future, which he saw as contingent on theirs. "I know what I want to do," he told me, "but I've got to face its implications for Diane and me. If we're going to team up, we'll have to get jobs near each other (and Africa sounds like non-starter)." In other words, he didn't see them going to Africa together, and so he'd have to see where she stood, perhaps even dissuade her. *But with what?* Some sort of a formal commitment seemed necessary – soon – or they were in danger of pursuing professional paths in widely separate locales for the foreseeable future. "I think it's time to get real," he said. He certainly was more (if not entirely) ready to get married just now, and it seemed as though he'd have to make a (positive) decision or foreclose the possibility altogether.

With regard to geography, his first choices for a post-doctoral program (in the Northeast) had ranked him highly. He might end up in Boston or she in New York, but the location didn't seem to bother him so long as they were *pretty* close. "Whatever I do, I'll have to triangulate my commitments – there's also my parents, and I'm sure they'll need me." He seemed anxious to resolve his situation *relative* to the people who concerned him, which I read as reassuring himself that he was a responsible adult with a coherent, stable identity. It was as if he were saying "Look, I've come this far, there is objective evidence." Making these commitments were acts of will, to demonstrate that he *could* act reliably, maturely – even conventionally.

Of course, nothing happened as smoothly as he'd hoped. The combined focus on Diane and his parents was a lot for Andy to handle.

He worried about lack of support. "My father's alone," he said, "and my mother met someone else." He worried about caring for his father as he aged. Over several sessions, he had reviewed his own academic accomplishments, but said he felt depressed about possibly winning an award. "I'll just have to live up to expectations," he said, "which is just one more commitment. Won't I already have enough?" Would he backtrack on all his commitments, telling himself that he was just too overwhelmed to be decisive about any of them? I'd seen that before with other patients on the brink of major decisions.

"You go back and forth about the idea that winning means that your father's losing," I said. "And when you're not winning – in the competition with your father for your mother's attention, for example – it discourages you."

Andy pushed back: "I don't need to be force-fed canned interpretations," he said. "I get the Oedipal aspects in my behavior, but how is that helpful?" Here we go again, I thought, a retreat in the guise of self-righteousness.

But still (and perhaps unwittingly), he was helping himself, since explaining the psychology behind his feelings was a way of owning them – in effect, of assuming responsibility. He didn't expect me to compliment him, but I did. He seemed flustered.

Over the next several weeks, however, he ramped up his complaining, and his depression deepened. When I stated the obvious – "You spend a lot of time being unhappy" – he got angry.

"Because *you're* not doing your job," he snapped, "which is to make me feel better." So much for our being peers, colleagues, collaborators. So much for his newfound self-confidence. With Andy, it was always too soon to pass judgment, to say "This is how he's come to terms with things, and we can go on from here." Andy was a moving target, always circling one conflict or another, entering and exiting transference based on whom he was thinking about with regard to that conflict. But at least he was more comfortable with expressing his anger toward me. Being able to feel angry and resolve differences is often part of a committed, loving relationship. I had to hope that some element of this would inflect how he felt about Diane and his parents.

But rather than accept the work of the end-phase of analysis, he complained some about it, even while recognizing that he complained "the way my father would about his job."

"Being like your father," I observed, "keeps you connected to him."

After reflecting a moment, he said, "That's it, I guess. If I'm less like him then I'm less like a man." He had trouble imagining manliness outside his father's version of it.

Finally, we were picking up where we'd left off before the break. Andy's aggressive criticism of me was how he rejected a passive, feminine identification. It was what his father would do.

"Being open and expressive," I said, "means you're not fully in charge anymore. You're sharing with someone else." If he came around to share my views, or at least acknowledge them enough to openly explore them, he'd cease to be the dominant actor. He might then be more open to hearing constructive feedback, rather than just plowing ahead like his father, blinded by his own desires.

But Andy willed himself into an impasse, still fighting to hold on to ideas of masculinity that prevented his coming to terms with his uniquely personal version of being a man.

His resurgent depression was also a way of putting me down, in effect by saying, *You're ineffective. We're right back where we started from.*

His anger at me was at heart competitive, where the patient eluded me as the doctor. By staying depressed, he showed me up; he defeated me. He was stronger, manlier.

It took time for Andy to realize that striving for manliness on these terms was self-defeating. What mattered most, in his frame of reference, was that he was defeating the efforts of a rival professional, a male in a position of authority. In this sense, depression gave him a buzz. The more he sought help with it, the more he'd try (in his conflicted way) to thwart me and remain depressed. He had power over me.

Continuing in analysis meant giving up control, which he equated with feeling female. So, he got the benefit of feeling masculine at the cost of remaining angry and depressed. But he could still turn on a dime, and blame me for leaving him during the break, and not caring enough to try my best. I never tested his logic to the point of saying "Well, if I'm not trying, then how are you such a powerful guy by defeating my best efforts?" Perhaps I should have called this aspect of his conflicts into the open, but it was all entangled with issues involving transference, and I thought we'd spend endless time pursuing those before we got back to why he needed to stymy the analysis. So, for a while, there seemed so many dead ends. I just wanted to see if, somehow, we could address his depression by rewriting the straitened ideas of toxic masculinity that he got from his father. If he could accept his own homoerotic tendencies, and define his own version of masculinity to include them, then I thought we had a chance.

We spoke for a while about what made him, at least in part, identify female.

There were a number of incidents, including urinating on himself and getting punched in the nose.

Andy continued to explore these issues through a couple of more sessions and, as he gained insight into how his sense of being female-identified was his own, arbitrary construction – not a judgment coming from outside – his depression let up somewhat. He still wanted to resist me but, when he understood that giving up arbitrary associations with "female" behavior would make him feel more male, his need to thwart me seemed less urgent. He'd have room to feel manlier while remaining in analysis.

Still, the struggle was far from over.

Liberation

A few months into his fourth year of his doctoral work, Andy began to talk about ending analysis. At first the issue came up only indirectly. His thoughts had returned to Diane, after what had seemed like a welcome hiatus, and he wondered whether he could measure up – to her or to anyone, including his ideas of himself. Still, he had embraced the idea of building a life together with her. They spoke about living together after he graduated, and they talked about how they'd make a good couple in raising children and having a family.

I agreed.

"Your MO has tended to be passive and to avoid discussing uncomfortable subjects with Diane, with me, and with everyone," I said. "Now you're having more direct conversations about issues that matter." I sensed that his original now-or-never sense of his own situation had resurfaced – that somehow he understood that he had to recognize himself as sufficiently heteronormative to get on with life professionally and emotionally. He'd seemed ready enough to more fully choose an identity, accept it, and accept the consequences.

He smiled, but cited a patient who was angry with him for not finishing a task.

"You tend to displace your anger onto physicians, supervisors, or patients at the hospital," I said.

My observation brought up situations over which he felt he'd had no control, such as wetting his bed as a child.

Throughout his treatment, he'd felt a need to defeat me, to put me down – the fact that I was a "real" doctor seemed to lessen him. He showed off his knowledge about psychology, acting like an accomplished practitioner who no longer needed me. At the same time, he talked about feeling that I was judging him.

By aggrandizing himself, he was diminishing patriarchal figures (like me). As he gained more clinical privileges, getting closer to graduation, he became cockier. He viewed his treatment's ending as a defeat for me, and interpreted whatever I said in defense as an attack on *him*.

"Your placement next year might force to you to drop out of analysis. I think it's worth exploring what that would mean to you."

"If I think about not coming back here," he said, "I get the feeling of being liberated."

"From me?"

"From authority."

Andy liked missing a session because he was "too busy with more important stuff." I was subordinated as the weak, ineffectual father, brought down to my proper place.

I felt frustrated and somewhat annoyed with him over the next few weeks. On the one hand, he claimed that analysis had been useful; after all, he was now getting his doctorate in a profession he found meaningful and hoped to move forward with Diane. But, on the other hand, his missing sessions felt dismissive. He was also talking about buying an apartment with Diane and moving in together, while he had fallen behind paying me. Despite the years we had put in together, he complained that I was never emotionally "involved." I felt that his parting shot tried to make me question myself – a final boost to his manly pride.

"So you resent me?" I asked.

"Well," he replied, "I feel guilty because I still owe you money, and anger's a way of distancing myself from the guilt. I can substitute your shortcomings for mine." Not a bad interpretation.

"This attitude of obligation – you *have* to come to treatment, you *have* to talk about different aspects of your sexuality – flared up in relation to leaving treatment and separating from me."

Separation would be *easier* if he was angry at me ("I never liked that guy anyway"). Moreover, he thought he'd feel even more like his own man once he cut the cord. He once admitted "I won't have to think about stuff that bothers me. I'll be in charge of what I think." In other words, if he wanted to repress thoughts of, say, homoeroticism, no one would call him out on it.

Ultimately, he chose to do his post-graduate training in Boston, and would simply *have* to give up analysis. But this also brought up new issues. He was now safely beyond the reach of authority, which included both his professors and me. He felt an impulse to rebel by not completing his remaining clinical rotation and blowing off sessions with me. In effect, he was tempted to objectify freedom by acting it out, showing all the patriarchs that he didn't need them (though I wondered how this attitude would fly once he took up the next phase of his professional work).

"You see yourself as a rebellious child who has to fight, rather than as an adult on equal footing with your peers," I observed.

This prompted him to recall a recent dream where I was disguised as his older brother.

"I kick your ass and pull your arms out of their sockets."

He still approached our relationship as competitive, although now he sensed that he had academic chops enough to win.

Finally, however, he made a few appreciative, albeit a bit grudging, concessions.

"I owe you some of the credit for my success," he said. "You helped me be more comfortable with myself. I was finally able to put more time into work – rather than just worrying all the time. I'm able to be in a committed relationship in a more intimate and loving way."

In effect, he was acknowledging that while the success was his, I had helped clear the way. Well, that *is* what I am supposed to do, since no one can live anyone else's life. Psychotherapists *help* people live their best lives. So, while he was trying to pay me a left-handed compliment, he recognized and said just what someone departing analysis would say if they *had* been helped.

I thought that he saw us as more collaborative peers, even if there were some competitive undercurrents.

But still, I did not want to let Andy end treatment without having some further resolve about the issues that brought him in to begin with (and that on some level, he wanted to avoid): his homoerotic tendencies and conflicting ideas about masculinity.

Crying is for wimps!

A dream captured themes from Andy's final stage of analysis: "I was tunneling up through a hill in the woods. The trees were like sticks. I had a place of my own there. Then the scene shifts. Diane and I are looking for a place to live in a flophouse with a nice lobby. Some clown is mistreating Diane and calling her 'honey.'"

He saw tunneling as a metaphor for growing up. Now that he was an adult and much bigger, the trees looked like sticks (he needed to see himself as big and strong in order to leave me). Climbing out in the sense of *emerging* contrasted with an earlier dream where he'd seen climbing as dangerous (he was killed in a fall). His association to the clown was to "a loud, tall man, like you." In other words, he still needed to see me as demanding and ineffectual, but he no longer feared me. Seeing me as powerless and denigrating me would make it easier to leave analysis – a necessary step to becoming his own man.

"Earlier in treatment, you saw me as an aggressive, threatening authority figure," I suggested.

"Well, I used to idolize psychiatrists," he replied, "but now I see them as human beings with their own faults."

However, being on equal footing – as just another flawed human being – still felt uncomfortable. Clearly, he wasn't quite fully where he wanted to be, but his considerable progress was apparent. Yet some of our following sessions had a one-foot-out-the-door quality. He avoided getting too deeply into his feelings and toyed with ways of running out the clock, including his imposition of a week's hiatus.

After Andy returned, he focused more on termination issues. He worried that he'd finish not having been completely analyzed. Yet he chewed up our sessions speculating about what defined a "cure." To me, it seemed like he'd found yet another, more intellectually refined way to express (rather than mitigate) his conflicts. He was giving in to his conflicts, almost as he said he would once he was "liberated" from authority figures like me.

Over the next few weeks, I experienced a type of boredom that wasn't just my usual tiredness from the late hour at which we met. Andy was apparently content to talk about how he wasn't talking about much of anything. At one point he said, "I know I'm resisting," as if by naming the problem he'd fulfilled his analytic responsibility. He treated talking about what was preventing him from opening up fully as an end in itself, rather than as a means of getting behind or around that defense. He associated intellectualizing with power and masculinity.

"Leaving treatment stirs up feelings that you are still covering up some things," I said. "Maybe you're still a bit worried that showing your feelings will feminize you."

Andy suddenly dropped his lassitude. He became emotional, describing how, when he cried, his father would shout, "Crying is for wimps!"

Bullseye, I thought.

Andy recounted the times when he'd cried over some past hurt and described the sense of vulnerability he'd felt after his father's angry reactions.

These emotional accounts of painful childhood incidents, and his father's impatience with tears, showed real progress but, like a crying fit, they ended soon enough and were followed by a withdrawal. Andy now reverted to talk about leaving.

"I'm so ready for this to be over," he said. "It really doesn't matter much whether I come for the last couple weeks or not."

Trying to guide the conversation back to his need to hide his emotions, I said, "Don't you think you're minimizing the emotional meaning of our relationship – *and* of its end?"

This got him talking about how vulnerable he felt lying on my couch. "It's like my mom's tucking me into bed." He imagined getting off the couch and looking me in the eyes, "face to face, like a man."

"We can do that," I said, feeling this is where we had come in almost four years earlier.

"I don't need you in the same way anymore," he said. "You're not quite disposable but less necessary. How could I be depressed if I'm having fun just thinking about leaving you, going on to my postdoc, and making a go of it with Diane?"

"When you first walked in here," I reminded him, "you didn't just want to eliminate your symptoms. You wanted to know why you were angry and depressed, why you felt guilty about enjoying yourself. Well, you're not so symptomatic anymore. And you have a better understanding of your issues, right?"

"Yeah," he said, picking up the gauntlet. "I was conflicted. I didn't know whether I was me or my father. And if I became more me and less him, that was knocking him aside, renouncing him. That made me a pussy. But if I wanted to be my own man, I *had* to reject him in some ways – his being unfaithful to my mom, the way he stamped on shows of emotion. Things like that had to go. The depression and anger came out of those conflicts."

"What about enjoying yourself?"

He thought for a moment. "I guess this comes down to my dad too. I always equated his unhappiness and his willingness to suffer with manhood."

I wanted to shout *exactly*! Or at least shout. But I didn't want the importance of this statement to come from me.

"Where does that leave you?" I asked.

"I internalized all this shit from my father, like being emotional makes you a pussy, suffering is what makes you a man, homosexuals were obnoxious ..." He trailed off. "And if I have bisexual tendencies what does that say about what my father thinks of me? And so, I ... I just denied that whole side of me. Who wants to repel their father like that?"

In those few sentences he'd captured so much of what we'd worked on. But verbalizing these things was one thing; adding them to his belief system, to the way he perceived himself and his circumstances, was another. I still had some doubts that he had but time would tell.

He had purchased a ring (an emerald cut, her favorite) so he could formally propose to Diane, and asked her parents for consent ("What an odd formality," he said, "but I think everyone was happy that I went along with the custom"). He told them that he loved her, and they said they would be delighted to have him as a son-in-law ("Can you imagine when people really sweated this stuff?" he asked, clearly relieved that he had gone through with it). One weekend when Diane was visiting, they were walking across the Brooklyn Bridge when he got down on one knee and proposed. "It was funny, I guess, but still a great moment. She agreed, and I couldn't have been happier."

We discussed his fear about how he still had some homoeroticism. Would it remain relatively recessive, or assert itself in some unexpected way? His not sharing had been a form of control that he tried to let go of with me. But might he hold onto it with Diane – not a good recipe for staying married, especially with Diane who was fully his peer and herself independent.

Only time would tell.

But shortly after this session, he had a dream suggesting that concerns about his identity had not just been skin-deep. There was a Lucite cutting board that stretched across the kitchen sink. The water from the faucet was too hot and melted it. His cat, Motor, was underneath the board, and when he pulled her out, she was sticky and gooey.

His associations to the cutting board were to old fears about analysis – the couch was like the cutting board or an operating table. The shape of the board reminded him of a tombstone and the impending "death" of his analysis. Like a penis, the board went from being stiff to flaccid. He now recalled how the night before he'd tried to masturbate but couldn't bring himself to orgasm.

"And Motor?" I asked. "Might she be a reminder of the times you mentioned feeling like a 'pussy' with me?"

Andy welled up in tears.

Until a few sessions ago, he'd always felt the need to cover up his emotions – in his view, his feminine side. The cat represented his soft underbelly: being intimate, crying, showing his fears. At last, I thought, we'd achieved something like a breakthrough. I'd seen tears from Andy before, but he'd always fought them. Not this time. With the end of analysis in sight, he had gone from being emotionally stoppered to crying when he spoke about "giving you [me] up" for the rest of his life. The tears seemed genuine.

By accepting his emotional side, he was accepting a sense of manhood that differed from his father's. It was not an iron-fisted, demeaning, emotionally stifled stereotype of manliness, but one that was more comfortable with "feminine" and possibly even homosexual traits.

Rites of passage

Leaving analysis was a kind of victory for Andy – that of a son over the father with whom he was competing – just as his triumph in acing his post-graduate placement had been. It was a rite of passage since, at least to an acceptable degree, he hoped he could now define his own manliness. I wasn't sure how this would ultimately play out with Diane, and I envisioned that down the road he might be amenable to couples' therapy. Diane had been willing to wait until he graduated and she completed her fellowship – perhaps there was some patient, indulgent love on her part in doing so.

"You feel that having come through therapy is a bit of a triumph over me," I observed, "but you also seem to recognize it some as a shared achievement."

Conceding, at least, the magnitude of the experience ("Well, we've been through a lot") helped him assuage a certain guilt that he felt over moving forward with his life.

He still recognized, however, that he hadn't fully explored some of his (I would say relevant if not pressing) issues relating to homoeroticism and fantasies (that he still had) of defiling women's bodies.

I also noted that he was still inclined to interpret feelings of vulnerability as weakness. This was to be expected. Years of thinking in a certain way create pathways, emotional and perhaps even neural, that therapy may not fully overcome by the time it terminates, if ever.

At some level, Andy knew that he was not really completely "finished," even if formally he was. He looked to me to tell him what to do. He wanted permission to leave, for me to "set" him free.

I answered obliquely, reminding him that issues always remained to be further explored, and that was true for all of us and part of what enriches our lives. Andy certainly had become more self-reflective and insightful and had acquired the basic tools for self-analysis, possibly even enough to continue the journey on his own.

He left his last scheduled session unclear as to whether I was fully satisfied with the place where he was.

Well, I thought as Andy walked out my door for the last time, *we've both come pretty far in four years.* On Andy's part, some of this progress was owing to a choice, an act of will on his part. He knew he wanted to move forward with his life, and so he decided to. If he hadn't perceived a crossroads in his relationship, he might not have acted. That is, he might have kept kicking the can down the road, risking that it might finally disappear altogether. But he didn't want to take that risk. He wanted to take the next step, and he liked how it felt – timely and affirmative. Psychoanalysis helped Andy, and pressure of time and place crystallized his current moment. To a degree, this is often the case with therapy. A patient's life catches up with it, and he or she displays emotional fortitude – that is, the acumen and understanding that they have been searching for all along.

This is not in the least to discount psychotherapy, but only to say that it is one piece of the puzzle of a mutidimensional life. It may not be entirely pivotal, but without it the puzzle might still be incomplete.

Reference

Bowlby, John. *Attachment and Loss* (New York: Penguin, 1969)

Conclusion

A different method

Case studies are basic to the "literature" of psychoanalysis. They are how practitioners convey what practice has taught them, and in this sense *Faces of Love* is not unique. Yet as I set out to write, I wanted to try a new form of presentation which, I hoped, would more adequately convey what actually happens when analyst and patient talk for hundreds of hours over several years. I wanted readers to *experience* how diagnoses develop over time, rather than simply reading about them as a Q.E.D. I wanted readers to appreciate how diagnoses and treatment, as well as the patient's insight and understanding, are produced by processes that may seem non-directional until the analysis is almost concluded. In other words, I felt that taking my "word" for what occurred throughout the process was not as useful a heuristic as actually involving the reader in the course of treatment.

Accordingly, *Faces* presents real-time exchanges between patient and analyst so that readers can follow the course of analysis. While most studies describe a case and then describe a diagnosis and treatment, *Faces* allows the reader to understand how – organically – a diagnosis emerges and a treatment develops. There is an interactive quality to this book, a simultaneity between what the patient says and what the therapist thinks, that is much closer to the reality of treatment than is typical of case studies. The organic nature of therapy governs the mode of presentation. It creates an immersive experience – that is, *Faces* instructs by allowing the reader to understand why the analyst thinks as he does in a particular moment. The reader can observe change, both in the patient and the clinician. The object is to bring a higher level of clarity to clinical and instructional material than has been available.

In *Faces*, theory and technique are integrated within this real-time presentation, so that readers can understand how theory informs technique as it is actually applied. The reader does not have to read through to the end of the case, and then follow up – after its dry exposition – with a discussion of facts that may have become fuzzy or distorted. This process-oriented case study renders the organic nature of treatment, where the analyst thinks along with,

DOI: 10.4324/9781003352624-6

prompts, and responds to the patient. It captures the nuances of the psycho-analytic setting, rather than finessing them for purposes of a smooth, after-the-fact discussion and summary. This is closer to reality. The reader is in the room, and *also* – simultaneously – in the therapist's head. I first pursued this method of presentation in *Psychotherapy and Personal Change: Two Minds in a Mirror* (2021). Here, I apply it in far more detail and, hence, with a degree of clarity that, I hope, enhances the book's instructional capabilities and contributes to the literature.

Of course, doing psychoanalysis and writing about it are very different – the one does not readily translate into the other. Thus, I've had to edit my notes substantially to provide a semblance of narrative coherence amidst all the circularity, backsliding, and general non-linearity (which even an indulgent reader could not be expected to endure). So, while I've tried to render the ambiguity, and even fogginess, of treatment, I have taken some poetic license. Finding the right compromise between my everyday grind (on the one hand) and the reader's capacity to absorb it (on the other) was a challenge. No matter how truthful these studies are, they do not – could not – achieve strict verisimilitude. Even during moments of stunning clarity, as when Jock openly acknowledges that he desires his sister, the story does not just fall into place. Too many fragments are still lurking in the unconscious, and we cannot just say "Okay, case closed." In writing about analysis, I have to keep up with the treatment and accept, simultaneously, that all I can do is render it at that moment and strive towards truth and reality. I can speculate and, in that sense, sometimes get ahead of the treatment – but I cannot ever suggest that the apparent course of treatment will remain apparent as we proceed. *Faces* is as close as I could get to leading the reader through what I have been through.

Finally, any discussion of my method in *Faces of Love* would not be complete without explaining how love underlies the book's structure. *Faces* synthesizes a vast amount of complex psychoanalytic material through the lens of love. From the perspective of love, it deals with issues such as repressed homosexuality, a taboo desire for a sibling, obsession with a fantasy, a complex Oedipus complex, and transferences that become resistance – and even an obstacle – to treatment until they are examined and understood. Issues that may seem to have little in common, at least with regard to treatment, emerge as having a substrate – in love – that draws them together, facilitating the reader's comprehension of these issues and their treatment. *Faces*' core insight, therefore, is that a patient's problematic relationship to love, however expressed, can be addressed over time by enabling them to understand how love functions in their lives. I sought to render how this understanding develops.

Psychoanalysis

The working title of the first draft of this book was *A Way with Words*, which was meant as a corrective to the diagnostic and psychopharmacological framework that dominates the field. Of course, pills are useful in treating symptoms and relieving suffering. Major psychiatric disorders such as schizophrenia, bipolar disorders, and attention deficit disorder as well as other conditions may require medication. They help correct neuronal imbalances. But psychoanalysis is not primarily about symptom relief. It's about reaching into the mind of human beings, and making it less likely that the causes of suffering and psychic pain (which may have deepened over decades) will persist. It recognizes that human nature is a constantly shifting constellation of conflicts and compromises. Ultimately, it aims at personal growth, increased self-understanding, and empathy toward oneself and others. *Faces of Love* embodies this approach.

Perhaps as psychoanalysts, we help people to love themselves and others by listening and providing empathy. These are aspects of love. Some psychoanalysts have postulated that psychoanalysis is a cure through love – not, perhaps, as patients would understand it, but certainly insofar as love implies a type of attuned attentiveness where the analyst responds to the patient with insight and an empathic assurance, allowing the patient to freely associate with less fear or inhibition. In this posture, love does the work of psychotherapy. It's liberating. It enables the patient to experience a type of sharing that may, until that point, have seemed beyond reach. In this sense, love teaches. Certainly, my own work has shifted toward the interpersonal (vs. the intrapsychic) because it is through a relationship – or, rather, the paradigmatic relationship between psychoanalyst and patient – that healing happens.

So, it's important to explain how I listen – that is, what I listen *for*. Initially, I try to identify what the patient is talking about (the subject, internal or external) and ask myself why they are talking about it with me. What are they actually signaling? What kind of response are they trying to elicit (interest, sympathy, a quick fix with a pill and a regimen)? But then I turn inward, and ask myself if I would understand their situation in the same way if I were in it. This helps to create grounds for empathy or, at least, to establish the distance between their experience and mine. If I am going to help, I need to have a point of reference – how much of my experience can I usefully bring to bear? Am I starting from scratch on *terra incognita*? It's no secret that psychoanalysts find sources of understanding in their own lives (though, of course, case studies like *Faces of Love* can help!). I compare our realities, augmented by the possible motivations of the patient and those around him or her. Ultimately, I try to understand the patient's struggles, underlying conflicts, and unconscious mental life.

Of course, everything I just said about listening must be "situated" – that is, understood in terms that reflect the specific moment during analysis in which it occurs. So, I ask myself why the patient is saying what they're saying *now*, at this moment, at this point in analysis. I think about whom I might represent to them, which can vary during the course of analysis (as we saw, for example, with Carol, for whom I was sometimes a father and at other times a lover). Are they looking for the sort of love they would receive or didn't receive from such a person in the past? Is there some sibling rivalry playing out, as in Bobby's case? This transferential aspect of the relationship often reveals psychodynamic aspects of the patient's life, and allows me to call their attention to aspects of themselves affecting their other relationships (which they may be repressing or, at least, are not fully aware of).

As I listen, and my thoughts toggle between the patient's history and my own experience, I pay attention to thoughts that stir up in me – it's as if I am free-associating in parallel with the patient. I ask what *I* am feeling at a specific moment, much as I would ask of the patient. It's a two-track tape, and I am listening to both. Both tracks inform what I say to the patient. I learn something about the patient and our relationship. The exchange between what each of us says and my own reflection is integral to the therapeutic work.

So, in psychoanalysis, and more broadly in psychotherapy, listening is really about what the therapist will finally say. It's the predicate to speaking efficaciously. In this regard, one persistent question in psychotherapy is "What really helps?" What should we listen for *especially* so that we can provide the best response? Are we interpreting conflicts to help patients form better compromise formations (insight and understanding) or are we providing a corrective emotional experience (empathy) so that a patient feels better? While it's probably some of both, the question is still relevant because it informs the therapeutic approach and technique – that is, it gets back to how we listen and process what we hear. Of course, different approaches may work for different people, or at different times, depending on the personalities and how they interact.

How does analysis end?

In *How Wars End: Why We Always Fight the Last Battle* (2010), Gideon Rose makes a claim that could easily apply to psychoanalysis (which, with some patients, can at times seem a lot like a war zone): "[W]ars are difficult to close out even when they are started well, and mistakes at the beginning complicate the job exponentially, no matter who is in charge later on." Who *is* really in charge during analysis, especially toward the end when the patient insists that it's time to leave? How can analysts make the most of this late-stage period so that, even if mistakes have been compounding, the patient walks away with some benefit – some insight and understanding that empowers him or her to think about any remaining issues so as to deal with them effectively? The point, as in a war, is to resolve what you can, and hope that the redistribution of power going forward (this time overwhelmingly in favor of the patient) will at least provide some stability. So, fundamentally, psychoanalysis is a collaborative activity, and the patient's coming to recognize and utilize it in that way is often part of the therapeutic process.

Of course, analysis is meant to have an ending ... albeit imperfect, as in these studies. This ending, often punctuated and drawn out, is known as the termination phase, a sort of conclusion that may recapitulate issues from the beginning (or anywhere during the course) of an analysis. In this sense, analysis is open-ended, somewhat free-form, but not interminable. Feelings of loss may come to the surface during this phase as well. Impending loss of the analyst and the analytic relationship (including what it represents to both analyst and patient) can become an important subject to explore.

Why, for example, does the idea – or fear – of loss matter to the patient? Why does a patient who wants to conclude his or her treatment also feel conflicted, and create occasions to prolong it? The termination phase can become a type of meta-analysis, where patient and analyst examine analysis itself as a means to examining the patient's relationship to him- or herself and the wider world. This can become a rabbit hole, a mise en abyme that both parties have to get their minds around and work through. Failure to end things somewhere during this spiral can lead to disappointment and recriminations.

But still, is analysis ever really completed? I've had patients return years after we'd both said good-bye. In Bobby's case, for example, we never adequately explored the Oedipal love for his mother, which to some extent remained the basis for his Oedipal dilemma. We resolved (or, rather, manageably resolved) his conflicts with the males in his family, but aspects of his relationship with his mother remained an issue. Thus, an important phase of his treatment remained for his subsequent weekly psychotherapy, which I have only briefly described but that still mattered profoundly for his overall continued progress. In most cases, even when analysis has ended, there is more to explore. Overcoming the patient's resistance post-termination may feel to the analyst just like more analysis – that is, as if analysis has merely become less intensive rather than having reached its end.

Thus, where analysis passes into less intensive psychotherapy, the ending may seem less formal, more like a phase change than a hard break. In any case, whatever form the ending finally takes, we hope that the patient has acquired the tools necessary for becoming more self-aware, and for cultivating an ability to be self-reflective. It resembles when an overweight patient has slimmed down enough to enter into a maintenance diet – and everyone hopes that he or she stays on it.

Libido and love

Faces of Love began with the concept of libido, and I think it's a good place to end (though, of course, the topic can be endless, much like a course of therapy that shifts from one gear into another but never really stops). I think it's safe to say, as Freud did, that at least in our fantasy lives we are all polymorphously perverse. Our fantasies can run from Oedipal to incestuous, and on into bisexuality, MILF, bondage and submission, threesomes … just visit a few porn sites to extend the options. Of course, this doesn't mean that we all have "tendencies," that we're all perverted or sexually obsessed. But it does indicate that our sexuality and sexual identity are complex. How we come to terms with such complexity – how we sort through it so as not to hurt others or bewilder ourselves – determines how we conduct our lives and maintain a degree of mental health.

So, libido is not simply the most elemental of drives but, rather, the driving force behind both our self-acceptance and adjustment to society. In this sense, libido is a big deal. It is nothing to be relegated to the dark places of our mind. It needs to be understood, the way hurricanes and volcanoes need to be understood if, as humans, we're going to be able to live with them.

Accordingly, curiosity about sex and sexuality is a normal part of childhood, adolescence, and adulthood. During each phase of our lives, starting in infancy, we display an interest in sex. We may even flaunt it, and use it as an instrument of power – or, perversely, as a reason to feel guilty, incompetent, or depressed. In the case of children, a curiosity about sex, and about their parents "having sex," can issue in fantasies on the one hand (what *are* they doing, and why does it exclude me?) and resentments on the other, which can have implications throughout later life. The studies in *Faces of Love* demonstrate some of these protracted implications.

In adulthood, sexuality can take so many forms – from bisexuality, to gender dysphoria, S&M, and the toe fetishes that led to ancient Chinese foot-binding – that the whole idea of normality seems bizarrely quaint. Most people now insist that what goes on in private is not to be judged or questioned, provided that no one is harmed. In psychotherapy, the object is to ensure that the patient learns to accept their sexuality but (and this is a big "but") not allow it to dislodge their hold on reality (as Jock's threatened to do) or stand in the way of their forming satisfying relationships (with their loved ones and with others).

An illustration of how libido has come out of the closet and into main-stream, popular, *open* conversation is that S&M is now a major element of the plot in the hit TV series *Billions* (2016–). Paul Giamatti's character, a prom-inent U.S. Attorney, engages in violent sex acts with his wife, who acts as dominatrix, while he also seeks out satisfaction in the seamier purlieus of New York City. He accepts his needs, and is willing to risk his reputation to pursue them. What's important is that, even while others may be aghast, the character likes himself as he is. In this sense, the series challenges us to under-stand that even the most high-functioning individuals can practice sex in ways that are normal for them, even if we would never go there. Would we fantasize about going there? Some people feel powerful enough to act on their fantasies and, so long as everyone involved is "consenting," would we really require them to refrain merely in the name of conformity? In subtle ways, the series suggests (along with an emerging consensus) that we shouldn't.

Of course, while libido is expressible in endless forms, it is subsumed in what we call "love," which is not exclusively physical but is equally intense. *Faces of Love* is not directly concerned with exploring romantic love, though its expression is present (at least peripherally) in all the studies. I have been more concerned with types of love that, at various times in a patient's life, become more prominent. These include, significantly, mother-love and self-love.

So much depends on a mother's love which – when it's present and unconstrained – can help the child build a reservoir of self-esteem, as well as trust in the wider world. It can provide a source of resilience. However, when it is absent or insufficient, the negative effects on attachments throughout the person's life can be profound. We've seen this in Carol's inability to sustain a healthy romance.

As I have suggested, there is a segue from a mother's love to self-love, which we may not immediately think of as a form of libido but, in fact, is just another shading of it. In *Faces of Love*, all of the patients suffer – to some degree – from deficits in self-love. Notably, narcissism gets a bad rap in psychoanalytic circles, but it's crucial if viewed simply as a healthy relationship to oneself. Think of Jock's suffering as a measure of how far it is possible to fall out of love with oneself, and how important it is to recover. If we cannot accept ourselves, we will be unable to trust anyone else. We will be too afraid of diminishing ourselves even further through acts of common generosity. We will withdraw, become unsociable, and alone with the selves that (in many ways) we dislike. So, perhaps the starting point for the individual, and the end-point for psychotherapy, is to produce (or, rather, enable) a workable version of self-love. We all know that we are imperfect, but self-acceptance is still a major driver of mental health. It is the basic condition from which all the other work can take its course.

Part of working toward self-love, within the psychoanalytic setting, is to help patients overcome their resistance to making the unconscious or subconscious conscious. The patient has to confront him- or herself before an adequate degree of self-love can develop. *Faces of Love* has sought to demonstrate how, in my practice, we tried to achieve this result. It remains disputable as to whether the intensive regimen of psychoanalysis is the best method for drawing a patient out. There are also disputes over whether patients should lie on a couch, staring at the ceiling, or sit opposite the analyst making constant eye contact. Eye contact is, after all, a form of physicality (even though it is remote) and, in that sense, it's a vehicle of libido and for expressing love. The patients whose cases I present here all lay on couches, at least during the intensive phases of their treatment. We nonetheless managed to form deep connections which, after all, was the objective, and instrumental to their treatment.

For me, *Faces of Love* is the outward face of my work. It's what I do. I have lived with it for a long time, and now it's hard to let go. As with these patients' ending their treatment (sort of), it's hard to contend with the loss. In writing

this book – that is, in assembling all the notes that make up the narratives –
I was reminded again and again of moments that meant so much to me as
I helped patients work through their issues. I stopped and thought about the
implications of those moments – could I have said something else? Should
I have just sat quietly and waited, hoping that the patient would finally offer
me a cue? Perhaps and perhaps. Second-guessing is a natural component of
psychotherapy, which is polymorphously imperfect. Just like us. As I noted
in "Gatsby," its rhythms reflect each patient's neuroses, and ebb and flow
along with them. But so long as we come out in a better place than where we
started – and as long as the patient feels that we have – then the process is justifiable, even therapeutic. *Faces of Love* demonstrates how, in some instances,
we arrived at that place.

References

Friedberg, Ahron, with Sandra Sherman. *Psychotherapy and Personal Change: Two
    Minds in a Mirror* (London: Routledge, 2021)
Koppelan, Brian, David Levien, and Andrew Ross Sorkin. *Billions* (New York:
    Showtime, 2016–)
Rose, Gideon. *How Wars End: Why We Always Fight the Last Battle* (New York: Simon
    & Schuster, 2010)

Index

9781032403434